Fina Accounting

Jim O'Neill BA,
Gordon Holmes BA, FCCA,
and Geoff Thornton BA, FCCA

Charles Letts & Co Ltd
London, Edinburgh and New York

First published 1989
by Charles Letts & Co Ltd
Diary House, Borough Road, London SE1 1DW

Text: © O'Neill, Holmes and Thornton 1989
Illustrations: © Charles Letts & Co Ltd 1989

British Library Cataloguing in Publication Data

O'Neill, J. (James), 1946–
    Financial accounting.
    1. Financial accounting–Questions &
    answers
    I. Title II. Holmes, Gordon III. Thornton,
    Geoffrey
    657'.48'076

    ISBN 0 85097 853 X

The book's authors

Jim O'Neill is senior lecturer in Business Studies at the Staffordshire Polytechnic.
Before becoming a lecturer, he was an accountant in industry for eight years. He is a
joint author of *Numeracy and Accounts* (Collins) and has also written a number of
specialist publications for use by accountants in industry.

Gordon Holmes and Geoff Thornton are also senior lecturers at Staffordshire Polytechnic. Gordon Holmes was previously a manager with Peat, Marwick, Mitchell,
while Geoff Thornton's career as an accountant included being an examiner in
bankruptcy for the Department of Trade and Industry.

Acknowledgements

The authors and publishers are grateful to the following organizations for
permission to reproduce copyright material:

The Association of Accounting Technicians
The Accounting Standards Committee
The Chartered Association of Certified Accountants
The Chartered Institute of Management Accountants
ICC Information Group Ltd
Imperial Chemical Industries PLC
The Association of British Factors
The Institute of Chartered Accountants in England and Wales
Her Majesty's Stationery Office.

Printed and bound in Great Britain by
Charles Letts (Scotland) Ltd

Contents

Preface

This book is intended primarily for first-year college and university students studying financial accounting on degree courses in Business Studies and Accounting, and all other degree courses with an accounting and business studies input. Additionally, students studying for the first year examinations of professional accounting bodies, such as the Chartered Association of Certified Accountants, or the Chartered Institute of Management Accountants, and students studying for the intermediate level of accounting qualifications, such as those of the Association of Accounting Technicians, will find this book particularly useful.

This book covers what the authors consider to be the common core when studying for any accounting examination. At the end of each chapter there are a number of questions, most of which are from recent examination papers. The questions are there to enable the student to assess whether or not he or she has achieved the required standard.

Introduction and guide to using this book

This book has been written to supplement lectures and tutorials which you either currently, or will in future attend. Superfluous explanations have been dispensed with to leave the essential elements contained in each topic. We have identified every topic which it is necessary for the student to understand in order to succeed in a financial accounting examination.

You may use this book in one of two ways. Firstly, if you are taking part in a formal course you may refer to the relevant chapter after attending the lecture and/or tutorial. You will find fairly brief, but succinct explanations to help your understanding. Every complication is covered. Go through each part of the chapter and then attempt the questions at the end. Remember these questions are not graded; you should already have attempted easier questions in your tutorials.

Secondly, if you are studying independently you will still find this book very useful. Read the recommended text(s) for your course, attempting two of the questions provided, then go through the relevant chapter in this book and attempt the questions. If you still have difficulties with particular topics, there are reading hints at the end of each chapter.

1 Study skills

It is essential to attend lectures on a regular basis, and notes should be taken of the main points covered. Some of the information will quite often be given in the form of written hand-outs.

Following on from the lecture you should read your notes carefully, rewriting and expanding, if necessary. You should also read any hand-outs and recommended reading. It may be desirable to make notes from the recommended reading, as well.

At tutorials you should first of all take the opportunity to clarify any points arising from the lecture. The tutorial is likely to be based on discussion and/or graded exercises, and you should try to be in a position to participate fully. It would be very useful to refer to this book at this stage, and then fully read and carry out the questions as soon as possible after the tutorials.

You will be required to answer some questions in essay form. Read such questions carefully, and plan your answer. Your plan should have an introduction, a development of the main arguments or points, and a conclusion. Write down the main points you wish to cover in each section, such as the introduction, development, and conclusion. Then each point should be developed, drawing upon lecture and tutorial notes and original sources, such as text books, newspapers, magazines, journals, government statistics, etc.

Each main point should be presented as a paragraph, which is firstly written out in draft form. Once this is done, read through the whole of the draft to ensure that the question set has been answered. Be careful with the conclusion, because this is often the weakest part of students' answers. Make sure that all sources are correctly referenced, and when someone else's words have been quoted, that you have given them credit. Once you are satisfied with the draft, write out the essay neatly and carefully.

It is easier to remember facts if they are constantly at the surface of your mind. Constant referral to topics learnt throughout the year is recommended, rather than leaving revision to near the end of the course and trying to relearn facts in a short period of time.

You must try and reduce each topic to 'remembrable chunks'. Take each topic and refer to this book for the main elements, writing these down, using no more than one-and-a-half sides of A4 paper. The following is an example of this approach from chapter 8 of this book, 'Accounting for depreciation'.

Accounting for depreciation

1 **Main purposes**	(i) Cost allocation/matching
	(ii) Loss in value
	(iii) Funds for replacement
	(iv) Non-cash expense
	(v) Cash expense
2 **Major methods**	(i) Straight line
	(ii) Reducing balance, including sum of digits
	(iii) Other methods
3 **Accounting entries —ledger**	(i) Asset account
	(ii) Provision for depreciation account

(cont'd.)

(*cont'd.*)

4 Accounting entries
  —income statement

  (i) Year's charge only

5 Accounting entries
  —balance sheet

  (i) Cost or valuation
  (ii) Depreciation to date (cumulative)
  (iii) Written-down value

6 Accounting entries
  —disposal of asset

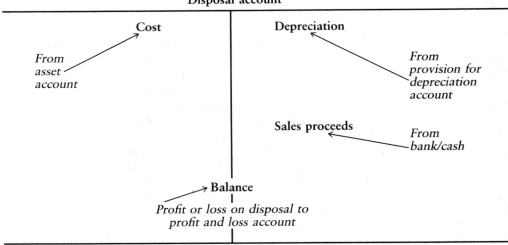

Disposal account

The next stage should be to rework the exercises given in the tutorials and finish by doing past examination questions. Repeat this process until you are able to answer examination questions without referring to your notes.

When tackling examination papers, read the examiner's instructions carefully, being careful to note any compulsory questions (which you should do first). Answer no more questions than the required number.

Divide the time between questions in proportion to marks awarded: if equal marks are awarded, devote equal time. Spend **no more** time on each question than the time you have allowed. Answer what you consider to be the easiest question first, to gain confidence, but any compulsory ones should be your priority.

When answering a question, show all workings, making sure that you are answering the question set and not a similar one that you may have revised. Indicate in the space provided on the answer sheet which question you are answering, and when your time is up, move on to the next question. If your answer does not balance, do not waste time trying to find the difference, you may lose marks through not having had enough time to answer another one.

Do not leave blank pages between your answers in the examination booklet. If you are unable to include everything in the time allocated, make brief notes, and if you have the time later, go back to these notes and complete your answer.

2 The balance sheet

This chapter examines the concept of the worth, or financial position, of a business. The function and derivation of the balance sheet is illustrated, and the idea of assets and liabilities is explained. The effect on the balance sheet of different forms of legal status is described and illustrated.

The balance sheet is an important financial statement of any business, and it is certain that candidates will be required to prepare at least one balance sheet under examination conditions. Most questions are linked to other topics, and it is unlikely that there would be a question simply on the balance sheet, at this level.

2.1 Worth of a business

The financial position of a firm at any specific point in time is calculated by deducting the value of everything that the firm owes from the value of everything that the firm owns, thus:

Assets – everything that the firm owns

less

Liabilities – everything that the firm owes

equals

Capital – the worth of the firm

The above is known as the 'accounting equation', and is an important part of accounting theory.

2.2 The basis of the balance sheet

The financial position of a firm is illustrated in the balance sheet. This statement is based upon the accounting equation, and comprises three parts: assets, liabilities and shareholders' funds.

Assets must have a money value, and can be tangible, like premises, or intangible, like patent rights. Assets are the firm's economic resources, which are used to increase the worth of the business. Fixed assets, such as land and machinery, are long-term assets, which are not usually held for resale. Current assets, such as debtors and stock, are short-term assets and are usually part of the manufacturing firm's production cycle. Liabilities also must have a money value, and they are what is owed by the firm. Current liabilities, such as bank overdraft, are due for repayment within one year. The repayment date for long-term liabilities is at least one year, usually more. Examples are loans and share capital. Shareholders' funds represent the share of the firm's assets that the owners hold. This share represents the worth of the business, and is calculated using the accounting equation thus:

Assets

minus

Liabilities

equals

Shareholders' funds

Creditors have prior claim upon the assets of a business, therefore the owners' claim is a residual one. If the owners decide to sell all the assets and discharge all the liabilities at the balance sheet values, the shareholders' funds would be what is left. Other names for shareholders' funds are 'net assets' and 'owners' equity'.

The accounting equation can be redrafted to show the basis of a balance sheet, as follows:

Assets ⟵——————— *Resources of the firm*
equals
Liabilities ⟵
and ⎫ *How the resources are financed*
Shareholders' funds ⟋

Consider a simple example: a manufacturer starts a new firm, buying £50,000 worth of machinery and renting a factory. The owner provides £15,000 of his own money and borrows the rest from the bank. The accounting equation would show this position.

	£
Assets	50,000
equals	
Liabilities	35,000
and	
Shareholders' funds	15,000

The balance sheet of this firm would be drawn up using the above as a basis. A number of rules have been developed to highlight certain aspects of a firm's affairs. A copy of the manufacturer's balance sheet is illustrated below:

**Balance sheet
as at 31 July**

	£
Fixed assets	
Machinery	<u>50,000</u>
Financed by:	
Shareholders' funds	15,000
Bank loan	<u>35,000</u>
	<u>50,000</u>

Note that the balance sheet actually balances, i.e., the total assets agree with the addition of the shareholders' funds and the bank loan. This is always the case, because of the accounting equation referred to earlier.

2.3 Modes of presentation

The legal status of a business determines, to a great extent, the way in which a balance sheet is presented. For our purposes the firm may be defined as a sole proprietor, or a partnership for a limited company. At each stage of the firm's life its financial position would be illustrated in a different way to reflect its changed legal status.

Consider the example of J. Horton, a sole trader who just completed one year' trading. His financial position is as follows:

	£
Premises	50,000
Machinery	25,000
Stock	15,000
Debtors	12,000
Bank balance	3,000
Bank loan	40,000
Creditors	28,000
Profit for the year	29,000
(after deducting all costs)	
Own funds used to start business	8,000

The balance sheet of Horton would be:

**Balance sheet
as at 31 July**

	£	£	£
Fixed assets			
Premises			50,000
Machinery			25,000
			75,000
Current assets			
Stock	15,000		
Debtors	12,000		
Bank	3,000	30,000	
Less Current liability			
Creditors		28,000	
Working capital			2,000
			77,000
Financed by:			
Capital account			
Balance at beginning		8,000	
Add Profit for year		29,000	37,000
Long-term liability			
Bank loan			40,000
			77,000

The assets are listed in descending order of liquidity, the most liquid item (bank) shown last and the least liquid item (premises) shown first. Liquidity in this context means nearness to cash. If you are not sure where a particular asset should be, consider how easily you may dispose of the asset in the event of a business being in trouble, without disrupting the business activity of the firm. The last asset you would dispose of would be the premises – without them the firm would be unable to continue.

Consider the effect if Horton were to have an equal partner, Jones. All the above details are the same, except the following:

		£
Capital	Horton	4,000
	Jones	4,000
Profits (shared equally)	Horton	14,500
	Jones	14,500

The assets and liabilities of the business are exactly the same. What has changed is the financing of the business by the owners, therefore the capital of the business is illustrated as thus:

Financed by:			
Capital account	Horton	Jones	
	£	£	£
Balances at beginning	4,000	4,000	
Add share of profits	14,500	14,500	
	18,500	18,500	37,000
Long-term liability			
Bank loan			40,000
			77,000

If the business is a limited company, then the capital at the beginning is divided, usually, into £1 parts, and becomes share capital. The owners become shareholders in the business, and the profits are kept in a reserve, normally called the profit and loss account. Thus the balance sheet of the business is illustrated as follows:

		£
Share capital		
8,000 Ordinary shares of £1 each		8,000
Reserves		
Profit and loss account (balance)		29,000
Shareholders' interest		37,000
Long-term liability		
Bank loan		40,000
Capital employed		77,000

A more detailed treatment of company accounts appears in chapter 10.

Summary

1 The balance sheet is a statement which illustrates the financial position of a business.

2 The economic resources of a business are known as assets.

3 The money value of what a firm owes is known as liabilities.

4 The accounting equation is used to calculate the worth of a firm.

5 The difference between the assets and the liabilities of a business is known as capital.

Links with other topics

Preparing a balance sheet is an essential task in virtually every topic of financial accounting. In company annual reports, analysis and interpretation, funds flow, financial structure, depreciation and incomplete records, it is essential to understand the effect that each topic has on the balance sheet. In some cases, such as will be shown in chapter 3 on the income statement, the balance sheet is slightly modified to cater for different types of business and ownership. In chapter 10, however, the company balance sheet is illustrated according to the Companies Acts. Finally, the inclusion and valuation of some balance sheet items is determined by the concepts and conventions described in chapter 7, and the accounting standards illustrated in chapter 9.

Sample questions

At this level, all balance sheet questions are linked to other topics. However, at this stage you will find it useful to attempt the following questions. Practice at drafting balance sheets is essential, and you will be able to concentrate more fully on subsequent topics if you become proficient at this stage.

Try the following short answer questions first. They will help to refresh your memory on the earlier parts of the chapter.

1 Fill in the missing word(s) from the following sentences:
(a) Current assets are .... – .... assets.
(b) Assets minus .... equals capital.
(c) A motor vehicle is a .... asset.
(d) Trade creditors are a .... liability.

2 True or false?
(a) Assets are listed in the balance sheet in order of liquidity.
(b) Liabilities are owned by the firm.
(c) Assets plus liabilities equals capital.
(d) The accounting equation explains why the balance sheet always balances.

Now attempt the following questions, which are designed to give you practice in preparing balance sheets of increasing complexity.

3 The following is a list of balances extracted from the books of Software Parts as at 31 December. Prepare a balance sheet as at that date.

	£
Premises	100,000
Machinery	45,000
Stock	22,500
Debtors	11,000
Bank loan (long-term)	40,000
Bank overdraft	3,250
Creditors	24,000
Profit for the year	65,000
Own funds used to start business	46,250

Answer

This is a simple variation of the first example, with just one new item, the bank overdraft. Whenever you encounter a new item, ask two questions: 'Is it an asset or a liability?' and 'Is it current or fixed?' Once you have decided, you can enter the item in the appropriate place. Your answer should appear as follows:

Software Parts Balance sheet
as at 31 December

	£	£	£
Fixed assets			
Premises			100,000
Machinery			45,000
			145,000
Current assets			
Stock	22,500		
Debtors	11,000	33,500	
Less Current liabilities			
Creditors	24,000		
Bank overdraft	3,250	27,250	
Working capital			6,250
			151,250
Financed by:			
Capital account			
Balance at beginning		46,250	
Add profit for year		65,000	111,250
Long-term liability			
Bank loan			40,000
			151,250

4 Prepare a balance sheet as at 30 June from the following list of balances extracted from the books of Ashton and Tate.

	£
Premises	250,000
Machinery	95,000
Fixtures and fittings	30,000
Motor vehicles	41,000
Stock	42,550
Debtors	15,000
Bank	12,345
Cash	1,090
Creditors	14,000
Expenses owing	5,140

(cont'd.)

(cont'd.)

	£
Share of profit for the year:	
Ashton	105,000
Tate	152,500
Capital accounts	
Balance at beginning of year:	
Ashton	80,345
Tate	130,000

Answer

Using the same advice as in the previous question, identify all the assets and liabilities, and classify them into either fixed or current. The illustration of net assets is now straightforward. As the business is a partnership, two capital accounts are required, one for Ashton and one for Tate. Illustrate them side by side, as in the earlier example of partnership accounts. Your answer should appear as follows:

Balance sheet
as at 30 June

	£	£	£
Fixed assets			
Premises			250,000
Machinery			95,000
Fixtures and fittings			30,000
Motor vehicles			41,000
			416,000
Current assets			
Stock	42,550		
Debtors	15,000		
Bank	12,345		
Cash	1,090	70,985	
Less Current liabilities			
Creditors	14,000		
Expenses owing	5,140	19,140	
Working capital			51,845
			467,845

Financed by:
Capital accounts

	Ashton	Tate	
Balances at beginning	80,345	130,000	
Add share of profits	105,000	152,500	
	185,345	282,500	467,845

Further reading

E. G. Bellamy, A. Colvin and J. O'Neill *Numeracy and Accounting* (Collins Educational), chapters 6 and 7.

3 The income statement

The income statement is a combination of two separate accounts, the **trading account** and the **profit and loss account**. It is still common for examiners, and textbook writers, to refer to both these accounts separately.

The balance sheet is limited in its utility as a provider of information about the financial position of a business. **Profit** is shown, but there is no information regarding the levels of expenses, total sales, or of any miscellaneous income received. In other words, there is no indication of how the profit was earned. This chapter explains the structure of the income statement, its presentation, and how the statement reflects the different forms of ownership a business may have, and the effect of the type of business activity. Also, adjustments to the payments and receipts in the income statement such as **accruals** and **prepayments** are explained.

Please note that a common collective term for the income statement and the balance sheet is the **final accounts**. The reader may initially find it confusing that the text refers to both the income statement and to the trading and profit and loss accounts. Remember that both these accounts are divisions of the income statement.

The most common type of examination question on this topic is for the student to be given a trial balance, then required to make adjustments to a number of items and to prepare an income statement and balance sheet. Other complications include **partnerships**, **non-profit making** and **manufacturing businesses**.

3.1 Structure of the income statement

3.1.1 The trader

Businesses such as newsagents, grocers and sports shops are known as **traders**; so are department stores and supermarkets. One thing that they have in common is the way in which they conduct their business: they buy goods from their suppliers at one price and sell the goods to their customers at a higher price. The difference between the two prices, the cost and selling prices, is known as **gross profit**. Of course, all traders have to pay other expenses such as rent, rates, heating and staff costs. Once the total of such running expenses has been deducted from the gross profit, the result is the **net profit** (or loss). The income statement illustrates the calculation of both profits thus:

Income statement
for the year ended 30 June

		£
Sales		100,000
Less cost of sales		45,000
Gross profit	*Day-to-day costs*	55,000
Less expenses ←	*such as rent etc.*	22,500
Net profit		32,500

This simple example shows the basic structure of the statement, and all subsequent examples will follow this pattern. There will be more detail, many adjustments to make for different forms of ownership and business activity, but this basic structure is used.

3.1.2 Cost of sales

For less complicated businesses, such as the sole trader, it is common to show how the cost of sales has been calculated. This is done by deducting the stock left unsold at the end of the year from the stock available for sale during the year thus:

Opening stock ⟵ *i.e. goods unsold at end of previous year*

add

Purchases ⟵ *i.e. goods bought during the year*

less

Closing stock ⟵ *i.e. goods unsold at end of current year*

equals

Cost of sales

Using the following figures:

	£
Opening stock	15,000
Purchases	50,000
Closing stock	20,000

the income statement is illustrated thus:

Income statement
for the year ended 30 June

	£	£
Sales		100,000
Less cost of sales		
Opening stock	15,000	
Purchases	50,000	
	65,000	
Closing stock	20,000	45,000
Gross profit		55,000
Less expenses		22,500
Net profit		32,500

The reason for illustrating the calculation is to show how the cost of sales is made up.

3.1.3 Revenue and capital expenditure

It is important to distinguish between expenditure which is entered on the income statement, and that which is entered on the balance sheet. **Capital expenditure** either increases or decreases the worth of a business, and should be entered on the balance sheet. Spending on assets and repayment of liabilities, therefore, is capital expenditure.

Revenue expenditure is expenditure on items which are used up during the business cycle within which the business operates. Either a gain or a loss is made on these items, and all such expenditure appears on the income statement.

Most items are easy to classify, but drawings are one with which many students have difficulty. Drawings represent a withdrawal of the owner's capital, and so always appear on the balance sheet. The effect of misclassifying expenditure is twofold: first, net profit is either over- or understated. Drawings or assets may be included as expenses, thus overstating the value of expenses. Secondly, the worth of the business may be incorrectly represented: assets and liabilities may be over- or understated.

3.2 The manufacturer

Many businesses transform raw materials into a finished product, using a manufacturing process. Thus there are two elements to the business: **manufacturing** and **trading**. This requires an additional statement, known as the **manufacturing account**. This account follows a formal structure encompassing the extra operations which take place in a manufacturing business. The purchases figure in the trading account is replaced by the production cost of finished goods, and stocks are divided into raw materials, work in progress (partly manufactured goods) and finished goods.

3.2.1 Prime cost

The cost of producing most products comprises raw materials, labour expenses, and overheads. Costs, such as operative's wages or royalties, which can be attributed directly to the making of an item, are known as direct costs. The total of the direct costs is known as the **prime cost**.

3.2.2 Overheads

All costs, other than direct costs, are known as overheads: for example rent, rates, light and heat. These costs are difficult to attribute to the production of a specific product.

3.2.3 The manufacturing account

**Manufacturing account
for the year ended 30 June**

Opening stock of raw materials
Add purchases of raw materials
Less closing stock of raw materials _____
Cost of raw materials consumed

Direct labour
Direct expenses
Prime cost _____

Add factory overheads
Rent
Rates
Power
Lubricants
Factory cost _____

Opening work-in-progress
Closing work-in-progress
Production cost of finished goods _____

Only those costs which are associated with the factory are entered in the manufacturing account. Other costs, such as administration and selling overheads, are entered in the income statement. The object of the manufacturing account is to calculate the production cost of finished goods, therefore no income is entered into this account. Production costs are transferred to the trading part of the income statement, replacing the purchases figure. Consider the following example:

	£
Trading costs:	
Opening stock of finished goods	60,000
Closing stock of finished goods	75,000
Sales	400,000
Manufacturing costs: raw materials	
Opening stock	33,000
Closing stock	42,000
Purchases	120,000
Direct labour	40,000
Direct expenses	2,000
Rent	24,000
Rates	12,000
Power	11,250
Lubricants	1,750
Work-in-progress	
Opening	26,000
Closing	30,000

Manufacturing account
for the year ended 30 June

	£	£
Opening stock of raw materials		33,000
Add purchases of raw materials		120,000
		153,000
Less closing stock of raw materials		42,000
Cost of raw materials consumed		111,000
Direct labour	40,000	
Direct expenses	2,000	42,000
Prime cost		153,000
Add factory overheads		
Rent	24,000	
Rates	12,000	
Power	11,250	
Lubricants	1,750	49,000
Factory cost		202,000
Add opening work-in-progress		26,000
		228,000
Less closing work-in-progress		30,000
Production cost of finished goods		198,000

Income statement
for the year ended 30 June

	£	£
Sales		400,000
Less cost of sales		
Opening stock	60,000	*From manufacturing*
Production cost of finished goods	198,000 ←	*account*
	258,000	
Closing stock	75,000	183,000
Gross profit		217,000

3.2.4 Complications

Examiners recognize that the structure of a manufacturing account is straightforward to learn, and that few students have any difficulty in memorizing the layout. Consequently, a number of complications are introduced to questions in order to test the understanding of the candidate.

The most common complication involves having to calculate the market value of finished goods. If a manufacturer were to purchase goods from outside sources, instead of manufacturing the goods himself, he would have to pay a higher price than his own production cost. The manufacturer might be said to make two gross profits, one on manufacturing and one on trading. Examination questions may either require you to calculate the market value, by increasing the production cost by a given percentage, or may alternatively give the market value and require you to deduct the production cost, to arrive at the gross profit on manufacture. Using the example shown earlier, with the firm making 10 per cent gross profit on manufacture, the calculation of market value would be as follows:

Extract from the manufacturing account

	£
Production cost of finished goods	198,000
Gross profit on manufacture (10%)	19,800
Market value of finished goods	217,800

The income statement appears as follows:

Income statement for the year ended 30th June

	£	£
Sales		400,000
Less cost of sales		
Opening stock	60,000	
Market value of finished goods	217,800	
	277,800	
Closing stock	75,000	202,800
Gross profit on trading		197,200
Gross profit on manufacture		19,800
Overall gross profit		217,000

Note that there is no change in the overall gross profit; the only difference is in the presentation of the gross profit and the market value of the finished goods.

The second type of complication is the calculation of factory managers' commission. This is often based upon the gross profit on manufacture, but sometimes the commission is expressed as a percentage of the profits which remain after charging the commission. In order to calculate the commission in the latter case, use the formula:

$$\frac{\text{percentage commission}}{100 + \text{percentage commission}} \times \begin{array}{l}\text{Profit before} \\ \text{commission}\end{array}$$

Using the previously derived gross profit on manufacture, and assuming a rate of commission of 5 per cent, the calculation is as follows:

$$\frac{5}{105} \times 19,800 = 943$$

Finally, some types of question may require you to apportion costs between the manufacturing account and the income statement. Only one figure will be given for costs such as rent and rates, and at the end of the question the required proportions of the division will be given.

3.3 Adjustments

3.3.1 Prepayments and accruals

The **matching** or **accrual concept** (see chapter 7) requires the matching of the revenue of a year with the costs incurred to generate that revenue. However, there are instances when not all the costs incurred within a period will have actually been paid. A good example is the payment of operatives' wages, which are often paid one week in arrears. Thus at the end of an accounting year, a business may owe one week's wages to its total labour force. By the same token, a business may make payments in advance, for example, rent for a factory or retail premises. In both cases, adjustments have to be made to the relevant accounts in order to show a true profit for the year. Costs which have to be included in the accounts, e.g. wages arrears, are known as accruals; costs which have to be excluded, e.g. rent paid in advance, are known as prepayments.

3.3.2 Illustration in the accounts

Using the example of the manufacturer, if the following adjustments have to be made:

	£
Direct labour wages in arrears	3,000
Rent paid in advance	5,000

The accounts in the general ledger would be:

Direct labour account

Debit			*Represents payments made this year*	Credit			
Date	*Details*	*Folio*	£	*Date*	*Details*	*Folio*	£
June 30	Balance	b/d ←	40,000	June 30	P & L acct.		43,000
" 30	Accrual	c/d	3,000				
			43,000				43,000
Paid in this year →	July 1	Accrual	b/d	3,000

The accrual represents a liability, therefore the balance is shown under current liabilities on the balance sheet. Note that both a debit and a credit have been made, thus the double-entry has been carried out.

Rent account

Debit				Credit			
Date	Details	Folio	£	Date	Details	Folio	£
June 30	Balance	b/d	12,000	June 30	Prepayment	c/d	5,000
				" 30	P & L acct.		7,000
			12,000				12,000
July 1	Prepayment	b/d	5,000				

The prepayment represents an asset, in that a cost has been paid in advance of its occurrence. Therefore, it is entered as a current asset in the balance sheet.

3.3.3 Provision for bad debts, discounts on debtors

In order to show a true and fair view of a firm's affairs, it is important to examine each asset to ensure that the value representing the asset is true. It is unlikely, for instance, that a firm will be able to collect all the debts owing: customers may move, become bankrupt or dispute a debt. Should a customer become bankrupt, any outstanding debt is written off to the income statement as an expense, although this only occurs when it is certain that the debt is irrecoverable. The ledger would appear as follows:

Assume total debtors balance of £15,000.

Customers account

Debit				Credit			
Date	Details	Folio	£	Date	Details	Folio	£
Dec 31	Balance	b/d	2,000	Dec 31	Bad debts acct.		2,000

Bad debts account

Debit				Credit			
Date	Details	Folio	£	Date	Details	Folio	£
Dec 31	Customer's acct.		2,000	Dec 31	P & L acct.		2,000

Of the remaining debtors, the owner may feel that a certain percentage, say 1 per cent, are likely to become bad in the foreseeable future. It is prudent for the owner to make a provision for future bad debts in the accounting period in which they have occurred, thus an account is opened and the provision is made on the new debtors figure after the bad debt has been written off. Entries in the ledger are as follows:

Provision for bad debts account

Debit				Credit			
Date	Details	Folio	£	Date	Details	Folio	£
Dec 31	Balance	c/d	180	Dec 31	P & L acct.		180
				Jan 1	Balance	b/d	180

Both bad debts and provision for bad debt appear as separate expenses in the income statement.

The balance on the provision for bad debts account is carried forward to the next year, when it may be either increased or decreased, according to economic conditions. In the balance sheet the balance is shown as a reduction in the debtors balance under current assets. It is important to note that once a balance has been established, only the increases in the balance are shown as an expense on the income statement; any decreases are shown as a gain after the gross profit.

A common complication in examinations is to show an existing balance in the trial balance, and ask a candidate to either increase, or more commonly decrease, the provision. Consider the following example, which is an extension of the previous illustration:

The provision for bad debts is to remain at 1 per cent of the total debtors each year. Calculate the amount to be provided for, and show the illustration in the income statement. Debtors for 1986 were £18,000, for 1987 £20,000 and for 1988 £19,000.

Set out the answer in tabular form:

	Debtors	Provision	Entry in the income statement	
			Expense	Gain
	£	£	£	£
1986	18,000	180	180	–
1987	20,000	200	20	–
1988	19,000	190	–	10

Once the provision is established, it is like a pool that is added to or taken from, depending upon whether debtors increase or decrease.

There is one further reason why the debtors figure may need adjusting: it is common for firms to offer a discount to encourage customers to settle their debts promptly; thus it is extremely unlikely that the full amount of all debts will be collected. So a further provision is made, for discounts on debtors, which operates in exactly the same way as the bad debts provision.

This variation hardly ever appears in an examination question, but you never know. The procedure for dealing with this provision is exactly the same: open an account, make the provision, and make a corresponding entry in the income statement and the balance sheet. Make sure, when you are calculating the discount, that you base your figure on the debtors **after** the bad debts provision has been deducted.

3.4 Partnerships

Final accounts should always cater for the changing circumstances of the business which is being reported on. If there is more than one owner in a business, profits must be shared; the exact proportion of the division will be determined by a partnership agreement. Any such agreement should cover the following accounting requirements:

1 capital to be contributed by each partner;

2 division of profits and losses;

3 interest to be charged on drawings;

4 interest to be charged on capital;

5 partners' salaries;

6 duration of partnership;

7 partners' drawings;

8 arbitration in the event of disputes.

If no partnership exists, then the Partnership Act 1890 Section 24 makes the following provisions:

1 profits and losses are to be shared equally;

2 no interest is allowed on capital;

3 no interest is charged on drawings;

4 salaries are not allowed;

5 partners are entitled to 5 per cent interest per annum on any advances made to the firm in excess of capital (i.e. loans).

The sharing of profits and losses, and other adjustments, are carried out on an additional statement, the **appropriation account**, attached to the end of the income statement. Using the figures from section 3.2.2, but introducing two partners, Horton and Jones, who share profits and losses equally, the illustration would be as follows:

Income statement
for the year ended 30 June

	£	£
Sales		100,000
Less cost of sales		
Opening stock	15,000	
Purchases	50,000	
	65,000	
Closing stock	20,000	45,000
Gross profit		55,000
Less expenses		22,500
Net profit		32,500
Share of profits:		
Horton	16,250	
Jones	16,250	32,500

} *Appropriation account*

All adjustments concerning the appropriation of profits are carried out in the appropriation account. Using the previous example, the following adjustments might be made:

		£
Interest on drawings:	Horton	1,200
	Jones	1,800
Interest on capital:	Horton	2,200
	Jones	3,000

These adjustments must be made before the profits are shared between the partners. Interest on drawings is charged to the partners, and so is an addition to the business profits. The appropriation account would then appear as follows:

	£	£
Net profit		32,500
Add interest on drawings:		
Horton	1,200	
Jones	1,800	3,000
Share of profits:		35,500
Less interest on capital:		
Horton	2,200	
Jones	3,000	5,200
		30,300
Horton	15,150	
Jones	15,150	30,300

Quite often, the partners will not actually receive or pay out cash; instead, their capital accounts are adjusted. In chapter 2, the capital account for a simple version of the Horton and Jones partnership was illustrated. The same format is used, except that the initial capital that the partners contributed is kept separate from the yearly increases and decreases which are entered in a current account. The balance sheet extract is as follows:

	Fixed £	£	£
Capital accounts			
Horton	4,000		
Jones	4,000		8,000

Current accounts	Horton	Jones	
Interest on capital	2,200	3,000	
Share of profit	15,150	15,150	
	17,350	18,150	
Less interest on drawings	1,200	1,800	
	16,150	16,350	32,500

3.5 Non-profit-making organizations

Social clubs, charities, etc., neither trade nor manufacture; nor do they aim to make a profit. Therefore, none of the statements shown so far are appropriate vehicles for reporting on the financial activities of these organizations. Instead, an **income and expenditure account** is used, to show a **surplus** or **deficit**, rather than a profit or loss. This account is similar to the profit and loss part of the income statement: capital is replaced by accumulated fund in the balance sheet, and surpluses are added to the balance and deficits deducted from it.

Consider the following example of the results extracted from the books of the Budgie Breeders' Society as at 31 July:

	£
Subscriptions received	1,200
Refreshment profits	67
Magazine purchases	250
Printing and stationery	123
Hall fees	150
Cost of prizes	54
Accumulated fund at start of year	1,369

Income and expenditure account for the year ended 31 July

Income	£	£
Subscriptions	1,200	
Refreshment profits	67	1,267
Expenditure		
Magazines	250	
Printing and stationery	123	
Hall fees	150	
Prizes	54	577
Surplus of income over expenditure		690

Balance sheet extract as at 31 July

Financed by accumulated fund	£	£
Balance at beginning	1,369	
Surplus for year	690	2,059

It is highly unlikely that the Treasurer or Secretary will have prepared full double-entry records for the club or society, therefore adjustments for incomplete records (which are examined in chapter 6) have to be applied.

The problems of accruals and prepayments are often examined, using subscriptions in arrear and advance to complicate matters. The subscriptions figure of £1,200 for the Budgie Breeders' Society was arrived at in the following way:

Subscriptions account

Debit				Credit			
Date	Details	Folio	£	Date	Details	Folio	£
June 1	Arrears	b/d	87	June 1	Advance	b/d	71

These balances brought down from the previous year's arrears are a debit, because they are owed to the society.

Subscriptions account

Debit				Credit			
Date	Details	Folio	£	Date	Details	Folio	£
June 1	Arrears	b/d	87	June 1	Advance	b/d	71
Dec 31	Advance	c/d	95	Dec 31	Cash Rec.		1,261
Dec 31	Inc. & Ex. acct.		1,200	Dec 31	Arrears	c/d	50
			1,382				1,382
June 1	Arrears	b/d	50	June 1	Advance	b/d	95

Although £1,261 was received during the year from members, £87 related to the previous year's accounts. This year, arrears are smaller, at £50. Last year some members' payments in advance amounted to £71, and this increased to £95 in the current year. Only those subscriptions relating to the current year are to be included in the income and expenditure account.

Some questions require a trading account to be shown, which calculates the profit on one of the club's activities, such as the bar. This may be in double-entry or vertical form, and must include sales, purchases, and opening and closing stocks. An example is given at the end of this chapter.

Summary

1 The income statement calculates gross and net profit.

2 Cost of sales is obtained by deducting the closing stock of goods from the cost of the goods available for sale.

3 Revenue expenditure is included in the income statement, and capital expenditure is included on the balance sheet.

4 A manufacturing account calculates the production cost of finished goods.

5 Prepayments are payments in advance; accruals are payment in arrears.

6 In order to show a true and fair view of debtors, provision must be made for bad debts and discounts on debts.

7 The distribution of partners' profits is carried out in the appropriation account.

8 Non-profit-making organizations use an income and expenditure account to record surpluses and deficits.

Links with other topics

The income statement is linked directly with the chapters on the balance sheet and the recording of transactions. The reasons for adjustments are based upon the accounting theory in chapter 7 on accounting concepts and conventions, and in chapter 9 on accounting standards. A sound knowledge of adjustments is required in incomplete records and funds flow statements.

Sample questions

1 The following trial balance has been extracted from the ledger of Mr Yousef, a sole trader.

Trial balance as at 31 May 1986

	Dr £	Cr £
Sales		138,078
Purchases	82,350	
Carriage	5,144	
Drawings	7,800	
Rent, rates and insurance	6,622	
Postage and stationery	3,001	
Advertising	1,330	
Salaries and wages	26,420	
Bad debts	877	
Provision for bad debts		130
Debtors	12,120	
Creditors		6,471
Cash on hand	177	
Cash at bank	1,002	
Stock as at 1 June 1985	11,927	
Equipment at cost	58,000	
accumulated depreciation		19,000
Capital		53,091
	216,770	216,770

The following additional information as at 31 May 1986 is available:

(a) Rent is accrued by £210.

(b) Rates have been prepaid by £880.

(c) £2,211 of carriage represents carriage inwards on purchases.

(d) Equipment is to be depreciated at 15 per cent per annum using the straight line method.

(e) The provision for bad debts is to be increased by £40.

(f) Stock at the close of business has been valued at £13,551.

Required:

Prepare a trading and profit and loss account for the year ended 31 May 1986, and a balance sheet as at that date.

AAT

Answer

Always read through a question, and mark by the side of each item where it should go – in the income statement or on the balance sheet. Next, go through the notes and jot down what is required for each adjustment. When you have done that, you are now ready to prepare the final accounts.

Carriage must be divided between the trading account for carriage inwards, and the profit and loss account for carriage outwards. This is because carriage inwards is part of the cost of purchases, and carriage outwards is a selling cost. There is one prepayment and one accrual; both are straightforward and require no special calculations. Provision for bad debts already exists at £130, and is to be increased by £40 to appear in the balance sheet at £170. Remember that only the amount of the increase is charged to the profit and loss account; this is because £130 was provided for in the previous accounting period.

Mr Yousef: Income statement for the year ended 31 May 1986

	£	£	£
Sales			138,078
Less cost of sales			
Opening stock		11,927	
Purchases	82,350		
Carriage inwards	2,211	84,561	
		96,488	
Less closing stock		13,551	82,937
Gross profit			55,141
Less expenses			
Carriage outwards		2,933	
Rent, rates and insurance		5,952	
Postage and stationery		3,001	
Advertising		1,330	
Salaries and wages		26,420	
Bad debts		877	
Increase in bad debts provision		40	
Depreciation		8,700	49,253
Net profit			5,888

Balance sheet as at 31 May 1986

Assets	Cost	Depreciation to date	Net
Fixed	£	£	£
Equipment	58,000	27,700	30,300
Current			
Stock	13,551		
Debtors	12,120		
Less provision	170	11,950	
Prepayments		880	
Bank		1,002	
Cash		177	27,560

(cont'd.)

(cont'd.)	Cost	Depreciation to date	Net
	£	£	£
Less current liabilities			
Creditors	6,471		
Accruals	210	6,681	
Working capital			20,879
Net assets			51,179
Financed by:			
Capital		53,091	
Balance as at 1 June 1985		5,888	
Net profit		58,979	
Drawings		7,800	51,179

2 Grahame, Margo and Raj set up in partnership together some years ago with capitals of £50,000, £30,000 and £15,000 respectively. The following are summaries of the partners' current accounts for the year ended 31 December 1985. Study these carefully and then answer the questions which follow.

Current account – Grahame

1985		£	1985			£
Dec 31	Drawings	13,031	Jan 1	Balance	b/d	366
Dec 31	Share of balance	200	Dec 31	Interest on capital		6,000
Dec 31	Balance c/d	135	Dec 31	Salary		7,000
		13,366				13,366

Current account – Margo

1985		£	1985			£
Dec 31	Drawings	10,640	Jan 1	Balance	b/d	264
Dec 31	Share of balance	120	Dec 31	Interest on capital		3,600
			Dec 31	Salary		6,500
			Dec 31	Balance	c/d	396
		10,760				10,760

Current account – Raj

1985		£	1985		£
Jan 1	Balance b/d	133	Dec 31	Interest on capital	1,800
Dec 31	Drawings	7,598	Dec 31	Salary	5,500
Dec 31	Share of balance	80	Dec 31	Balance	511
		7,811			7,811

Required:

(a) Reconstruct the appropriation scheme, Grahame, Margo and Raj have agreed for the division of profits and losses.

(b) Calculate the net profit of the partnership for the year ended 31 December 1985.

(c) How would the partners have shared this profit had they made no formal agreement as to the division of profits?

(d) What would the partners' shares in profit have been had the net profit for the year ended 31 December 1985 been £60,000? *AAT*

Answer

Part (a)

The use of the term 'appropriation scheme' is misleading; an appropriation account is not required. Instead, you have to work out how the profits are shared, how much interest on capital is to be received by the partners, their salaries and the profit sharing ratio.

By examining each current account, partners' salaries can be seen to be:

Grahame   £7,000
Margo   £6,500
Raj   £5,500

Interest on capital is £6,000 for Grahame on a capital figure of £50,000; therefore the interest rate is 12 per cent.

Total profits received are £400, Grahame receiving £200 (.5), Margo receiving £120 (.3), and Raj receiving £80 (.2). Therefore the profit-sharing ratio is 5:3:2 respectively. No interest is charged on drawings.

Note that the profit share is a debit, which means that it is actually a loss.

Part (b)

By totalling each appropriation, profit can be calculated thus:

	£
Interest on capital	11,400
Salary	19,000
Share of balance	(400)
	30,000

Part (c)

Profits would have been shared equally.

Part (d)

	£	£	£
Net profit			60,000
Less: Interest on capital:			
Grahame	6,000		
Margo	3,600		
Raj	1,800	11,400	
Salaries: Grahame	7,000		
Margo	6,500		
Raj	5,500	19,000	30,400
			29,600
Share of profits:			
Grahame	14,800		
Margo	8,880		
Raj	5,920		29,600

3 The following balances as at 31 December 1985 have been extracted from the books of William Speed, a small manufacturer:

		£
Stocks at 1 January 1985:	Raw materials	7,000
	Work in progress	5,000
	Finished goods	6,900
Purchases of raw materials		38,000
Direct labour		28,000
Factory overheads:	Variable	16,000
	Fixed	9,000
Administrative expenses:	Rent and rates	19,000
	Heat and light	6,000
	Stationery and postage	2,000
	Staff salaries	19,380
Sales		192,000
Plant and machinery:	At cost	30,000
	Provision for depreciation	12,000
Motor vehicles (for sales deliveries):		
At cost		16,000
Provision for depreciation		4,000

(cont'd.)

	£
Creditors	5,500
Debtors	28,000
Drawings	11,500
Balance at bank	16,600
Capital at 1 January 1985	48,000
Provision for unrealized profit at 1 January 1985	1,380
Motor vehicle running costs	4,500

Additional information:

1 Stocks at 31 December 1985 were as follows:

	£
Raw materials	9,000
Work in progress	8,000
Finished goods	10,350

2 The factory output is transferred to the trading account at factory cost plus 25 per cent for factory profit. The finished goods stock is valued on the basis of amount transferred, to the debit of the trading account.

3 Depreciation is provided annually at the following percentages of the original cost of fixed assets held at the end of each financial year:

Plant and machinery	10%
Motor vehicles	25%

4 Amounts accrued due at 31 December 1985 for direct labour amounted to £3,000 and rent and rates prepaid at 31 December 1985 amounted to £2,000.

Required:
Prepare a manufacturing, trading and profit and loss account for the year ended 31 December 1985 and a balance sheet as at that date.
Note: The prime cost and total factory cost should be clearly shown.

AAT Intermediate

Answer

This question contains two complications, the first of which is depreciation. In the answer, calculate depreciation and include the plant in the manufacturing account and the motor vehicles in the profit and loss account. See chapter 5 for a detailed treatment of the subject.

Provision for unrealized profit arises when the value of finished goods includes a profit element. It is prudent not to allow an unrealized profit, i.e. a profit on goods not yet sold, to be included. However, as factory profit is included in the trading account to be consistent so should finished goods stock. So the profit element is excluded at the profit and loss account stage, and the amount of the profit is carried forward in the balance sheet to the next accounting period. The provision for unrealized profit account in this question appears as follows in the ledger:

Provision for unrealized profit account

Debit				**Credit**			
Date	Details	Folio	£	Date	Details	Folio	£
1985				1985			
Dec 31	Balance	c/d	2,070	Jan 1	Balance	b/d	1,380
				Dec 31	Profit and loss account		690
			2,070				2,070
				1986			
				Jan 1	Balance		2,070

The new balance for 1985 is arrived at by multiplying £10,350 by $\frac{25}{125}$. The provision is then deducted from the value of finished goods in stock, in the balance sheet, in order to bring the stock back to cost. There is one accrual and one prepayment, which are fairly straightforward.

William Speed—Manufacturing, trading and profit and loss account for the year ended 31 December 1985

	£	£
Materials consumed:		
Opening stock	7,000	
Purchases	38,000	
	45,000	
Less: Closing stock	9,000	36,000
Direct labour (£28,000 + £3,000)		31,000
Prime cost		67,000
Factory overheads:		
Variable	16,000	
Fixed	9,000	
Depreciation—Plant and machinery	3,000	28,000
		95,000
Add: Opening work in progress		5,000
		100,000
Less: Closing work in progress		8,000
Factory cost		92,000
Factory profit (25% of factory cost)		23,000
Market value of finished goods		115,000
Sales		192,000
Less: cost of sales—opening stock	6,900	
Market value of finished goods	115,000	
	121,900	
Less: Closing stock	10,350	111,550
Gross profit on trading		80,450
Gross profit on manufacture		23,000
		103,450
Administrative expenses:		
Rent and rates (£19,000 − £2,000)	17,000	
Heat and light	6,000	
Stationery and postage	2,000	
Staff salaries	19,380	
Motor expenses	4,500	
Depreciation	4,000	
Increase in provision for unrealized profit	690	53,570
Net profit		49,880

Balance sheet as at 31 December 1985

	£	Cost £	Aggregate £	Depreciation £
Fixed assets				
Plant and machinery		30,000	15,000	15,000
Motor vehicles		16,000	8,000	8,000
		46,000	23,000	23,000
Current assets:				
Stocks of raw materials		9,000		
Work in progress		8,000		
Finished goods	10,350			
Less: Provision for unrealized profit	2,070	8,280		
Debtors		28,000		
Amounts prepaid		2,000		
Balance at bank		16,600		
		71,880		

(cont'd.)

(*cont'd.*)

	£	£	£	£
Less current liabilities:				
Creditors	5,500			
Accrued charges	3,000	8,500		
Working capital				63,380
				86,380
Net assets				
Capital account:				
At 1 January 1985			48,000	
Add: Net profit for year			49,880	
			97,880	
Less: Drawings			11,500	86,380

4 The Treasurer of the Mells Social Club has extracted the following information from records that he has kept for the year to 31 July 1984. *ACCA Level 1*

1 Subscriptions received in cash from members during the year amounted to £97,000. At 31 July 1983, members had paid subscriptions in advance totalling £200, and £400 was in arrears. At 31 July 1984, £600 had been paid in cash for subscriptions in advance, whilst £300 of subscriptions were in arrears.

2 The club had sent four cheques to the Electricity Board during the year, amounting to £2,400. However, at 31 July 1983 the club owed the Board £700, and at 31 July 1984 there was an outstanding invoice for £500.

3 Bar purchases amounted to £5,000 paid in cash during the year, and £64,000 paid for by cheque. At 31 July 1983, £1,000 was owing to the brewery for bar purchases, and £1,600 was owing at 31 July 1984. Bar stocks were valued at £4,500 at 31 July 1983, and at £6,600 at 31 July 1984.

4 Cash sales at the bar were banked weekly, and no cash payments were made out of them. For the year to 31 July 1984, the total amount banked was £101,270.

5 Credit was very rarely allowed at the bar, but at 31 July 1983 the President owed £70 (which the club received on 31 August 1983) and at 31 July 1984 the new President owed £50.

You are required to:

Write up the following accounts in double entry format for the Mells Social Club:

(a) Subscriptions; (b) Electricity; and (c) Bar Trading.

Answer

Part (a)

This question is very similar to the 'Budgie Breeders' Society' example in the text, and should present no problems to you.

Subscriptions account

1983			£	1983			£
Aug 1	Arrears	b/d	400	Aug 1	Advance	b/d	200
1984				1984			
July 31	Income and expend. acct.		9,200	July 31	Cash		9,700
July 31	Advance	c/d	600	July 31	Arrears	c/d	300
			10,200				10,200
1984				1984			
Aug 1	Arrears	b/d	300	Aug 1	Advance	b/d	600

Part (b)

A simple accrual brought forward and a further adjustment to be made in this year's account.

Electricity Account

1984			£	1983				£
July 31	Bank		2,400	Aug 1	Accrual	b/d		700
				1984				
July 31	Accrual	c/d	500	July 31	Income and expend. acct.			2,200
			2,900					2,900
				1984				
				Aug 1	Accrual	b/d		500

Part (c)

Bar purchases—don't forget to adjust for the previous year's accrual as well as this year's. Bar Sales require adjusting for £70 received from the President, and the £50 owing by the new President.

Bar purchases account

1984			£	1983			£
July 31	Cash		5,000	Aug 1	Credits b/d		1,000
July 31	Bank		64,000	1984			
July 31	Credits		1,600	July 31	Trading a/c		69,600
			70,600				70,600
				1984			
				Aug 1	Creditors b/d		1,600

Bar sales account

1983			£	1984			£
Aug 1	Debitor b/d		70	July 31	Bank		101,270
1984				July 31	Debitor c/d		50
July 31	Trading account		101,250				
			101,320				101,320
1984							
Aug 1	Debitor b/d		50				

Bar trading account

		£	£
Sales			101,250
Less cost of sales			
Opening stock		4,500	
Purchases		69,600	
		74,100	
Closing stock		6,600	67,500
Bar profit			33,750

5 The following summarized trial balance as at 31 December 1986 has been extracted from the books of John Twigg and Raymond Branch trading as Treetop Stores:

	£	£
Fixed assets	55,000	
Current assets	30,000	
Current liabilities		17,000
Capital accounts:		
John Twigg at 1 January 1986		25,000
Raymond Branch at 1 July 1986		10,000
Net profit for the year ended 31 December 1986		42,000
Drawings: John Twigg	4,000	
Raymond Branch	5,000	
	94,000	94,000

Raymond Branch was admitted as a partner on 1 July 1986 when he paid into the business bank account £20,000 for the credit of his capital account. Unfortunately, only £10,000 was credited to the capital account, the balance was credited to the sales account. After the preparation of the above trial balance, it has been discovered that accounting entries have not been made for the following matters agreed upon the admission of Raymond Branch as a partner:

1 The valuation of land owned by John Twigg and included in the business accounts should be increased by £5,000.

2 Goodwill was valued at £17,000; however it is agreed that a goodwill account should not be opened in the business books.

3 John Twigg's capital account balance as from 1 July 1986 should be £35,000 credit, any excess being transferred to a John Twigg loan account.

The partnership agreement provides for:
1 Interest at 10 per cent per annum to be credited to partners for any loans to the business.

2 Raymond Branch to be credited with a partner's salary of £9,000 per annum.

3 Interest at 5 per cent per annum to be credited to partners on the balances of their capital accounts.

4 The balance of profits and losses to be divisible between John Twigg and Raymond Branch in the proportions 3/5ths and 2/5ths, respectively.

Note: It can be assumed that the net profit shown in the above trial balance accumulated uniformly throughout 1986.

Required:
(a) Prepare the capital accounts of John Twigg and Raymond Branch up to 31 December 1986. Note: Assume that current accounts are being maintained for each partner.
(b) Prepare the partnership profit and loss appropriation account for the period from 1 July to 31 December 1986.

AAT

Answer

Part (a)

Capital account – John Twigg

		£			£
1986			*1986*		
July 1	J. Twigg Loan	1,800	Jan 1	Balance b/d	25,000
July 1	Balance c/d	35,000	July 1	R. Branch (Goodwill)	6,800
			July 1	Land (revaluation)	5,000
		36,800			36,800
			July 1	Balance b/d	35,000

Capital account – Raymond Branch

		£			£
1986			*1986*		
July 1	J. Twigg Capital		July 1	Balance b/d	10,000
	(Goodwill)*	6,800	July 1	Sales	10,000
July 1	Balance c/d	13,200			
		20,000			20,000
			July 1	Balance b/d	13,200

*Goodwill adjustment = 2/5ths × £17,000 = £6,800.

Part (b) Net profit is adjusted as follows:

	£
Net profit 1 July to 31 December 1986	
Net profit for 1986 per trial balance at 31 December 1986	42,000
Less: transferred to Raymond Branch capital account	10,000
	32,000

(cont'd.)

(*cont'd.*)

		£
Adjusted net profit for six months ended 31 December 1986 before interest on partner's loan account		
		16,000
Less: Interest on John Twigg's loan account		90
		15,910

Appropriation account	£	£
Net profit		15,910
Less:		
Salary (Branch)	4,500	
Interest on capital:		
Twigg	875	
Branch	330	5,705
		10,205
Share of profits:		
Twigg	6,123	
Branch	4,082	10,205

6 Alan Smith is a director of Broadbent Limited, for which he receives an annual salary of £15,000 and owns half the share capital of the company. Alan's brother Norman is trading in partnership with Joseph Pain; under the partnership agreement Norman receives a partner's salary of £15,000 per annum and 50 per cent of the balance of the net profit or net loss. The partners withdraw from the partnership all partners' salaries and all shares of profits immediately these are computed on the last day of the relevant financial period. It is generally agreed that Norman Smith's services to the partnership business are worth £16,000 per annum. The summarized balance sheets as at 31 October 1987 of the company and partnership are as follows:

Broadbent Limited

	£
Net assets	160,000
Capital – ordinary shares of 50p each fully paid	100,000
Retained profits	60,000
	160,000

Notes:

1) Provision has been made in the accounts for the year ended 31 October 1987 for a proposed final dividend of 10p per share.

Note: The company does not pay interim dividends.

2) The company's net profit, after tax, for the year ended 31 October 1987 is £26,000.

3) Broadbent Limited did not issue any shares during the year ended 31 October 1987.

Norman Smith and Joseph Pain trading in partnership

	£
Net assets	160,000
Capital Accounts	
Norman Smith	80,000
Joseph Pain	80,000
	160,000

Note: The net profit for the year ended 31 October 1987 of the partnership is £36,000.

Required:

(a) Prepare the summarized balance sheet as at 31 October 1986 of Broadbent Limited.

(Note – Use a similar layout to that given in the question.)

(b) Prepare statements of the financial benefits which each of Alan and Norman Smith received from their respective businesses for the year ended 31 October 1987.

(c) Assuming that the partnership had been a limited company during the year ended 31 October 1987, paying market salary rates for all its staff, prepare a statement of its net profit for that year.

(d) Alan Smith has the opportunity to convert his shareholding in Broadbent Limited into £50,000 10 per cent Loan Stock in the company.

Using appropriate computations as necessary, advise Alan Smith of the advantages and disadvantages to him of converting his shareholding to loan stock.

AAT

Answer

Part (a)

Read this question carefully! You are required to prepare the summarized balance sheet as at **1986**. The 1987 appropriation of profit has to be reconstructed as follows:

	£
Net profit year ended 31 October 1987	26,000
Less: Dividend year ended 31 October 1987	20,000
Add: To retained profits	6,000

The 1986 retained profits can then be calculated:

	£
Retained profits at 31 October 1987	60,000
Less: Addition year ended 31 October 1987	6,000
Retained profits at 31 October 1986	54,000

Thus, the 1986 summarized balance sheet is as follows:

Broadbent Limited as at 31 October 1986

	£
Net assets	154,000
Capital – ordinary shares of 50p each fully paid	100,000
Retained profits	54,000
	154,000

Part (b)

Benefits year ended 31 October 1987

(NB Tax ignored)

	£
Alan Smith	
Director's salary	15,000
Dividends	10,000
	25,000

	£
Norman Smith	
Partner's salary	15,000
Half share balance of profits	10,500
	25,500

Part (c) Assuming partnership had been a limited company during year ended 31 October 1987:

	£
Net profit per partnership accounts	36,000
Less: Salary of Norman Smith at market rate	16,000
Net profit for company	20,000

Note: It is assumed that all salaries other than that of Norman Smith were considered at market rates in the original calculation of net profit.

Part (d) Benefits accruing to Alan Smith if shareholding converted to £50,000 10 per cent loan stock holding in Broadbent Limited:

Interest receivable £5,000 per annum regardless of net profit of company; the loa stock interest is a liability which the company has to honour. The option has possible attractions if the future stability of the company's profit is doubtful. However, otherwise the option may have fewer attractions for Alan Smith as it may not reflect the company's success.

7 The following trial balance as at 30 September 1987 has been extracted from the books of River, Stream and Pool who are trading in partnership:

	£	£
Freehold land and buildings – net book value	42,000	
Fixtures and fittings – net book value	16,000	
Stock	9,000	
Debtors	6,000	
Balance at bank	2,000	
Creditors		7,000
Capital accounts as at 1 October 1986:		
River		30,000
Stream		20,000
Pool		15,000
Current accounts as at 1 October 1986:		
River		1,000
Stream		700
Pool		—
Drawings:		
River	21,000	
Stream	13,000	
Pool	11,000	
Net profit for the year ended 30 September 1987 per draft accounts		46,300
	120,000	120,000

Pool joined River and Stream in partnership on 1 October 1986 under an agreement which included the following terms:

1 Pool to introduce £15,000 cash to be credited to his capital account.

2 The goodwill of the business of River and Stream as at 1 October 1986 to be valued at £28,000, but a goodwill account is not to be opened.

3 The value of the stock of River and Stream as at 1 October 1986 to be reduced from £9,000 to £7,000.

4 £10,000 is to be transferred on 1 October 1986 from River's capital account to the credit of a loan account; River to be credited with interest at the rate of 10 per cent per annum on his loan account balance.

5 Pool to be credited with a partner's salary of £11,000 per annum.

6 Interest at the rate of 5 per cent per annum to be credited to partners in respect of their adjusted capital account balances at 1 October 1986.

7 The balances of profits and losses to be shared between River, Stream and Pool in the ratio 5:3:2 respectively.

It now transpires that effect has not yet been given to the above terms **2** to **7** inclusive in the partnership books.

Up to 30 September 1986, River and Stream had no formal partnership agreement.

Required:
(a) Prepare the partnership profit and loss appropriation account for the year ended 30 September 1987.

(b) Prepare the partners' capital and current accounts for the year ended 30 September 1987.

AAT

Answer

Notes **3** and **4** affect the net profit, which must be adjusted as follows:

	£
Net profit for the year ended 30 September 1987 per draft accounts	46,300
+ Adjustment re-reduction in valuation of stock 1 October 1986 (Note 3)	2,000
	48,300
− Interest on River's loan account for year ended 30 September 1987 10% pa on £10,000 (Note 4)	1,000
	47,300

Part (a)

River, Stream and Pool
Profit and loss appropriation account
for the year ended 30 September 1987

	£		£		£
Partner's salary — Pool		11,000	Net profit b/d		47,300
Interest on partners' capital @ 5% pa					
River	950				
Stream	1,230				
Pool	470	2,650			
Balance — Divisible					
River	16,825				
Stream	10,095				
Pool	6,730	33,650			
		47,300			47,300

Part (b)

Goodwill is an intangible asset which is often used to compensate existing partners for their work prior to the admission of a new partner. The partners' capital accounts are used to make the adjustments. Goodwill in this case is calculated as follows:

Goodwill at 1 October 1987

	Old partnership £		New partnership £		Net effect (on capital balances) £	
River	14,000	Cr	14,000	Dr	Nil	
Stream	14,000	Cr	8,400	Dr	5,600	Cr
Pool	—		5,600	Dr	5,600	Dr
	28,000		28,000		—	

Partners' capital accounts
for the year ended 30 September 1987

	River £	Stream £	Pool £		River £	Stream £	Pool £
Adjustment Stock valuation	1,000	1,000		Balance b/f			
Goodwill			5,600	per draft accounts	30,000	20,000	15,000
Transfers to				Goodwill		5,600	
loan a/c	10,000						
Balances c/d	19,000	24,600	9,400				
	30,000	25,600	15,000		30,000	25,600	15,000
				Balances b/f	19,000	24,600	9,400

Partners' current accounts
for the year ended 30 September 1987

	River £	Stream £	Pool £		River £	Stream £	Pool £
Drawings	21,000	13,000	11,000	Balance b/f	1,000	700	—
Balance c/d			7,200	Loan interest	1,000		
				Interest on partners' capital @ 5%	950	1,230	470
				Partner's salary			11,000
				Balance of profit	16,825	10,095	6,730
				Balances c/d	1,225	975	—
	21,000	13,000	18,200		21,000	13,000	18,200
Balances b/d	1,225	975		Balances b/d			7,200

8 The following trial balance as at 31 March 1987 has been extracted from the books of the Skymaster Manufacturing Company Limited:

	£	£
Market value of goods manufactured	80,000	
Profit on goods manufactured		14,000
Provision for unrealized profit on goods manufactured at 31 March 1986		1,365
Stock of raw materials at 31 March 1987	5,000	
Stock of finished goods at 31 March 1986	7,800	
Work in progress at 31 March 1987	9,100	
Plant and machinery:		
at cost	29,000	
provision for depreciation at 31 March 1987		16,400
Shop fixtures and fittings:		
at cost	49,000	
provision for depreciation at 31 March 1986		9,800
Sales		130,000
Debtors/Creditors	12,700	8,000
Shop rent and rates	3,900	
Shop light and heat	7,600	
Shop salaries	11,700	
Balance at bank	4,300	
Share capital: ordinary shares of 50p each: fully paid		30,000
Retained earnings		10,535
	220,100	220,100

Additional information:

1 The stock of finished goods at 31 March 1987 has been valued, at market value, at £6,600.

Note: The company only sells goods it manufactures.

2 The provisions for unrealized profit on goods manufactured at 31 March 1987 is to be £1,155.

3 Depreciation is to be provided on shop fixtures and fittings at the rate of 10 per cent of the cost of assets held at the accounting year end.

4 Provision is to be made for a proposed dividend of 10p per ordinary share.

Required:

(a) Prepare a trading and profit and loss account for the year ended 31 March 1987 of the Skymaster Manufacturing Company Limited.

(b) A balance sheet as at 31 March 1987 of the Skymaster Manufacturing Company Limited.

AAT

Answer

There is no need to prepare a manufacturing account as the market value of goods manufactured is given. The provision for unrealized profit is dealt with as follows:

Provision for unrealized profit account

	£		£
Balance c/d (Note 2)	1,155	Balance b/d	1,365
Profit and loss account (balancing figure)	210		
	1,365		1,365
		Balance b/d	1,155

Part (a) **The Skymaster Manufacturing Company Limited Trading and profit and loss account for the year ended 31 March 1987**

	£	£
Sales		130,000
Less: Cost of sales:		
Opening stock of finished goods	7,800	
Market value of goods manufactured	80,000	
	87,800	
Less: Closing stock of finished goods	6,600	81,200
Gross profit		48,800
Less: Shop: salaries	11,700	
rent and rates	3,900	
light and heat	7,600	
Depreciation of shop fixtures and fittings	4,900	28,100
Net profit on sales		20,700
Profit on goods manufactured		14,000
Reduction in provision for unrealized profit on goods manufactured		210
Profit for the year		34,910
Retained earnings at 31 March 1986		10,535
		45,445
Proposed dividend of 10p per share		6,000
Retained earnings at 31 March 1987		39,445

Part (b)

Balance sheet as at 31 March 1987

	At cost	Aggregate depreciation	Net
	£	£	£
Assets			
Fixed			
Plant and machinery	29,000	16,400	12,600
Shop fixtures and fittings	49,000	14,700	34,300
	78,000	31,100	46,900
Current			
Stocks: raw materials	5,000		
finished goods*	5,445		
Work in progress	9,100	19,545	
Debtors		12,700	
Balance at bank		4,300	
		36,545	
Less current liabilities			
Creditors	8,000		
Proposed dividends	6,000	14,000	22,545
			69,445 (cont'd.

(contd.)

		£
Represented by:		
Share capital: ordinary shares of 50p each, fully paid		30,000
Retained earnings		39,445
		69,445

*Closing stock at market value (£6,600) less new provision for unrealized profit (£1,155).

9 The following receipts and payments account for the year ended 31 December 1986 for the Springtime Gardeners' Club has been prepared by the club's treasurer:

	£		£
Opening bank balance	876	National Gardening Show:	
Seed sales	1,684	purchase of tickets and	
National Gardening Show:		brochures	3,600
ticket sales to		Seed purchases	1,900
non-members	400	Lawn mower purchases	5,400
Lawn mower sales	3,800	Coaches to National	
Subscriptions received	7,190	Gardening Show	490
Closing bank overdraft	270	Club premises – rent	500
		Gardening magazines for	
		members' use	390
		Secretarial expenses	940
		Proposed new club building plans –	
		architect's fees	1,000
	14,220		14,220

The club's executive committee has now decided that members should receive an income and expenditure account for the year ended 31 December 1986 and a balance sheet as at that date.

Accordingly, the following additional information has been given:

1 Club assets and liabilities, other than bank balances or overdrafts:

As at:	1 January 1986	31 December 1986
	£	£
Plot of land for proposed new club building, bought 1 January 1980 for £2,000; current market value	5,000	5,500
Stocks of seeds, at cost	250	560
Debtors – lawn mower sales	400	1,370
Membership subscriptions received in advance	240	390
Creditors – lawn mower supplier	800	170
seed growers	110	340

2 The club sells lawn mowers at cost price to members; however the club never holds any stock of unsold lawn mowers.

3 Membership benefits include a ticket and transport to the National Gardening Show.

Required:

(a) Prepare the club's accumulated fund as at 1 January 1986.

(b) Prepare the club's income and expenditure account for the year ended 31 December 1986.

(c) Prepare the club's balance sheet as at 31 December 1986.

AAT

Answer

Adjustments have to be made to seed purchase, National Gardening Show tickets and subscriptions received. These adjustments are illustrated vertically, rather than horizontally, in the ledger accounts to show an alternative method of presentation.

	£
Seed purchases	
Cash paid	1,900
Less creditors at 1 January 1986	110
	1,790
Add creditors at 31 December 1986	340
	2,130
Less stock increase (£560 − £250)	310
	1,820
National Gardening Show	
Purchase of tickets and brochures	3,600
Coaches	490
	4,090
Less ticket sales to non-members	400
	3,690
Subscriptions	
Cash received	7,190
Add subscriptions paid in advance at 1 January 1986	240
	7,430
Less subscriptions paid in advance at 31 December 1986	390
	7,040

Part (a)

Springtime Gardeners' Club
Accumulated fund as at 1 January 1986

	£		£
Membership subscriptions		Bank	876
in advance	240	Debtors—	
Creditors—		lawn mower sales	400
lawn mower supplier	800	Stocks of seeds, at cost	250
seed growers	110	Land, at cost	2,000
Balance c/d	2,376		
	3,526		3,526
		Balance b/d	2,376

Part (b)

Income and expenditure account
for the year ended 31 December 1986

Income	£	£
Subscriptions		7,040
Less expenditure		
Loss on seed sales:		
Sales	1,684	
Less cost of sales	1,820	
	136	
National Gardening Show	3,690	
Garden magazines	390	
Secretarial expenses	940	
Rent of club premises	500	5,656
Excess of income over		
expenditure		1,384

Part (c)

Balance sheet as at 31 December 1986

	£	£	£
Fixed assets			
Land at cost		2,000	
Architect fees		1,000	3,000
Current assets			
Stocks of seeds, at cost		560	
Debtors – lawn mower sales		1,370	
		1,930	
Less current liabilities			
Creditors – Lawn mower supplier	170		
seed growers	340		
Membership subscriptions in advance	390		
Bank overdraft	270	1,170	760
			3,760
Represented by:			
Accumulated fund: at 1 January 1986			2,376
Add: Excess of income over expenditure for 1986			1,384
			3,760

10 (a) The balance sheet as at 31 December 1985 of Zoom Products Limited included:

Trade debtors   £85,360

The account for the year ended 31 December 1985 included a provision for doubtful debts at 31 December 1985 of 3 per cent of the balance outstanding from debtors. During 1986, the company's sales totalled £568,000 of which 90 per cent, in value, were on credit and £510,150 was received from credit customers in settlement of debts totalling £515,000. In addition, £3,000 was received from K. Dodds in settlement of a debt which had been written off as bad in 1985; this receipt has been credited to K. Dodd's account in the debtors' ledger.

On 30 December 1986, the following outstanding debts were written off as bad:

J. Sinder   £600
K. Lambert   £2,000

Entries relating to bad debts are passed through the provision for doubtful debts account whose balance at 31 December 1986 is to be 3 per cent of the amount due to the company from debtors at that date.

Required:

(i) Write up the provision for doubtful debts accounts for the year ended 31 December 1986 bringing down the balance at 1 January 1987.

(ii) Prepare a computation of the amount to be shown as 'trade debtors' in the company's balance sheet at 31 December 1986.

(b) On 1 January 1985, J. Cort Limited purchased the following fixed assets upon the opening of a new department producing cakes:

Cake mixing machine   £20,000
Delivery vehicle   £25,000

Provision for depreciation for these assets was made as follows:

Cake mixing machine   10% per annum reducing balance method

Delivery vehicle   20% per annum straight line method

On 1 January 1987, the company closed the cake department and sold the cake mixing machine and delivery vehicle to Creamy Cakes Limited for £23,000, payment to be made on 1 March 1987.

The 'accounting year end of J. Cort Limited is 31 December.

A sale of cake department fixed assets account is to be opened in the books of J. Cort Limited.

Required:

Prepare the journal entry (or entries) recording the disposal of the cake department fixed assets, on 1 January 1987.

AAT

Note: Journal entries should be supported by narratives.

Answer

1 Trade debtors as at December 1985 per balance sheet (£85,360) are after deduction of the provision for doubtful debts; £85,360 is therefore 97 per cent of the debtors outstanding at 1 December 1985. Therefore:

	£
Debtors outstanding at 31 December 1985	88,000
Less provisions for doubtful debts (3%)	2,640
Debtors at 31 December 1985 per balance sheet	85,360

2

Debtors' ledger for the year ended 31 December 1986

1986		£	1986			£
Jan 1	Balance b/d	88,000	Dec 31	Bank		510,150
Dec 31	Sales		Dec 31	Discounts allowed		4,850
	(90% × £568,000)	511,200	Dec 31	Bank (K. Dodds)		3,000
Dec 31	Provision for		Dec 31	Provision for		
	doubtful debts			doubtful debts		
	(K. Dodds)	3,000		(£600 + £2,000)		2,600
			Dec 31	Balance c/d		81,600
		602,200				602,200

1987			
Jan 1	Balance b/d	81,600	

Provision for doubtful debts at 31 December 1986 = 3% × £81,600 = £2,448

Part (a) (i)

Zoom Products Limited
Provision for doubtful debts account
for the year ended 31 December 1986

1986			£	1986			£
Dec 30	Debtors' ledger			Jan 1	Balance b/d 1		2,640
	account:			Dec 31	Debtors ledger –		
	J. Sinder		600		K. Dodds		3,000
	K. Lambert		2,000				
Dec 31	Balance c/d 2		2,448				
			5,048				
Dec 31	Profit and loss						
	(balancing figure)		592				
			5,640				5,640

1987			
Jan 1	Balance b/d		2,448

(ii) Zoom Products Limited Balance Sheet as at 31 December 1986 will include Trade debtors £79,152 (81,600 less £2,448)

Part (b)

J. Cort Limited
Journal entries

1987		£	£
Jan 1	Cake mixing machine provision for		
	depreciation*	3,800	
	Delivery vehicle provision for		
	depreciation*	10,000	
	Sale of cake department fixed assets	31,200	
	Cake mixing machine at cost		20,000
	Delivery vehicle at cost		25,000
	being transfer of assets sold upon		
	closure of cake department		

(cont'd.

*For a detailed explanation of depreciation, see chapter 8, Accounting and depreciation.

(cont'd.)

			£	£
Jan 1	Creamy Cakes Limited		23,000	
	Sale of cake department fixed assets			23,000
	Being sale of cake department fixed assets; settlement to be on 1 March 1987			
Jan 1	Profit and loss			8,200
	Sales of cake department fixed assets		8,200	

11 In 1983 Keith Maltby had bought a café which he re-opened under the name 'Keith's Kaff'.

In February 1985, he rented a grocery shop which he renamed 'Keith's Larder'.

Notes on the operations of the businesses:

1 The annual rental of the grocery shop is £3,200, payable quarterly in advance on the last day of March, June, September and December.

2 The shop buys food in bulk both for resale to the public and for supply to the café. Food is transferred to the café at cost.

3 Each establishment is under the control of a manageress who is paid a basic salary plus a commission of 10 per cent (calculated to the nearest £1) of the net profit of her establishment *before* charging the commission (see note **9** but after crediting the Enterprise Grant instalment (see note **11**).

4 The office work for both establishments is carried out by the shop manageress who receives an annual payment of £600 for the extra responsibility. Two-thirds of this sum is charged to the café (see note **9**).

5 Maltby's accounting year runs from 1 April to 31 March and he accounts for the café and the shop as separate departments.

6 The shop manageress lives above the shop in self-contained accommodation for which she pays an inclusive rental of £60 per month, payable one month in arrears (see note **9**).

7 Depreciation of fixed assets is provided on the reducing balance method at the following rates:

	%
Premises	2
Fixtures, etc.	20
Vehicles	20

8 Closing stocks at 31 March 1987, at cost

	£
Food – café	3,513
– shop	1,774
Cleaning materials – café	30
– shop	24
Wrapping materials – café	10
– shop	12

9 At 31 March 1987

Electricity accrued – café	131
– shop	78
General expenses accrued – café	46
– shop	68
Shop manageress' office allowance due	600
Shop manageress' accommodation rent receivable	60
Commission – café manageress	to be calculated
– shop manageress	to be calculated
Rent payable prepaid – shop	800

10 On 31 March 1986, Maltby had obtained a Business Development Loan for the café, to be repaid in one lump sum in 1991, at a concessionary rate of interest (10 per cent per annum), payable half yearly on 30 August and 31 March.

11 Maltby has also been awarded an Enterprise Grant of £5,000 for the café, with effect from 1 April 1986. He has decided to hold this sum in suspense and to credit it to the café profit and loss account in five equal instalments in the years ended

31 March 1987 to 1991, inclusive. However, at 31 March 1987 the £5,000 had not yet been received.

12 The sales of both the shop and the café are for cash, except that the café has a contract to supply meals to a local factory which is then invoiced with the cost, for which seven days' credit is allowed.

13 The overdraft finances Maltby's operations in general but is accounted for as a liability of the shop.

At 31 March 1987, the following balances were extracted from the ledger.

	Café £	Shop £
Premises (at cost)	25,000	—
Fixtures, fittings (at cost)	7,500	—
Vehicles (at cost)	—	6,000
Provisions for depreciation at 1 April 1986:		
Premises	6,000	—
Fixtures, fittings	1,600	—
Vehicles	—	1,000
Rent paid (see note 1)	—	4,000
Manageresses' salaries and related charges (see notes 3 and 9)	4,200	3,900
Assistants' wages and related charges	2,100	900
Electricity charges	1,874	851
Telephone charges	209	411
Stationery (see note 4)	—	126
Turnover	36,791	27,430
Food transferred from shop to café (see note 2)	19,427 (debit)	19,427 (credit)
Stocks at 1 April 1986:		
Food	1,272	303
Cleaning materials	44	32
Wrapping materials	27	28
Purchases:		
Food (see note 2)	—	30,432
Cleaning materials	71	68
Wrapping materials	45	53
Loan interest paid (see note 10)	700	—
Business development loan (see note 10)	7,000	—
Bank overdraft (seee note 13)	—	2,209
Bank overdraft interest (see note 13)	—	37
Creditors:		
Food	—	4,582
Other items	15	6
Rates (general and water)	2,943	1,864
General expenses	605	756
Cash	109	155
Rent receivable (see note 6)	—	660
Debtors:		
Trade (see note 12)	1,312	—

The only other balances are the personal accounts of the proprietor and are not allocated to departments:

	£
K. Maltby:	
Capital	9,000
Current account	1,634 (credit)

Required:
Prepare a departmental trading and profit and loss account for year ended 31 March 1987 and a departmental balance sheet at that date, in each case using separate columns for the café, the shop and the total business.

ACCA Level 1

Answer

This question requires the final accounts to be presented in tabular form, thus:

	Café		Shop		Total	
	£	£	£	£	£	£

There is a large volume of information which must be read through carefully. Approach this question systematically – make careful note of accruals, prepayments and any apportionments to be made between the café and the shop and between years, e.g. the Enterprise Grant.

K. Maltby
Trading and profit and loss account for year ended 31 March 1987

	Café		Shop		Total	
	£	£	£	£	£	£
Turnover		36,791		27,430		64,221
Less cost of sales						
Opening stock	1,272		303		1,575	
Purchases	—		30,432		30,432	
Transfers	19,427		(19,427)		—	
Closing stock	(3,513)	17,186	(1,774)	9,534	(5,287)	26,720
Gross profit		19,605		17,896		37,501
Add:						
Enterprise Grant (1/5 × 5,000)		1,000				1,000
Rent receivable (660 + 60)				720		720
		20,605		18,616		39,221
Less:						
Salaries, etc.:						
Manageresses	4,200		3,900		8,100	
Assistants	2,100		900		3,000	
Electricity (1,874 + 131; 851 + 78)	2,005		929		2,934	
Telephones	209		411		620	
Office allowance	400		200		600	
Rent payable (4,000 − 800)	—		3,200		3,200	
Stationery	—		126		126	
Cleaning materials (44 + 71 − 30; 32 + 68 − 24)	85		76		161	
Wrapping materials (27 + 45 − 10; 28 + 53 − 12)	62		69		131	
Development loan interest	700				700	
Overdraft interest	—		37		37	
Rates	2,943		1,864		4,807	
General expenses (605 + 46; 756 + 68)	651		824		1,475	
Depreciation:						
Premises (2% × 19,000)	380		—		380	
Fixtures, etc. (10% × 5,900)	590		—		590	
Vehicles (20% × 5,000)	—	14,325	1,000	13,536	1,000	27,861

(cont'd.)

(cont'd.)

	£	£	£
Net profit before commission	6,280	5,080	11,360
Commission (10%)	628	508	1,136
Net profit	5,652	4,572	10,224

K. Maltby
Balance sheet as at 31 March 1987

	Café		Shop		Total	
	£	£	£	£	£	£
Fixed assets						
Premises (cost)	25,000					
Less depreciation (6,000 + 380)	(6,380)	18,620		—	18,620	
Fixtures/fittings (cost)	7,500					
Less depreciation (1,600 + 590)	(2,190)	5,310		—	5,310	
Vehicles			6,000			
Less depreciation (1,000 + 1,000)			(2,000)	4,000	4,000	
		23,930		4,000		27,930
Current assets						
Stock:						
Food	3,513		1,774		5,287	
Cleaning materials	30		24		54	
Wrapping materials	10		12		22	
	3,553		1,810		5,363	
Debtors:						
Trade	1,312		—		1,312	
Rent receivable	—		60		60	
Enterprise Grant	5,000		—		5,000	
Prepaid rent	—		800		800	
Cash	109		155		264	
	9,974		2,825		12,799	
Less current liabilities						
Creditors:						
Food	—		4,582		4,582	
Other items	15		6		21	
Office allowance	—		600		600	
Commission	628		508		1,136	
Accruals (131 + 46; 78 + 68)	177		146		323	
Bank overdraft			2,209		2,209	
	820		8,051		8,871	
Working capital		9,154		(5,226)		3,928
Net assets employed		33,084		(1,226)		31,858

Further reading

A. Rowe *An Outline of Accounting Method* (Gee & Co), chapters 4, 9 and 10.
F. Wood *Business Accounting 1* (Pitman), fifth edition, chapters 7, 9, 21, 22 and 24.

4 Recording business transactions

Every time a firm buys an item, pays a bill or receives cash, this is known as a **transaction**. The recording of transactions is the theme of this chapter. The business of James Ferguson is used to illustrate the function of a 'T' account. The idea of a **debit** and **credit** is explained, and the balancing-off procedure is demonstrated. Finally, the duality of transactions is explained.

The recording of transactions is an integral part of any accounts course. Although the computer has replaced the repetitive recording that any junior clerk had to carry out in the past, examiners require the student to be able to open ledger accounts, record events accurately, and carry out checks on the validity of a business's records.

4.1 The account

In chapter 2, the use of the balance sheet to illustrate the worth of the firm was shown. If there were only a few purchases and sales in a year, a balance sheet could be drawn up after each transaction. This would indicate to the owner the firm's financial position, and would illustrate whether the worth of the firm had changed.

However, most firms carry out many transactions each day. Imagine the number made by ICI, for instance.

Therefore, it is impractical to draw up a balance sheet after each transaction. Also, a record of how much each customer owes, or how much is owed to each supplier, is required. So, every time a transaction occurs it is recorded in an **account**. This is a record of the date and value of a transaction, and an example is shown below:

Debit	Description of transaction		Reference No.					Credit		
Date	Details	Folio	£	p	Date	Details	Folio	£	p

Note that there are two sides to the account. The **debit** side is on the left, and the **credit** side is on the right. One side of the account, the debit, is used to record the **ins**, and one side, the credit, is used to record the **outs**.

Using the Ferguson transactions, listed below, it is possible to illustrate the use of accounts.

On 1 August the following cash transactions occurred:

	£
Sales	395.01
Rent	107.12
Gas	50.67
Electricity	61.13
Repairs	25.56
Insurance	100.43
Purchases	263.12

The first account to be opened is the **sales account**. All sales are recorded on the credit side of the account. This is because the credit side is the giving side. The cash account will receive the sale on its debit side. The entry is thus:

Debit						Sales account			Credit	
Date	Details	Folio	£	p	Date	Details	Folio	£	p
					Aug 1	Cash		395	01

All sales, whether cash, bank or credit, are entered on the credit side of the sales account.

Each account is separate, usually on an individual card or page. Only transactions involving sales are recorded in the sales account.

The rent value is entered on the debit side of the rent account. All costs are entered on the debit side, because they are the opposite to sales. The rent account appears as follows:

Debit						Rent account			Credit	
Date	Details	Folio	£	p	Date	Details	Folio	£	p
Aug 1	Cash		107	12					

Now use the accounts given below for each of the remaining costs. Record each transaction, and remember that all **costs** are recorded on the **debit** side of the account.

If you are unsure about a transaction, look at the answer at the end of the chapter for guidance.

Debit						Gas account			Credit	
Date	Details	Folio	£	p	Date	Details	Folio	£	p

Debit						Electricity account			Credit	
Date	Details	Folio	£	p	Date	Details	Folio	£	p

Debit						Repairs account			Credit	
Date	Details	Folio	£	p	Date	Details	Folio	£	p

Debit						Insurance account			Credit	
Date	Details	Folio	£	p	Date	Details	Folio	£	p

Debit						Purchases account			Credit	
Date	Details	Folio	£	p	Date	Details	Folio	£	p

4.1.1 Balancing off

At the end of each month, every account is closed and the balance is carried down to the next month, to become the opening balance. Then additional transactions in that month are added to that opening balance. Look at Ferguson's complete sales account for August:

Debit					Sales account				Credit	
Date	Details	Folio	£	p	Date	Details	Folio		£	p
					Aug 1	Goods			395	01
					6				472	12
					10				512	12
					12				256	95
					18				190	10
					26				403	60
					30				198	83

The object is to make the value of both sides of the account agree, i.e. the account **balances**.

Steps in balancing the account are as follows:

1 Rule off both sides on the same line after the last value, thus:

Debit					Sales account			**Credit**	
Date	Details	Folio	£	p	Date	Details	Folio	£	p
					Aug 1			395.01	
					6			472.12	
					10			512.21	
					12			256.95	
					18			190.10	
					26			403.60	
					30			198.83	

← Rulings are → level

2 Add up both sides and insert in the rulings the value of the greatest side:

Debit					Sales account			**Credit**	
Date	Details	Folio	£	p	Date	Details	Folio	£	p
					Aug 1			395.01	
					6			472.12	
					10			512.21	
					12			256.95	
					18			190.10	
					26			403.60	
					30			198.83	
			2,428.82					2,428.82	

← Totals → agree

3 Insert the difference between the two sides and describe it as balance:

Debit					Sales account			**Credit**	
Date	Details	Folio	£	p	Date	Details	Folio	£	p
Aug 31	Balance	c/d	2,428.82		Aug 1	Goods		395.01	
					6			472.12	
					10			512.21	
					12			256.95	
					18			190.10	
					26			403.60	
					30			198.83	
			2,428.82					2,428.82	

4 Bring down the balance on the opposite side:

Debit					Sales account				Credit	
Date	Details	Folio	£	p	Date	Details	Folio	£	p	
Aug 31	Balance	c/d	2,428.82		Aug 1	Goods		395.01		
					6			472.12		
	carried				10			512.21		
	down				12			256.95		
					18			190.10		
					26			403.60		
					30			198.83		
			2,428.82					2,428.82		
						brought				
						down				
					Sept 1	Balance	b/d	2,428.82		

When there is only one entry in the account, the account is still balanced off. The rent is balanced as follows:

Debit				Rent account				Credit	
Date	Details	Folio	£ p	Date	Details	Folio	£ p		
Aug 1	Cash		107.12	Aug 31	Balance		107.12		
Sept 1	Balance	b/d	107.12						

Now balance off all the other Ferguson accounts. Compare your answer with the one shown at the end of the chapter.

4.1.2 The dual aspect of transactions

In the example of Ferguson, all the transactions were cash transactions, so all items were entered in their respective accounts, e.g. sales, rent, etc. However, these transactions also affected the cash balance held by Ferguson. Some items increase the cash balance, and some items reduce the cash balance.

A record has to be kept of the value of the cash balance, and this done in the **cash account**. So each transaction has to be entered twice: once in its respective account, and once in the cash account. There are always two entries, and this is known as the **double-entry system**.

In the cash account, the second part of each transaction is entered. If an item increases the cash balance, it is entered on the debit side of the account; if it reduces the cash balance, it is entered on the credit side. Thus for each transaction there is a debit and a credit entry.

The cash account is illustrated below (assume an opening cash balance of £500):

Debit					Sales account				Credit	
Date	Details	Folio	£	p	Date	Details	Folio	£	p	
Aug 1	Balance	b/d	500.00		Aug 1	Rent		107.12		
1	Sales		395.01		1	Gas		50.67		
6	Sales		472.12		1	Electricity		61.13		
10	Sales		512.21		1	Repairs		25.56		
12	Sales		256.95		1	Insurance		100.43		
18	Sales		190.10		1	Purchases		263.12		
26	Sales		403.60		31	Balance	c/d	2,320.79		
30	Sales		198.83							
			2,928.82					2,928.82		
corresponding entry in sales account					*corresponding entry in purchases account*					
Sept 1	Balance	b/d	2,320.79							

4.1.3 Debit or a credit?

There are a number of rules which will help you to decide on which side of the account a transaction should be recorded.

1 **Cash and bank payments** are recorded on the **credit** side of the cash/bank account.

2 **Cash and bank receipts** are recorded on the **debit** side of the cash/bank account.

3 All **sales** are recorded on the **credit** side of the sales account.

4 All **purchases** are recorded on the **debit** side of the purchases account.

5 All **assets** are recorded on the **debit** side of the asset account.

6 All **liabilities** are recorded on the **credit** side of the liability account.

4.2 The ledger

As each account is a separate card or sheet, they are kept together in what is known as a ledger. This usually comprises a hardback binder containing a separate sheet for each account.

4.2.1 Division of the ledger

As there are many hundreds of transactions happening in a firm each week, a simple double-entry system using 'T' accounts would not be able to cope. Some accounts, such as cash, sales, and purchases, would be many pages long and the owner would have considerable difficulty in identifying individual totals for items such as discounts.

Therefore, the busy accounts are taken out and worked upon separately. The ledger is divided as follows:

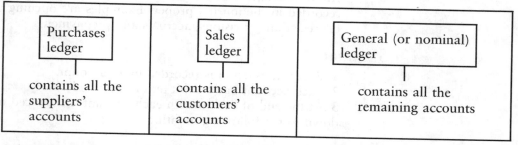

A further sub-division of the general ledger occurs as the firm increases in size, and it becomes impractical to record every single transaction in the general ledger. Thus the general ledger is divided:

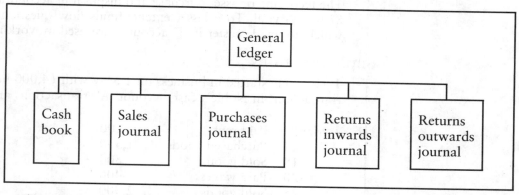

The cash book contains the receipts and payments for both cash and bank. An example of the ruling is shown below.

Debit
receipts

Credit
payments

Date	Details	Folio	Discount	Cash	Bank	Date	Details	Folio	Discount	Cash	Bank

The most frequently occurring entries in the sales and purchases accounts, namely the recording of invoices, is taken from the ledger and entered in the journals. Thus credit sales are recorded in the sales journal and credit purchases are recorded in the purchases journal. Only the entry which would have been recorded in the sales or purchases account is entered in the respective journal.

In the purchases journal all the purchases invoices are listed and then totalled, usually for the month. This total is then transferred to the debit side of the purchases account in the general or nominal ledger. The individual purchases invoices are posted to the respective suppliers accounts in the purchases ledger.

In the sales journal, all the sale invoices are listed and then totalled, usually for the month. This total is then transferred to the credit side of the sales account in the general or nominal ledger. The individual sales invoices are posted to the respective suppliers' accounts in the sales ledger.

A typical journal is as follows:

Date	Details	Folio	Net amount	VAT	Total	Analysis columns	

Purchase and sales returns, known as **returns outwards** and **inwards** respectively, are recorded in their own separate journals. The monthly totals are then posted to the relevant accounts in the general ledger.

4.2.2 The journal proper

All transactions which cannot go through the aforementioned ledgers and journals are recorded in the journal proper. Examples are opening entries, correction of errors, depreciation provisions, accruals and prepayments.

Summary

1 Every transaction is recorded in an account.
2 Each account has a debit and a credit side.
3 At the end of each month each account is balanced off and the balance is carried down to the following month.

Links with other topics

This topic underpins the whole of the course. A full understanding of double-entry is required in the verification of records (chapter 5), and incomplete records (chapter 6). The recording of asset purchase and disposal in accounting for depreciation (chapter 8) is also vital. To a lesser extent, funds flow questions require some calculations which are made easier if 'T' accounts are used in workings.

Sample questions

1 C. Noble started in business on 1 May with £4,000 in cash. Record the following transactions in Noble's cash account. All transactions are in cash:

		£
May 7	Paid rent	200
14	Purchased goods	1,300
18	Sold goods	800
20	Paid wages	400
25	Sold goods	2,900
28	Purchased goods	550
31	Paid wages	40

Now complete the double-entry by opening accounts for all the above transactions in the ledger.

Staffordshire Polytechnic

Understanding the question

This is a simple, straightforward question, which is designed to give you practice in the opening of accounts and carrying out double-entry.

Neat and accurate work is required at this stage. Make sure that you rule off and carry down the balances correctly.

Answer

Debit					Cash Account				Credit	
Date	Details	Folio	£	p	Date	Details	Folio	£	p	
May 7	Balance	c/d	4,000.00		May 7	Rent		200.00	
18	Sales		800.00		14	Purchases		1,300.00	
25	Sales		2,900.00		20	Wages		400.00	
					28	Purchases		550.00	
					31	Wages		40.00	
					31	Balance	c/d	5,210.00	
			7,700.00					7,700.00	
June 1	Balance	b/d	5,210 .00						

Sales account

May 31	Balance c/d	3,700		May 18	Cash	800	
				May 25	Cash	2,900	
		3,700				3,700	
				June 1	Balance b/d	3,700	

Rent account

May 7	Cash	200		May 31	Balance c/d	200
June 1	Balance b/d	200				

Purchases account

May 14	Cash	1,300		May 31	Balance c/d	1,850
May 28	Cash	550				
		1,850				1,850
June 1	Balance b/d	1,850				

Wages account

May 20	Cash	400		May 31	Balance c/d	440
May 31	Cash	40				
		440				440
June 1	Balance b/d	440				

2 T. Burn started in business with £20,000 in cash and £50,000 in the bank. Record the following transactions in the ledger:

			£
April	1	Bought goods by cheque	10,000
	3	Paid rent by cheque	2,000
	5	Sold goods for cash	8,000
	8	Paid wages in cash	1,200
	9	Sold goods by cheque	4,300
	12	Bought goods by cash	1,000
	14	Sold goods by cheque	9,000
	15	Paid wages in cash	1,200
	20	Printing expenses cash	150
	21	Bought goods by cash	2,500
	22	Paid wages by cash	1,200
	26	Sold goods by cheque	4,000
	28	Bought goods by cheque	2,000
	29	Paid wages by cash	1,200
	30	Sold goods for cash	500

Staffordshire Polytechnic

Understanding the question

This question introduces receipts and payments made through the bank for which a separate account is required. Otherwise there are no complications.

Answer

The balances on each account should be:
purchases £15,500, rent £2,000, wages £4,800, printing £150, sales £25,800, cash £20,050, bank £53,300.

Answer to first example:

Debit				Sales account			Credit
Date	*Details*	*Folio*	*£ p*	*Date*	*Details*	*Folio*	*£ p*
Aug 31	Balance	c/d	395.01	Aug 1	Goods		395.01
				Sept 1	Balance	b/d	395.01

Debit				Rent account			Credit
Date	*Details*	*Folio*	*£ p*	*Date*	*Details*	*Folio*	*£ p*
Aug 1	Cash		107.12	Aug 31	Balance	c/d	107.12
Sept 1	Balance	b/d	107.12				

Debit				Gas account			Credit
Date	*Details*	*Folio*	*£ p*	*Date*	*Details*	*Folio*	*£ p*
Aug 1	Cash		50.67	Aug 31	Balance	c/d	50.67
Sept 1	Balance	b/d	50.67				

Debit				Electricity account			Credit
Date	*Details*	*Folio*	*£ p*	*Date*	*Details*	*Folio*	*£ p*
Aug 1	Cash		61.13	Aug 31	Balance	c/d	61.13
Sept 1	Balance	b/d	61.13				

Debit				Repairs account			Credit
Date	*Details*	*Folio*	*£ p*	*Date*	*Details*	*Folio*	*£ p*
Aug 1	Cash		25.56	Aug 31	Balance	c/d	25.56
Sept 1	Balance	b/d	25.56				

Debit				Insurance account			Credit
Date	*Details*	*Folio*	*£ p*	*Date*	*Details*	*Folio*	*£ p*
Aug 1	Cash		100.43	Aug 31	Balance	c/d	100.43
Sept 1	Balance	b/d	100.43				

Debit				Purchases account	Credit		
Date	*Details*	*Folio*	*£ p*	*Date*	*Details*	*Folio*	*£ p*
Aug 1	Cash		263.12	Aug 31	Balance	c/d	263.12
Sept 1	Balance	b/d	263.12				

Further reading

E. G. Bellamy, A. Colvin and J. O'Neill *Numeracy and Accounting* (Collins Educational), chapters 4 and 5.

5 Verification of records

Once the transactions of a business have been recorded, there must be checks to ensure that the entries are correct and that the double-entry has been carried out. The **trial balance** is a check on the double-entry, sometimes used in conjunction with **control accounts**. The **bank reconciliation** verifies the bank balance in the cash book, and the **suspense account** is used as a holding account until errors are corrected.

Most questions on verification of records are of a practical nature; figures are given then errors must be discovered, corrected and/or balances verified. Some questions may combine two topics, usually the correction of errors and control accounts. Occasionally, some explanation may be required, for instance, of the functions of a trial balance or a suspense account.

5.1 The trial balance

At the end of an accounting period a list of all the balances is extracted from the ledger. This list is not part of the double-entry, so each debit balance in the ledger is entered in the debit column, and each credit entry is entered in the credit column. This list is known as a trial balance. If the total values of the two columns agree then the trial balance balances. This means that, all things being equal, the double-entry has been carried out correctly: there have been no incorrect additions, entries on one side of the books only, or a different amount entered on one side than on the other. However, this does not mean that no errors have been made; there are some errors which are not revealed by a trial balance. These are:

1 error of omission;
2 error of commission;
3 error of original entry;
4 error of principle;
5 compensating error;
6 complete reversal of entries.

5.1.1 Error of omission

This occurs when an entry is completely omitted from the books. Neither the debit nor credit sides are affected.

5.1.2 Error of commission

The correct double-entry has been carried out but the wrong person's account has been used, e.g. A. Smith instead of B. Smith.

5.1.3 Error of original entry

The double-entry is carried out correctly but the figure used is incorrect. A purchase invoice amounting to 110 is entered as 100. Everything is correct except the original amount.

5.1.4 Error of principle

If the purchase of fixtures is entered in the purchase of goods account, but correctly debiting and crediting.

5.1.5 Compensating error

An error on one side of an account is compensated, in value, by one or more errors on the other side.

5.1.6 Complete reversal of entries

If the debit and credit entries are reversed, as long as equal amounts are entered, then the trial balance will be unaffected.

5.2 Control accounts

In chapter 4 the division of the ledger was discussed. If one combined trial balance was extracted for all the different ledgers, i.e. general sales and purchases, every ledger would have to be checked if the trial balance did not balance. Therefore a type of trial balance is extracted for both the sales and purchases ledger. This is known as a control account, and is used primarily to verify each ledger.

Consider the following transactions for the month of January:

Jan 10 Sold goods on credit to R. Bailey £10,000
Jan 15 Sold goods on credit to J. Rowley £5,000
Jan 26 Sold goods on credit to G. Bancroft £3,000
Jan 28 Received £4,000 by cheque from R. Bailey
Jan 31 Received £4,800 from J. Rowley in full settlement

The entries in the sales ledger would be as follows:

Debit   **Credit**

R. Bailey account

Date	Details	Folio	£	Date	Details	Folio	£
Jan 10	Sales		10,000	Jan 28	Bank		4,000
				Jan 31	Balance	c/d	6,000
			10,000				10,000
Feb 1	Balance	b/d	6,000				

J. Rowley account

Date	Details	Folio	£	Date	Details	Folio	£
Jan 15	Sales		5,000	Jan 28	Bank		4,800
				Jan 31	Discount		200
			5,000				5,000

G. Bancroft account

Date	Details	Folio	£	Date	Details	Folio	£
Jan 26	Sales		3,000	Jan 31	Balance	c/d	3,000
Feb 1	Balance	b/d	3,000				

Normally a person in a responsible position, usually the sales ledger supervisor, prepares the control account for the sales ledger. In practice, there would be many, many more customer accounts than in this example. Independently of the individual accounts, the supervisor will use the totals entered in the sales ledger. In our example, the totals are:

Credit sales	£18,000
Receipts from customers	£ 8,800
Discounts allowed	£ 200
Balances	£ 9,000

These totals are taken from the sales journal and the cash book, in practice. The supervisor is now able to prepare a control account, which is an account containing the totals of all the individual accounts in the sales ledger. This account is balanced off, and the balance should agree with the total of all the individual balances extracted from the sales ledger. If the two figures agree then it can be assumed that the double-entry has been carried out correctly, as this is the equivalent of the trial balance balancing. The sales ledger control account is as follows:

Debit   **Credit**

Sales ledger control account

	£			£
Credit sales	18,000	Receipts from customers		8,800
		Discounts allowed		200
		Balances	c/d	9,000
	18,000			18,000
Balances	b/d	9,000		

If the balances do not agree, then the ledger is checked, the error located, and the control account is corrected.

There are three main uses of control accounts:

1 Location of errors

Mistakes can be traced to individual ledgers if the control accounts do not agree. This saves time, otherwise all ledgers have to be checked, if only a combined trial balance is extracted.

2 Prevention of fraud

Control accounts help to reduce the chances of fraud occurring. The control account is prepared by someone who is not involved in the day-to-day entries in the ledger. Any transfers to cover up fraud should be revealed by the control account. Collusion would be required in order to carry out fraud.

3 Ascertaining debtors and creditors

If these balances are required in a hurry, it is possible to use the totals only without waiting for the individual extraction of the balances.

When answering control account questions, there are two different approaches to adopt. In double-entry terms, a total goes on the same side in the control account as it does in the individual ledger. This applies to both sales and purchases ledger control accounts. An alternative approach is to start with the opening balances and take each item in turn, and work out its effect on the opening balances. If opening balances are increased by the item, then it is entered on the same side, and vice versa.

5.2.1 Complications

Firstly, the principles involved with purchase ledger control accounts are exactly the same, except items swap sides. Credit purchases are on the credit side and bank payments are on the debit side. Opening and closing balances are brought down on the credit side.

Secondly, there are a number of items which crop up that are intended to test the student's double-entry knowledge. The most common of these, and their treatment, are listed below:

Item	Effect on balances	Treatment in control account
Purchases returns	decrease	Debit
Sales returns	decrease	Credit
Discounts received	decrease	Debit
Discounts allowed	decrease	Credit
Bad debt written off	decrease	Credit
Customer's cheque dishonoured	increase	Debit
Interest charged on debtors	increase	Debit
Set-offs (contras)	decrease	Credit (sales)
		Debit (purchases)

5.3 Bank reconciliation statements

It is rare for the cash book balances to agree with the bank statement balance. This is because of differences in procedure between the bank and the firm's cashier or bookkeeper. Payments and receipts are entered in the cash book as soon as they arise, but the bank statement balance is not affected until a cheque passes through the clearing system. Also, some charges made by the bank are not communicated to the cashier until the bank statement is received.

The main items which have to be dealt with are:

1 Unpresented payments

Cheques sent to creditors which have not yet passed through the clearing system and been presented to the bank. They have, however, reduced the bank balance in the cash book.

2 Unpresented receipts

Cheques received from customers which have not yet been entered on the bank statement, but have increased the cash book bank balance.

3 Payments on the bank statement but not in the cash book

Items such as direct debits, standing orders and bank charges.

4 Receipts shown on the bank statement but not in the cash book

Dividends or interest received directly by the bank.

In order to ensure that any difference between the cash book and bank statement balances is because of procedural reasons and not error, a **bank reconciliation statement** is drawn up. This is an arithmetic proof which begins with either the bank statement or cash book balances, and adjustments are made for any discrepancies. Consider the following example:

J. Straw cash book (bank columns only)

Receipts				Payments				
			£					£
Feb 1	Balance	b/d	2,500	Feb 2	Green			135.80
Feb 10	Rice		149.75	Feb 14	Cray			250.50
Feb 17	Bloggs		230	Feb 19	Brown			117
				Feb 28	Balance	c/d		2,376.45
			2,879.75					2,879.75
	Balance	b/d	2,376.45					

Bank statement

Date	Details	Withdrawals	Deposits	Balance
		£		£
Feb 1				2,500.00
Feb 2		135.80		2,364.20
Feb 12	cc		149.75	2,513.95
Feb 16	00479	250.00		
Feb 16	Bank charges	155.00		2,108.45
Feb 17	cc		230.00	2,338.45

What to do:

Compare the cash book and bank statement, and note all the items of disagreement. Adjust all the items that can be put right in the cash book. Reconcile the rest in a reasonable statement, starting with one balance and finishing with the other.

The differences are:

1 Unpresented payment to Brown appears in the cash book, but not in the bank statement.

2 Bank charges on the bank statement, but not in the cash book.

The corrected balance on the cash book is:

			£				£
Feb 28	Balance	b/d	2,376.45	Feb 16	Bank charges		155
				Feb 28	Balance	c/d	2,221.45
			2,376.45				2,376.45
Mar 1	Balance	b/d	2,221.45				

Now the reconciliation of the two balances:

Bank reconciliation statement as at 28 Feb

	£
Corrected cash book balance	2,221.45
Add unpresented payment	117.00
Bank statement balance	2,338.45

It is possible to start off with the bank statement balance and arrive at the cash book balance, thus:

Bank reconciliation statement as at 28 Feb

	£
Bank statement balance	2,338.45
Less unpresented payment	117.00
Corrected cash balance	2,221.45

Both these statements verify the cash book balance. The differences between the cash book and bank statement balance arise out of procedural factors and are not errors.

5.3.1 Complications

Whichever balance you start with, you must consider the effect of each item on that balance. The following list is a guide to the treatment of the most common complications:

Item	Starting with cash book balance	Starting with bank statement balance
Unpresented receipts	deduct	add
Unpresented payments	add	deduct
Dishonoured cheques	enter in the cash book	
Standing orders	enter in the cash book	
Credit transfers	enter in the cash book	

The only other complication you are likely to encounter is the bank overdraft. When this occurs, the opposite treatment for the unpresented items applies.

5.4 The correction of errors and the suspense account

On a number of occasions it may not be possible to know how to treat a transaction. An amount received may be correctly debited, but the credit entry may be difficult to make because of uncertainty surrounding the customer.

It is also possible that a trial balance or a control account will not balance first time. If the discrepancy is not material, it is pointless to waste time looking for the reason. In both these cases, there are amounts which are 'looking for a home'. That home is a temporary account called the **suspense account**. It is used until either errors are discovered and corrected, or a place is found for the unidentified debit or credit. Once this is done, entries are required in the journal in order to clear the item(s) from the suspense account.

The journal is used to indicate the accounts which have been debited and credited, each set of entries accompanied by an explanatory narrative.

Consider the following example:

A trial balance did not agree, the credits exceeding the debits by £2,200, and immediately a suspense account was opened. Upon investigation, the following errors were discovered:

1 The purchase of a piece of equipment for £6,000 had been posted to the purchases account, instead of to the plant and machinery account.

2 The sales journal had been understated when totalled, by £4,000.

3 The payment of rent, £2,000, had been incorrectly entered in the rent account as £200.

Only those errors which prevent the trial balance balancing are entered in the suspense account. All other errors are corrected by journal entries only.

The first step is to open the suspense account, and enter the £2,200.

Suspense account

Error	2,200

Only errors 2 and 3 affect the trial balance, and their effect on its agreement must be assessed. One entry is required in the suspense account itself, and another entry is required to correct the error in the account affected. When the correction has taken place, the total debits must equal the total credits.

What has happened in error 2?

The sales are understated by £4,000. To correct this the sales account must be credited with £4,000 and, to complete the double-entry, the suspense account must be debited thus:

	£		£
Sales account	4,000	Error	2,200

What has happened to error?
The rent has been understated by £1,800. To correct this, the rent account must be debited and the suspense account credited, thus:

Suspense account

	£		£
Sales account	4,000	Error	2,200
		Rent account	1,800

Error 1 is an error of principle, and is corrected through the two accounts, purchases and plant and machinery, supported by entries in the journal. The suspense account is now clear and should be balanced off thus:

Suspense account

	£		£
Sales account	4,000	Error	2,200
		Rent account	1,800
	4,000		4,000

The journal is now used to support all the corrections which have taken place. It is traditional to use the debit column first. Each correction must have both a debit and a credit entry.

Journal

	Debit	Credit
	£	£
Plant and machinery account	6,000	
Purchases account		6,000
Correction of incorrect posting		
Suspense account	4,000	
Sales account		4,000
Undercasting of sales corrected		
Rent account	1,800	
Suspense account		1,800
Understating of purchases corrected		

Summary

1 The trial balance is used to verify that the double-entry has been carried out correctly. However, there are some errors which are not revealed by a trial balance.
2 A control account is a type of trial balance which is used to check whether the double-entry has been carried out correctly in both the sales and the purchase ledgers.
3 The bank reconciliation statement is used to verify the cash book balance.
4 The suspense account is a holding account for entries yet to be identified, or the balancing figure on a trial balance.
5 The journal is used to correct errors.

Links with other topics

All three topics are linked with chapter 4 (the recording of transactions). The correction of errors is linked to accounting concepts, such as matching.

Sample questions

1 The bank reconciliation statement as at 19 September 1986 for the account number 0439567 of John Henry Limited with Industrious Bank Plc showed that the difference between the cash book and bank statement was due entirely to four unpresented cheques, numbers 765417 to 765420 inclusive.

The cash book, bank columns, for the period from 19 September to 30 September 1986, for John Henry Limited is as follows:

1986	£	1986	Cheque	£
23 Sept B. Main	692.30	19 Sept Balance b/fwd		21.00
23 Sept T. Patrick	27.24	22 Sept S. Salter Ltd.	765421	25.67
25 Sept S. Saunders	410.00	22 Sept Sway District Council	765422	275.10
26 Sept P. King	400.00	23 Sept North South Electricity	Direct	
26 Sept K. Plunket	39.60	Authority	debit	316.50
28 Sept J. Lim	324.92	23 Sept John Peters Ltd.	765423	18.34
30 Sept S. Balk	220.39	24 Sept Furniture Trade	Standing	
		Association	order	45.00
		24 Sept K. Patel	765424	19.04
		25 Sept Cash (petty cash)	765425	50.00
		26 Sept J. Green Ltd.	765426	45.00
		26 Sept G. Glinker	765427	174.00
		29 Sept Deposit account		600.00
		29 Sept Wages	Transfer	390.00
		30 Sept Balance c/d.		134.80
	2,114.45			2,114.45
1 Oct Balance b/fwd	134.80			

Early in October 1986, John Henry Limited received the following statement from Industrious Bank Plc.

John Henry Ltd
Statement of account with Industrious Bank Plc
East Road, Streamly

Account number 0439567

Date 1986	Particulars	Payments £	Receipts £	Balance £
19 Sept	Balance			453.26
22 Sept	765419	138.35		314.91
23 Sept	Sundry credits		719.54	1,034.45
23 Sept	Direct debit	316.50		717.95
24 Sept	765421	25.67		692.28
24 Sept	Standing order	45.00		647.28
25 Sept	765420	160.04		487.24
26 Sept	765422	275.10		212.14
26 Sept	Sundry credits		400.00	612.14
26 Sept	Bank Giro credit		410.00	1,022.14
29 Sept	Bank Giro credit		334.92	1,357.06
29 Sept	765418	21.69		1,355.37
29 Sept	765424	19.04		1,316.33
29 Sept	Transfer to Deposit account	600.00		716.33
29 Sept	Transfer	390.00		326.33
29 Sept	765425	50.00		276.33
29 Sept	As advised		65.00	341.33
29 Sept	Bank Giro credit		39.60	380.93
30 Sept	Loan account interest	41.25		339.68
30 Sept	Bank charges	16.70		322.98

The following additional information is given:

1 The amount received from J. Lim on 28 September 1986 was £334.92 not £324.92;

2 The amount credited in the bank statement on 29 September 1986 and shown 'As advised £65.00' concerned dividends received;

3 John Henry Limited has written to the bank complaining concerning the bank charges of £16.70; the company's view is that no charges should arise for the month of September. The bank has a reputation for not cancelling bank charges.

Required:

(a) Prepare a bank reconciliation statement as at 30 September 1986.

Note: Indicate the amount which should be included in the balance sheet as at 30 September 1986 of John Henry Limited for the company's account number 0439567 with Industrious Bank Plc.

(b) What are the major uses of a bank reconciliation statement?

AAT Intermediate

Answer

(a) Adopting the approach recommended for this type of question, compare the cash book and bank statement and identify the differences. You may find it useful to tick each item that appears on both. Remember to tick off those cheque numbers 765417 to 765420 inclusive that refer to the previous bank reconciliation. 765417 is missing. It is important to work out the amount involved. The question states that the differences between the opening balance in the cash book (overdraft) and the bank statement balance is due to those unpresented cheques. So calculate that difference and deduct the total value of those cheques already presented to discover the value of the still unpresented cheque. Attempt this, and then compare your answer with the one in the reconciliation.

The differences are:

unpresented payments –	18.34	
	45.00	
	174.00	237.34
unpresented receipts –		220.39

Items on bank statement but not on cash book:

loan account interest –	41.25
bank charges	16.70
dividends received	65.00
one correction to make to a receipt in the cash book	
receipt	10.00

The next step is to correct the cash book:

Sept 30	balance b/d	134.80	Sept 30	Loan account		41.25
Sept 30	J. Lim	10.00		interest		
	(correction)		Sept 30	Bank charges		16.70
Sept 29	Dividends	65.00	Sept 30	Balance	b/d	151.85
		209.80				209.80

Oct 1	Balance b/d	151.85

Finally the reconciliation statement:–

Bank reconciliation statement as at 30 September

	£	£
Corrected cash book balance		151.85
Add unpresented payments	18.34	
	45.00	
	174.00	
from previous period	*154.18	391.52
		543.37
Less unpresented receipt		220.39
Bank statement balance		322.98
	21.69	
	138.35	
	160.04	320.08
		154.18

---

* Difference between two balances is £474.26 (£453.26 + £21.00, £474.26 less cheques already presented).

The amount to include in the balance sheet as at 30 September 1986 is the corrected cash book balance of £151.85.

(b) The two main uses of a reconciliation statement are the detection of errors and the verification of the cash book bank balance.

2 The bookkeeper of Excel Stores Ltd prepared a schedule of balances of individual suppliers' accounts from the creditors' ledger at 30 June 1984 and arrived at a total of £86,538.28.

He passed the schedule over to the accountant who compared this total with the closing balance on the creditors' ledger control account reproduced below:

Creditors' Ledger Control

1984		£	1984			£
June 30	Purchases returns	560.18	June 1	Balance b/d		89,271.13
30	Bank	96,312.70	30	Purchases		100,483.49
30	Balance c/d	84,688.31	30	Discount received		2,656.82
			30	Debtors ledger control (contras)		3,049.75
		192,561.19				195,261.19
			July 1	Balance b/d		84,688.31

During his investigation into the discrepancy between the two figures, the accountant discovered a number of errors in the control account and the individual ledger accounts and schedule. You may assume that the total of each item posted to the control account is correct except to the extent that they are dealt with in the list below:

(1) One supplier has been paid £10.22 out of petty cash. This had been correctly posted to his personal account but has been omitted from the control account.

(2) The credit side of one supplier's personal account had been under-added by £30.00.

(3) A credit balance on a supplier's account had been transposed from £548.14 to £584.41 when extracted on to the schedule.

(4) The balance on one supplier's account of £674.32 had been completely omitted from the schedule.

(5) Discounts received of £12.56 and £8.13 had been posted to the wrong side of two individual creditors' accounts.

(6) Goods costing £39.60 had been returned to the supplier but this transaction had been completely omitted from the returns day book.

Required:

(a) Prepare a statement starting with the original closing balance on the creditors' ledger control account, then identifying and correcting the errors in that account and concluding with an amended closing balance, and

(b) Prepare a statement starting with the original total of the schedule of individual creditors, then identifying and correcting errors in that schedule and concluding with an amended total. *ACCA Level 1*

Answer

This question uses the medium of control accounts to test the candidates' ability to detect and correct errors. This combines the topics of control accounts and the correction of errors.

	£	£
Original balance on control account at 30 June 1984		84,688.31
Error in deriving closing balance		11,000.00
		95,688.31
Items posted to wrong side of account:		
Discount received	2,656.82	
	2,656.82	
Contras	3,049.75	
	3,049.75	*(cont'd.)*

(*cont'd.*)		(11,413.14
		84,275.17
Purchase returns omitted		(39.60
		84,235.57
Error in credit side total		200.00
(195,461.19 − 195,261.19)		84,435.57

	£	£
Transposition error in debit side total		2,700.00
(195,261.19 − 192,561.19)		87,135.57
Petty cash payment omitted		(10.22
Amended balance on control account		87,125.35

		£
Original total of schedule of individual creditors at 30 June 1984		86,538.28
Item no.		
Add:		
(1) No effect		
(2)	30.00	
(4)	674.32	
		704.32
		87,242.60
Less:		
(3) (584.41 − 548.14)	36.27	
(5) (12.56 + 8.13)	20.69	
	20.69	
(6)	39.60	
Amended total of schedule of individual creditors		(117.25
at 30 June 1984		£87,125.35

3 Mainway Dealers Limited maintains a debtors' (sales) ledger and a creditors' (purchases) ledger.

The monthly accounts of the company for May 1986 are now being prepared and the following information is now available:

	£
Debtors' ledger as at 1 May 1986: Debit balances	16,72(
Credit balances	1,14(
Creditors' ledger as at 1 May 1986: Debit balances	28(
Credit balances	7,47(
Credit sales May 1986	19,38(
Credit purchases May 1986	6,70(
Cash and cheques received May 1986: Debtors' ledger	15,49'
Creditors' ledger	13(
Cheques paid May 1986: Debtors' ledger	47(
Creditors' ledger	6,32(
Credit notes issued May 1986 for goods returned by customers	1,19'
Credit notes received from suppliers May 1986 for goods returned by Mainway Dealers Limited	24(
*Cheques received and subsequently dishonoured May 1986: Debtors' ledger	32(
Discounts allowed May 1986	43(
Discounts received May 1986	33?
Bad debts written off May 1986	13
*Bad debt written off in December 1985 but recovered in May 1986 (R. Bell)	14?
Debtors' ledger as at 31 May 1986: Debit balances	To be determined
Credit balances	67(
Creditors' ledger as at 31 May 1986: Debit balances	36?
Credit balances	To be determined

It has been decided to set off a debt due from a customer, L. Green, of £300 against a debt due to L. Green of £1,200 in the creditors' ledger.

*Included in cash and cheques received May 1986 £15,497.

The company has decided to create a provision for doubtful debts of 2½ per cent of the amount due to Mainway Dealers Limited on 31 May 1986 according to the debtors' ledger control account.

Required:

(a) Prepare the debtors' ledger control account and the creditors' ledger control account for May 1986 in the books of Mainway Dealers Limited.

(b) An extract of the balance sheet as at 31 May 1986 of Mainway Dealers Limited relating to the company's trade debtors and trade creditors.

AAT

Answer

The information provided combines both sales and purchases ledger figures. Allocation of figures to the correct control accounts is essential.

(a) There are opening credit and debit balances for each control account. You have to determine the closing debtors and creditors after preparing the control accounts. Make sure that you do not include any irrelevant figures. Remember the provision for doubtful debts!

Mainway Dealers Limited
Debtors' Ledger Control Account May 1986

	£		£
Balance b/fwd	16,720	Balance b/fwd	1,146
Credit sales	19,380	Bank	15,497
Bank	470	Sales returns	1,198
Bank –		Discounts allowed	430
Cheques dishonoured	320	Bad debts written off	131
Bad debts recovered		Creditors' ledger control	
(R. Bell)	142	(Re. L. Green)	300
Balance c/d	670	Balance c/d	19,000
	37,702		37,702
Balance b/d	19,000	Balance c/d	670

Creditors' Ledger Control Account May 1986

	£		£
Balance b/fwd	280	Balance b/fwd	7,470
Bank	6,320	Credit purchases	6,700
Purchases returns	240	Bank	130
Discounts received	338	Balance c/d	365
Debtors' ledger control			
(Re. L. Green)	300		
Balance c/d	7,187		
	14,665		14,665
Balance b/d	365	Balance b/d	7,187

(b) Once the control accounts have been prepared you have to state the values of the trade creditors and debtors to appear in the balance sheet. Don't forget the provision for bad debts! Also a debit balance in the purchases ledger control account is a debtor, and vice versa.

Balance Sheet as at 31 May 1986 (Extract)

	£
Current Assets	
Trade Debtors	18,890
(£19,000 − £475*) + £365	
(*2½% × £19,000)	
Current Liabilities	
Trade Creditors	7,857
(£670 + £7,187)	

4 Allan Smith, an inexperienced accounts clerk, extracted the following trial balance, as at 31 March 1986, from the books of John Bold, a small trader:

	£	£
Purchases	75,950	
Sales		94,650
Trade debtors	7,170	
Trade creditors		4,730
Salaries	9,310	
Light and heat	760	
Printing and stationery	376	
Stock at 1 April 1985	5,100	
Stock at 31 March 1986		9,500
Provision for doubtful debts	110	
Balance at bank	2,300	
Cash in hand	360	
Freehold premises:		
At cost	22,000	
Provision for depreciation	8,800	
Motor vehicles:		
At cost	16,000	
Provision for depreciation	12,000	
Capital at 1 April 1985		23,096
Drawings		6,500
Suspense		21,760
	160,236	160,236

In the course of preparing the final accounts for the year ended 31 March 1986, the following discoveries were made:

(1) No entries have been made in the books for the following entries in the bank statements of John Bold:

1986	Payments	£
March 26	Bank charges	16
March 31	Cheque dishonoured	25

Note: The cheque dishonoured had been received earlier in March from Peter Good debtor.

(2) In arriving at the figure of £7,170 for trade debtors in the above trial balance, trade creditor (Lionel White £70) was included as a debtor.

(3) No entries have been made in the books for a credit sale to Mary Black on 29 March 1986 of goods of £160.

(4) No entries have been made in the books for goods costing £800 withdrawn from the business by John Bold for his own use.

(5) Cash sales of £700 in June 1985 have been posted to the credit of trade debtors accounts.

(6) Discounts received of £400 during the year under review have not been posted to the appropriate nominal ledger account.

(7) The remaining balance of the suspense account is due to cash sales for January and February 1986 being posted from the cash book to the debit of the purchase account.

Required:
(a) The journal entry necessary to correct for item 7 above.
Note: A narrative should be included.

(b) Prepare a corrected trial balance as at 31 March 1986. *AA*

Answer

This question requires a great deal of working out in order to answer part (a). The corrected trial balance is fairly straightforward.

The original balance on the suspense account is £21,760. However, the trial balance total is incorrect, because of the errors that have been made. So, the effect of those errors on the totals has to be calculated next:

Adjustments	Debits		Credits	
	+	−	+	−
	£	£	£	£
Provision for doubtful debts		110	110	
Stock at 31 March 1986				9,500
Freehold premises:				
Provision for depreciation		8,800	8,800	
Motor vehicles:				
Provision for depreciation		12,000	12,000	
Lionel White, trade creditor		70	70	
Drawings	6,500			6,500
	6,500	20,980	20,980	16,000
Net adjustments		14,480	4,980	

	£	£
Original trial balance totals (incorrect)	160,236	160,236
Net adjustments (see above)	−14,480	+4,980
	145,756	165,216
Less original suspense account balance (per trial balance)		−21,760
		143,456
Corrected suspense account balance		+2,300
	145,756	145,756

Suspense account	£		£
Discounts received	400	Balance per trial balance	2,300
Sundries			
(see journal entry below)	1,900		
	2,300		2,300

The new suspense account balance of £2,300 is corrected by the following journal entry:

John Bold

	Dr	Cr
	£	£
Suspense	1,900	
Sales		950
Purchases		950

Being correction of posting error; cash sales for January and February 1986 previously posted to debit of purchases.

John Bold
Trial Balance as at 31 March 1986 (corrected)

	£	£
Purchases (£75,950 − £800 − £950)	74,200	
Sales (£94,650 + £160 + £950 + £700)		96,460
Trade debtors (£7,170 + £25 + £700 − £70 − £160)	7,985	
Discounts received		400
Trade creditors (£4,730 + £70)		4,800
Salaries	9,310	
Light and heat	760	
Bank charges	16	
Printing and stationery	376	
Stock at 1 April 1985	5,100	
Provision for doubtful debts		110
Balance at bank (£2,300 − £16 − £25)	2,259	
Cash in hand	360	(cont'd.)

	£	£
Freehold premises: At cost	22,000	
Provision for depreciation		8,800
Motor vehicles: At cost	16,000	
Provision for depreciation		12,000
Capital at 1 April 1985		23,096
Drawings (£6,500 + £800)	7,300	
	145,666	145,666

5 A sales ledger control account and a purchase ledger control account are maintained as integral parts of the accounting records of James Swift Limited. The following information is relevant to the business of James Swift Limited for the year ended 30 November 1987.

1 Balances at 1 December 1986:

	£
Sales ledger	10,687 debit
	452 credit
Purchases ledger	1,630 debit
	9,536 credit

2 Sales totalled £130,382 whilst sales returns amounted to £1,810.

3 £127,900 was received from debtors in settlement of accounts totalling £130,650. In addition, £1,200 was received for a debt which had been written off as irrecoverable in the year ended 30 November 1986.

4 A debt of £350 due from J. Hancock was transferred to the purchases ledger and set off against a debt of £1,100 due to J. Hancock.

5 An amount of £560 due to James Swift Limited for goods supplied to T. Dick was written off as bad in November 1987.

6 Purchases amounted to £99,000 at list prices and purchases returns totalled £600 at list prices. All purchases and purchases returns were subject to a trade discount of 10 per cent.

7 £83,500 was paid to suppliers in settlement of debts due of £85,000.

8 Balances at 30 November 1987 included:

	£
Sales ledger	1,008 credit
Purchases ledger	760 debit

Required:
Prepare the following accounts for the year ended 30 November 1987 in the books of James Swift Limited:

(a) Sales ledger control

(b) Purchases ledger control

AA

Answer

Part (a)   **James Swift Limited year ended 30 November 1987**
Sales ledger control account

	£		£
Balance b/f	10,687	Balance b/f	452
Sales	130,382	Sales returns	1,810
Bad debt recovered	1,200	Discounts allowed	
Balance c/f	1,008	(£130,650 − £127,900)	2,750
		Cash received	127,900
		Cash received	
		(re. bad debt)	1,200
		Transfer to purchases	
		ledger	350

(cont'd.)

(cont'd.)

	£		£
		Bad debts written off	560
		Balance c/f	8,255
	143,277		143,277
Balance b/f	8,255	Balance b/f	1,008

Part (b)   **Purchases ledger control account**

	£		£
Balance c/f	1,630	Balance c/f	9,536
Purchases returns		Purchases	
(£600 less 10%)	540	(£99,000 less 10%)	89,100
Transfer from sales			
ledger	350		
Cash paid	83,500		
Discounts received	1,500		
Balance c/f	11,876	Balance c/f	760
	99,396		99,396
Balance c/f	760	Balance c/f	11,876

6 The draft balance sheet as at 31 August 1987 of Leslie Rivers Limited is as follows:

Fixed assets	Cost	Aggregate depreciation		Capital and reserves	
	£	£	£		£
Freehold property	20,000	11,550	8,450	Ordinary	
Motor vehicles	19,000	11,400	7,600	shares of	
	39,000	22,950	16,050	£1 each	
				issued and	
				fully paid	25,0(
Current assets				Profit and loss	
Stock		12,000		account	5,1(
Debtors		9,200			
Balance at bank		2,360			
		23,560			
Less creditors:					
Amounts falling due within one year					
Trade creditors	3,800				
Accrued charges	710	4,510	19,050		
			35,100		
Less creditors:					
Amounts falling due after more than one year					
Bank loan			5,000		
			30,100		30,1(

Notes:

1 The stock at 31 August 1987 includes goods received in July 1987 from Worldwide Products Limited on a sale or return basis. These goods, which remained unsold at 31 August 1987, had been recorded as purchased from the supplying company at the pro forma invoice price of £1,000.

2 A debt of £300 due to the company from Cable Products Ltd is now regarded as irrecoverable. However, this debt has been included in the debtors in the above draft balance sheet.

3 The company's directors have decided that a provision for doubtful debts of 3 per cent of debtors at 31 August 1987 is to be created.

4 A payment in August 1987 of £900 to K. Bream, trade creditor, has been posted from the cash book to the printing and stationery expenses account.

5 Provision is to be made for a proposed dividend for the year ended 31 August 1987 on the ordinary shares of 10p per ordinary share.

6 It can be assumed that a purchases ledger control account is not maintained.

Required:
(a) Prepare the corrected balance sheet as at 31 August 1987 of Leslie Rivers Limited.

(b) Prepare the journal entry (or entries) necessary for any corrections required for Note **1** above. Narratives are required.

AAT

Answer

Part (a)

Leslie Rivers Limited
Corrected balance sheet as at 31 August 1987

Fixed assets	Cost	Aggregate depreciation	
	£	£	£
Freehold premises	20,000	11,500	8,450
Motor vehicles	19,000	11,400	7,600
	39,000	22,950	16,050
Current assets			
Stock (£12,000 − £1,000)		11,000	
Debtors (£9,200 − £300 − £267)		8,633	
Balance at bank		2,360	
		21,993	
Less creditors:			
Amounts falling due within one year			
Trade creditors	1,900		
(£3,800 − £1,000 − £900)			
Accrued charges	710		
Proposed dividends	2,500	5,110	16,883
			32,933
Less: creditors:			
Amounts falling due after more than one year			
Bank loan			5,000
			27,933
Capital and reserves			
Ordinary Shares of £1 each issued and			
fully paid			25,000
Profit and loss account			
(£5,100 − £300 − £267 + £900 − £2,500)			2,933
			27,933

Part (b)

	Dr	Cr
	£	£
Worldwide Products Limited	1,000	1,000
Purchases		
Being correction of entry recording goods as purchased which had been received as 'on sale or return basis'.		
Profit and loss a/c (for the year ended 31 August 1987)	1,000	
Stock a/c		1,000
Being deletion from stock on 31 August 1987 of goods held at that date 'on sale or return basis'.		

7 The trial balance as at 30 April 1987 of Timber Products Limited was balanced by the inclusion of the following debit balance:

Difference on trial balance suspense account £2,513.

Subsequent investigations revealed the following errors:

1 Discounts received of £324 in January 1987 have been posted to the debit of the discounts allowed account.

2 Wages of £2,963 paid in February 1987 have not been posted from the cash book.

3 A remittance of £940 received from K. Mitcham in November 1986 has been posted to the credit of B. Mansell Limited.

4 In December 1986, the company took advantage of an opportunity to purchase a large quantity of stationery at a bargain price of £2,000. No adjustments have been made in the accounts for the fact that three quarters, in value, of this stationery was in stock on 30 April 1987.

5 A payment of £341 to J. Winters in January 1987 has been posted in the personal account as £143.

6 A remittance of £3,000 received from D. North, a credit customer, in April 1987 has been credited to sales.

The draft accounts for the year ended 30 April 1987 of Timber Products Limited show a net profit of £24,760.

Timber Products Limited has very few personal accounts and therefore does not maintain either a purchases ledger control account or a sales ledger control account.

Required:

(a) Prepare the difference on trial balance suspense account showing, where appropriate, the entries necessary to correct the accounting errors.

(b) Prepare a computation of the corrected net profit for the year ended 30 April 1987 following corrections for the above accounting errors.

(c) Outline the principal uses of trial balances.

AAT

Answer

Part (a)

Timber Products Limited
Difference on trial balance suspense account

	£		£
Balance per trial balance	2,513	Wages	2,963
Discounts allowed	324	J. Winters (£341 − £143)	198
Discounts received	324		
	3,161		3,161

Part (b) Computation of corrected net profit for the year ended 30 April 1987:

	£	£	£
Net profit per draft accounts			24,760
	Decreases	Increases	
1 Discounts		648	
2 Wages	2,963		
3 Remittance from K. Mitcham	No effect		
4 Stationery stock		1,500	
5 Payment to J. Winters	No effect		
6 Remittance from N. North	3,000		
	5,963	2,148	−3,815
Corrected net profit			20,945

71

Part (c) Principal uses of trial balances:

Evidence of accuracy of accounting records, subject to entries being completely omitted, compensating errors and postings to wrong accounts.

Useful source document for preparation of annual accounts.

Useful control document.

Further reading

F. Wood *Business Accounting 1* (Pitman), fifth edition, chapters 6, 29, 30 and 31.

6 Incomplete records

The owners of small businesses often have neither the time nor the expertise to keep a full set of **double-entry records**, and often there is not enough money for them to employ a bookkeeper to write up the records to the degree which we examined in chapter 4.

Other reasons for records being incomplete may be loss due to fire or theft, or the retirement or death of the bookkeeper. However, some records will have been kept, even if they are incomplete, and it is up to the accountant to derive a full set of final accounts from these records. This topic requires an application of all the knowledge gained so far.

Incomplete records are a popular subject area for examiners, because double-entry knowledge can be tested without requiring the candidate to write out all the accounts. Some questions ask just for a calculation of profit from given ratios, or changes in assets and liabilities; some questions require the preparation of a full set of final accounts.

6.1 Statement of affairs

It is possible to calculate the profit or loss made by a business by comparing the opening and closing assets and liabilities within an accounting period. The capital is calculated at the beginning and end of the period; any increase is attributed to a profit, any decrease is attributed to a loss. Consider the following list of assets and liabilities:

	1 January	31 December
	£	£
Motor van	4,500	4,050
Stock	2,900	3,200
Creditors	1,920	1,821
Debtors	4,190	2,050
Bank	2,900	–
Cash	136	245
Bank overdraft	–	198

A list of the opening assets and liabilities, known as a **statement of affairs**, is drawn up, and the opening capital is calculated. A closing statement of affairs is then drawn up, and the closing capital is calculated. The statements appear as follows:

Statement of affairs as at 1 January

	£	£	£
Assets:			
Fixed			
Motor van			4,500
Current			
Stock	2,900		
Debtors	4,190		
Bank	2,900		
Cash	136	10,126	
Less current liabilities			
Creditors		1,920	
Working capital			8,206
			12,706
Financed by:		*Balancing*	
Capital		*figure* →	12,706

The statement of affairs is similar to a balance sheet, except that no balances exist in a business which does not keep ledger accounts. The accounting equation still applies when calculating the capital. The closing statement of affairs is as follows:

Statement of affairs as at 31 December

Assets:
Fixed

The reduction in value must be because of depreciation ↘

	Cost £	Depreciation £	Net £
Motor van	4,500	450	4,050

Current

Stock	3,200	
Debtors	2,050	
Cash	245	5,495

Less current liabilities

Creditors	1,821	
Bank overdraft	198	2,019
Working capital		3,476
		7,526

Financed by:

Capital as at 1 January	12,706	Net
Less loss for the year	5,180	loss 7,526

In this example, the worth or capital of the business has fallen during the year. As the owner has not introduced any capital, nor have there been any drawings during the year, the reduction must be because of a net loss made.

6.2 Business ratios

More detail about the affairs of a business may be discovered by using some of the ratios examined in chapter 12. They are calculated as follows:

Term	Definition	Formula
Mark-up	Gross profit as a percentage of cost of sales	$\dfrac{\text{Gross profit}}{\text{Cost of sales}} \times 100$
Margin	Gross profit as a percentage of sales	$\dfrac{\text{Gross profit}}{\text{Sales}} \times 100$
Stockturn	The number of times the average stock is sold	$\dfrac{\text{Cost of sales}}{\text{Average stock}}$

These ratios are useful when trying to obtain a missing figure. For example:

What are a business's sales during the year if the firm adds $33\frac{1}{3}$ per cent to its cost of sales, which amounted to £60,000?

Answer:
First write down the mark-up formula, inserting the known figures:

$$\frac{\text{Gross profit}}{60,000} \times 100 = 33\tfrac{1}{3}\% \qquad \text{or} \qquad \frac{\text{Gross profit}}{60,000} = \tfrac{1}{3}$$

∴ Gross profit = £20,000

Then sales = gross profit + cost of sales = £80,000

Use exactly the same method to derive the margin and the stockturn, as follows:

A firm has a stockturn of 10 and an average stock of 35,000. What is its cost of sales?

Write down the relevant formula, using the known figures

$$\frac{\text{Cost of sales}}{35,000} = 10$$

Therefore cost of sales = £350,000.

6.3 Cash and bank summary

The more complete the information given, the more comprehensive a set of final accounts you can prepare. If a trader has kept a record of the total receipts and payments, classified into sales, purchases, rent, rates, etc., it is possible to determine the closing bank and cash balances, and to prepare an income statement. The structure of the **cash and bank summary** is as follows:

Receipts			Payments		
Description	*Cash*	*Bank*	*Description*	*Cash*	*Bank*
Opening balances			Purchases		
Sales			Expenses		
Other income			Closing balances		

The summary is similar to a combined cash and bank account, and it follows the same rules, except that only totals are used. It is used to calculate the closing bank and cash balances and to collect together all the ingredients of the final accounts.

6.4 Other adjustments and missing figures

Once the cash and bank summary is completed, adjustments such as prepayments and accruals have to be made. You may find it useful to set out your workings as they would appear in the books. For example:

A firm owed £6,000 to its trade suppliers at the beginning of the year and £7,200 at the end. During the year the cashier paid £45,000 to suppliers, receiving a credit note for faulty goods amounting to £120. If opening stock is £9,200 and closing stock is £10,100, calculate the value of purchases and cost of sales.

Answer:
As the only record available is the amount paid for purchases, the amounts owing at the beginning and end of the year have to be taken into account. Consider the effect of the amount owing at the beginning of the year: this relates to purchases received and mostly sold during last year. These creditors have been paid this year, and are included in this year's amount paid, therefore they must be excluded, by being entered on the credit side. Closing creditors, however, relate to the present accounting period, and therefore must be included by being entered on the debit side. The purchases account would be as follows:

Purchases account

Debit	£	**Credit**	£
Paid	45,000	Closing creditors	6,000
Closing creditors	7,200	Trading acct.	46,200
	52,200		52,200

To obtain the cost of sales:

	£	£
Opening stock		9,200
Purchases	46,200	
Less returns	120	46,080
		55,280
Less closing stock		10,100
Cost of Sales		45,180

A popular adjustment is to include payments made, usually, from cash takings. This is a common practice in many businesses, and the total of these payments must be added back to the takings to obtain the total sales for the year. See question 2 for a practical example.

Summary

1 The statement of affairs is a list of assets and liabilities of a firm as at a specific date, and is used to calculate the capital of a business.

2 Accounting ratios can be used to discover missing figures.

3 The cash and bank summary is used to collect all the payments and receipts together, and to calculate the closing cash and bank balances.

Sample questions

1 The following receipts and payments account for the year ended 31 October 1980 has been prepared from the current account bank statements of the Country Cousins Sports Club:

1979		£	1980		£
1 Nov	Balance b/fwd	1,700	31 Oct	Clubhouse:	
1980					
31 Oct	Subscriptions	8,600		Rates and insurance	380
	Bar takings	13,800		Decorations and repairs	910
	Donations	1,168		Annual dinner catering	650
	Annual dinner			Bar purchases	9,200
	Sale of tickets	470		Stationery and printing	248
				New sports equipment	2,463
				Hire of films	89
				Warden's salary	4,700
				Petty cash	94
				Balance c/fwd	7,004
		25,738			25,738

The following additional information has been given:

At 31 October:	1979	1980
	£	£
Clubhouse, at cost	15,000	15,000
Bar stocks, at cost	1,840	2,360
Petty cash float	30	10
Bank deposit account	600	730
Subscriptions received in advance	210	360
Creditors for bar supplies	2,400	1,900

It has been decided to provide for depreciation annually on the clubhouse at the rate of 10 per cent of cost, and on the new sports equipment at the rate of $33\frac{1}{3}$ per cent of cost.

The petty cash float is used exclusively for postages.

The only entry in the bank deposit account during the year ended 31 October 1980 concerns interest.

One-quarter of the warden's salary, and one-half of the clubhouse costs, including depreciation, are to be apportioned to the bar.

The donations received during the year ended 31 October 1980 are for the new coaching bursary fund, which will be utilized for the provision of training facilities for promising young sportsmen and sportswomen. It is expected to make the first award during 1981.

Required:

(a) An account showing the profit or loss for the year ended 31 October 1980 on the operation of the bar.

(b) An income and expenditure account for the year ended 31 October 1980, and a balance sheet at that date for the Country Cousins Sports Club.

(c) Outline the advantages and disadvantages of apportioning costs in accounting.

ACCA Level 1

Answer

This question combines the concept of incomplete records with the requirements of non-profit-making organizations.

The receipts and payments account is given, thus eliminating the need to prepare a cash and bank summary. The first step is to prepare a statement of affairs as at 1 September 1979, in order to calculate the accumulated fund. Don't forget to include the opening balance in the bank current account.

**Statement of affairs
as at 1 September 1979**

	£	£	£
Assets:			
Fixed			
Clubhouse at cost			15,000
Current			
Bar stocks	1,840		
Bank deposit account	600		
Bank current account	1,700		
Petty cash float	30	4,170	
Less current liabilities			
Creditors for bar supplies	2,400		
Subscriptions in advance	210	2,610	
Working capital			1,560
			16,560
Accumulated fund			16,560

Now the first part of the question can be answered:

Part (a)

Bar purchases are arrived at by using an account:

Bar purchases account

Debit	£	Credit	£
Paid	9,200	Opening creditors	2,400
Closing creditors	1,900	Trading acct.	8,700
	11,100		11,110

One quarter of the warden's salary and one half of the clubhouse costs are to be apportioned to the bar thus:

	£	£
Clubhouse costs are: Rates and insurance		380
Decorations and repairs		910
Clubhouse depreciation		1,500
		2,790
Apportioned: Bar half	1,395	
Other half	1,395	2,790

Bar trading and profit and loss account
Year ending 31 October 1980

	£	£
Sales		13,800
Less cost of sales:		
Opening stock	1,840	
Purchases	8,700	
	10,540	
Less closing stock	2,360	8,180
Gross profit		5,620
Less expenses:		
Proportion of warden's salary	1,175	
Proportion of clubhouse costs	1,395	2,570
Net profit		3,050

Part (b)

Before the income and expenditure account can be prepared, adjustments must be made to subscriptions, postage and the annual dinner figures.

Subscriptions account

		£			£
Advance	c/d	360	Advance	b/d	210
Income and expenditure		8,450	Receipts		8,600
		8,810			8,810

The postages adjustment is as follows:

Postages account

		£			£
Float	b/d	30	Income and expenditure acct.		114
Transfers during year		94	Float	c/d	10
		124			124

For the annual dinner:

	£
Ticket sales	470
Less catering expenses	650
Loss on dinner	180

The final item to consider, before preparing the income and expenditure account, is the treatment of the donations received for the coaching bursary fund. Is it capital or revenue expenditure? As the fund is for a specific purpose, to be used as and when required, it is capital expenditure and must be shown on the balance sheet.

Income and expenditure account
for the year ended 31 October 1980

	£	£
Income		
Subscriptions	8,450	
Bar profit	3,050	
Bank interest	130	11,630
Expenditure		
Clubhouse costs	1,395	
Warden's salary	3,525	
Loss on annual dinner	180	
Sports equipment depreciation	821	
Film hire	89	
Stationery and printing	248	
Postages	114	6,372
Surplus of income over expenditure		5,258

The balance sheet can now be prepared; don't forget that all the adjustments made earlier, such as the subscriptions in advance, must also be included at this stage.

Balance sheet
as at 31 October 1980

Assets:
Fixed

	Cost	Depreciation to date	Net
	£	£	£
Clubhouse	15,000	1,500	13,500
Sports equipment	2,463	821	1,642
	17,463	2,321	15,142

Current

Bar stocks	2,360	
Bank: deposit account	730	
current account	7,004	
Petty cash float	10	10,104

Less current liabilities:

Creditors	1,900		
Subscriptions in advance	360	2,260	
Working capital			7,844
Net assets			22,986

Financed by:
Accumulated fund

Balance as at 1.9.79	16,560	
Surplus of income over expenditure	5,258	21,818
Coaching bursary fund		1,168
		22,986

Part (c)

The objective in apportioning costs to a specific activity is to provide a complete picture of the benefit received from that activity. This is an application of the accounting concept of matching costs incurred in generating revenue. The problem associated with apportionment is that of subjectivity. Many assessments of proportions are arbitrary.

2 Jean Smith, who retails wooden ornaments, has been so busy since she commenced business on 1 April 1985 that she has neglected to keep adequate accounting records. Jean's opening capital consisted of her life savings of £15,000, which she used to open a business bank account. The transactions in this bank account during the year ended 31 March 1986 have been summarized from the bank account as follows:

Receipts:	£
Loan from John Peacock, uncle	10,000
Takings	42,000

Payments:	
Purchases of goods for resale	26,400
Electricity for period to 31 December 1985	760
Rent of premises for 15 months to 30 June 1986	3,500
Rates of premises for the year ended 31 March 1986	1,200
Wages of assistants	14,700
Purchase of van, 1 October 1985	7,600
Purchase of holiday caravan for Jean Smith's private use	8,500
Van licence and insurance payments covering a year	250

According to the bank account, the balance in hand on 31 March 1986 was £4,090 in Jean Smith's favour. Whilst the intention was to bank all takings intact, it now transpires that, in addition to cash drawings, the following payments were made out of takings before banking:

	£
Van running expenses	890
Postages, stationery and other sundry expenses	355

On 31 March 1986, takings of £640 awaited banking: this was done on 1 April 1986. It has been discovered that amounts paid into the bank of £340 on 29 March 1986 were not credited to Jean's bank account until 2 April 1986, and a cheque for £120, drawn on 28 March 1986 for purchases, was not paid until 10 April 1986. The normal rate of gross profit on the goods sold by Jean Smith is 50 per cent on sales. However, during the year a purchase of ornamental goldfish costing £600 proved to be unpopular with customers and therefore the entire stock bought had to be sold at cost price.

Interest at the rate of 5 per cent per annum is payable on each anniversary of the loan from John Peacock on 1 January 1986.

Depreciation is to be provided on the van on the straight line basis: it is estimated that the van will be disposed of after five years' use for £100.

The stock of goods for resale at 31 March 1986 has been valued at cost at £1,900.

Creditors for purchases at 31 March 1986 amounted to £880 and electricity charges accrued due at that date were £180.

Trade debtors at 31 March 1986 totalled £2,300.

Required:
Prepare a trading and profit and loss account for the year ended 31 March 1986 and a balance sheet as at that date.
AAT

Answer

Read through the question carefully and identify where adjustments have to be made, whether there are any red herrings and where you need to start. Remember that the normal procedure is: statement of affairs, cash and bank summary and then adjustments. Some information is included to distract you; try to identify this early on! In this case there is no need to prepare a statement of affairs, because there is only one asset – the bank balance of £15,000, which also represents the opening capital of the business – so the first step is to prepare a cash and bank summary, as follows:

Receipts Description	Cash £	Bank £	Payments Description	Cash £	Bank £
Opening balance		15,000	Purchases		26,520
Loan		10,000	Electricity		760
Cash banked		42,340	Rent		3,500
Cash sales	48,100		Rates		1,200
			Wages		14,700
			Van		7,600
			Caravan		8,500
			Van expenses	890	250
			Postage, stationery etc	355	
			Banked	42,340	
			Drawings (balancing figure)	3,875	
			Closing balances	640	4,310
	48,100	67,340		48,100	67,340

Notes:
The closing cash balance represents the takings not banked at the end of the year. The closing bank balance of £4,090 has to be increased by £340 unpresented receipts and reduced by the unpresented payment of £120.

Cash banked is £42,000 + £340, and represents a cash payment and a bank receipt. It is a contra entry. The purchases account is as follows:

Purchases account

		£		£
Bank		26,520	Trading account	27,400
Creditors	b/d	880		
		27,400		27,400
			Creditors b/d	880

The final accounts are as follows:

**Trading and profit and loss account
for the year ended 31 March 1986**

	£	£	£
Sales			50,400
Less: Cost of sales		27,400	
Closing stock		1,900	25,500
Gross profit (£25,500 − £600)			24,900
Rent (£3,500 − £700)	2,800		
Rates	1,200		
Electricity (£760 + £180)	940	4,940	
Postages, stationery and other sundry expenses		355	
Wages		14,700	
Van	890		
Van licence and insurance (£250 − £125)	125		
Van depreciation	750	1,765	
Loan interest		125	21,885
Net profit			£3,015

Balance sheet as at 31 March 1986

Assets:	Cost	Depreciation to date	Net
Fixed	£	£	£
Motor van	7,600	750	6,850
Current			
Stock	1,900		
Debtors	2,300		
Prepayments (£700 + £125)	825		
Bank	4,310		
Cash	640	9,975	
Less current liabilities			
Creditors	880		
Accruals (£125 + £180)	305	1,185	
Net assets			8,790
			15,640
Financed by:			
Capital account			
Balance as at 1 April 1985		15,000	
Net profit		3,015	
		18,015	
Less drawings (£3,875 + £8,500)		12,375	5,640
Loan from uncle			10,000
			15,640

3 The following summary for the year ended 31 October 1987 has been prepared from the cash book of Jean Black, a retailer.

1986	Receipts	Cash £	Bank £
November 1	Balances brought forward	142	2,830
	Cash sales	390	9,200
	Credit sales	110	37,500
	Cash from bank	748	
	Legacy from late aunt's estate		8,000
	Sale of motor vehicle		500
1987			
October 31	Balance carried forward		1,400
		1,390	59,430

	Payments	Cash £	Bank £
	Purchasers of goods for resale		24,300
	Wages		7,400
	General expenses	240	6,510
	Cash from bank		748
	Drawings	900	10,600
	Purchase of motor vehicle		9,872
1987			
October 31	Balance carried forward	250	
		1,390	59,430

Unfortunately Jean Black does not keep a full set of accounting records. However the following additional information has been obtained for the accounting year ended 31 October 1987:

1 Jean Black's assets and liabilities, other than cash and bank balances, were:

As at	1 November 1986 £	31 October 1987 £
Motor vehicle valued at	300	7,404
Stock valued at	1,900	2,500
Trade debtors	3,100	3,900
General expenses – prepaid	390	—
– accrued due	82	36
Wages: accrued due	—	810
Trade creditors	2,100	5,400

2 During the year ended 31 October 1987, Jean Black withdrew goods costing £800 from the business for her own use.

3 The above cash book summary does not include bank charges of £40 debited to Jean Black's account by the bank on 31 October 1987.

Required:
(a) Prepare Jean Black's trading and profit and loss account for the year ended 31 October 1987.
(b) Prepare Jean Black's balance sheet as at 31 October 1987.

AAT

Answer

Part (a)

The cash and bank summaries have already been prepared. Note the bank overdraft.

The sales account is prepared as follows:

Sales account

	£		£
Balance b/d	3,100	Cash sales	390
Trading a/c	48,000	" "	9,200
		Credit sales	110
		" "	37,500
		Balance c/d	3,900
	51,100		51,100

Don't be confused by the way the sales receipts are illustrated in the question. The total sales figures are important, not the way the monies were received.

The purchase account is prepared as follows:

Purchases account

	£		£
Bank	24,300	Balance b/d	2,100
Balance c/d	5,400	Trading a/c	27,600
	29,700		29,700

Accruals and prepayments are included in the general expenses account:

General expenses account

	£		£
Prepaid b/d	390	Accrual b/d	82
Cash	240	Profit and loss a/c	7,094
Bank	6,510		
Accrual c/d	36		
	7,176		7,176

Opening capital is calculated as follows:

	£	£
Motor vehicle		300
Stock		1,900
Trade debtors		3,100
Amounts prepaid		390
Balance at bank		2,830
Cash in hand		142
		8,662
Less: Accruals	82	
Creditors	2,100	2,182
		6,480

Goods for own use represent withdrawals of capital and are therefore included in the drawings account:

Drawings account

	£		£
Cash	900	Capital account	12,300
Bank	10,600		
Own use of goods	800		
	12,300		12,300

Jean Black
Trading and profit and loss account
for the year ended 31 October 1987

	£	£	£
Sales			48,000
Less: Cost of sales:			
Opening stock		1,900	
Purchases		27,600	
		29,500	
Less goods for own use		800	
		28,700	
Less closing stock		2,500	26,200
Gross profit			21,800
Less: Wages (£7,400 + £810)		8,210	
General expenses		7,094	
Motor vehicles:			
Depreciation	2,468		
Less 'Profit' on sale	200	2,268	
Bank charges		40	17,612
Net profit			4,188

Part (b)

Balance sheet as at 31 October 1987

	£	£	£
Assets:			
Fixed			
Motor vehicles valued at			7,404
Current			
Stock		2,500	
Trade debtors		3,900	
Cash in hand		250	
		6,650	
Less current liabilities:			
Creditors	5,400		
Accruals (£810 + £36)	846		
Bank overdraft (£1,400 + 40)	1,440	7,686	(1,036)
			6,368
Represented by:			
Capital account:			
At 1 November 1986			6,480
Add: Legacy			8,000
Net profit for the year			4,188
			18,668
Less: drawings			12,300
			£6,368

Further reading

A. Rowe *An Outline of Accounting Method* (Gee & Co), chapters 5 and 6.
F. Wood *Business Accounting 1* (Pitman), fifth edition, chapter 33.

7 Concepts and conventions

By its very nature, accounting information is financial data expressed in units of money such as pounds, dollars, francs, etc.

The question may be asked, 'How shall a fixed asset such as a building be recorded?' The simple answer is, 'At its value.' It is precisely there that the problem begins. Values can change over time, particularly with assets, and this makes the recording of accounting data rather difficult, because value can mean different things to different people, depending on the circumstances prevailing at the time.

For example, the following are ways of valuing a commercial aircraft:

1 **Historic cost:** The amount spent when the asset was purchased. This is the amount as originally recorded in the accounts.

2 **Book value:** This is historic cost less depreciation to date.

3 **Going concern value:** What the asset is worth to the company that owns it.

4 **Scrap value:** What the asset is worth at break-up value.

5 **Replacement value:** The cost of another aeroplane to do the same job.

6 **Market value:** The value another airline would be willing to pay.

7 **Opportunity cost:** The value placed on the asset if used for another purpose – say, carrying freight instead of passengers.

It will be apparent that if different values were to be used in the balance sheet at either end of a given accounting period, the profit and loss account could show a misleading profit/loss. For profits to be meaningful from one year to another, similar treatment must be given to assets etc. at both the beginnings and ends of accounting periods.

In this chapter, the problem of value and income is explored, and we will discuss how accountants treat accounting data in varying circumstances.

It is quite usual to find questions on concepts and conventions in examination papers, which usually require a prose discussion rather than a numerical answer. Typical questions are where the treatment of items in the profit and loss account and balance sheet is disclosed, and comments are invited as to whether the treatment is in accordance with best accounting practice.

7.1 Value and income

The problem of expressing value and income is difficult, and various assumptions and conventions have been made by accountants over time as to the best way of treating certain data. Since 1970, Statements of Standard Accounting Practice (SSAPs) have gone a long way to standardize the presentation of data in accounts (see chapter 9) and the 1985 Companies Act sets down rigid formats within which balance sheets and profit and loss accounts must be produced.

Public limited companies, such as ICI, are expected to disclose their accounting policies on the way certain accounting data are treated, notably depreciation, foreign currency, goodwill, government grants, leases, research and development, stock valuation and taxation. This facilitates the understanding of the figures and how they compare with similar companies.

7.1.1 Objectives and problems of measuring profit and value

These can be divided into three areas:

Assumptions

1 Entity;
2 going concern;
3 money measurement;
4 periodicity.

Conventions

1 Conservatism;
2 materiality;
3 realization;
4 business practice.

Principles

1 Consistency;
2 disclosure;
3 matching;
4 objectivity.

During the preparation of final accounts, procedures are adopted to put the above into practice, particularly in respect of asset valuation.

7.2 Assumptions

7.2.1 Entity

With limited companies, the law is quite clear. They are separate legal entities, quite distinct from the people who own shares in them.

In the case of a sole proprietor, there is again an assumption that there is a clear distinction between those assets held by the business, and those assets and transactions completed by the proprietor privately. For example, if Mr Smith pays £100 for a dress for his wife, this is obviously private. Although, for convenience, it may be paid out of his business account, it must nevertheless be regarded as money drawn out for his personal use.

There are, however, cases of expenditure on items which are used for both business and private purposes. The best example, perhaps, is the use of a company motor car, which is used ostensibly for business, but almost inevitably is used for personal journeys. (For taxation assessment, travelling from home to work and back is considered to be a non-business expense.) The usual way to deal with these types of expenditure is to treat assets and related expenses as business-related, then making an adjustment in the accounts for non-business use.

7.2.2 Going concern

This assumption considers entity from another viewpoint. Not only is a business separate from its owners or shareholders, but it is also considered to have a perpetual life. When the balance sheet is reviewed, the assets are valued at what they are worth to that particular active business.

At the time of writing, all limited companies, whether PLCs or not, must have a statutory audit undertaken by an independent accountant (this requirement for the private limited companies may change in the future, however). One of the major considerations of the auditor when making his report to the accounts and stating, as is usual, that they give 'a true and fair view', is that the company is viable financially and can continue into the foreseeable future on a sound basis. The audit report implies that this is so, unless a statement is made to the contrary in the form of a 'qualified' audit report.

Good examples of companies which would not be financially sound without continued backing from their directors are many of the Football League clubs. If such financial support was to be discontinued, in all probability many would be insolvent, and certainly not 'going concerns'.

7.2.3 Money measurement

Value and profit must be measured, and a standard by which this can be accomplished must be adopted. Money is considered to be the most consistent standard, although this has drawbacks, if, say, one compares the results of one year with another, when the impact of inflation on the figures shown in the accounts must be considered (see chapter 18).

7.2.4 Periodicity

To know exactly what profit has been made by a business, one could look at the total life of the concern, from commencement to cessation. It is not usually possible, however, to wait for the indefinite life of a business to monitor performance. A year is a more useful period.

This annual review corresponds with the scheme of yearly assessment for taxes, renewal of banking facilities based on forecasts as well as previous results, and most importantly, allows shareholders to assess the progress of the concern in which they have invested and to receive some reward (probably dividends) for the risk taken.

Obviously, business continues from day to day, and the production of accounts at a particular date is somewhat artificial. The skill of 'matching' revenues and expenditures (see later in this chapter) for a particular period is fundamental to accountancy training.

7.3 Conventions

7.3.1 Conservatism

This is not, as is sometimes imagined, 'understating' value and profit. An understatement could not be regarded as 'true and fair'. It is best to regard conservatism as the practice by accountants of taking the lower, rather than the higher, of a range of likely values. If after taking a lower figure a business has still made a profit, an accountant can be more confident about the reality of the profit.

This idea is manifested in the fact that profit is taken only at point of sale in most transactions, and stock is shown in the balance sheet always at the lower of cost or market value. No anticipation of future profits is made.

7.3.2 Materiality

Errors will occur even in the best-run accounting systems. Auditors cannot possibly check every item in a company's records, when undertaking an audit assignment, so the total of errors found, provided that they do not exceed certain percentages of either sales or pre-tax profit, may well be considered not to be 'material' to the truth and fairness of the figures. Because so much judgment is required when accounts are prepared (e.g. bad debts provision), and accounts seen by shareholders are often stated to the nearest thousand pounds for convenience, small errors may have no effect on the overall position of the profit/loss and balance sheet. What percentage of either sales or profits is considered material is a matter of professional judgment, based on the previous history of the particular company's internal control and the results of sampling techniques employed by the auditors.

Example of materiality

A large textile company has £400 of petrol in stock at the end of its accounting year. Although, to be strictly accurate, this could be shown as an asset in the balance sheet, convention dictates that the petrol will be used shortly, and therefore there is no need to account for it when preparing the accounts. Materiality is relative. An item of £400 would of course be material to a company with a turnover of, say, £4,000.

7.3.3 Realization

The general rule that profit should not be taken until realized, which is usually at point of sale, is fundamental to accountancy practice.

There are certain exceptions to this rule, however, and amongst these are the following:

1 Accretion – or ageing process. Applicable to whisky distilleries, timber growing.

2 Interest on loans and hire-purchase agreements. Profit spread over life of loan or agreement.

3 Long-term contracts. Very often, civil engineering works last for many years, and profit is uncertain until the latter stages of work are completed.

Other types of exception can be found.

The reason why stocks are carried forward from one year to another at cost derives from this principle.

Example of realization

Main car dealers often sell cars to garages on a 'sale or return' basis. Only when vehicles are actually sold by the garage in question does the main dealer accept the profit.

7.3.4 Business practice

Certain practices and conventions have grown up in particular industries and trades, and accountants must recognize these, so as to provide values and information that will be acceptable to those that use them.

7.4 Principles

7.4.1 Consistency

There are often several accounting methods of valuing a particular good or service. For example, valuation of stock can be made on FIFO, LIFO and weighted average methods, and similarly there are many ways of providing for depreciation. If comparison of figures is to be meaningful from year to year, consistency of treatment of such items is essential. Auditors and Inland Revenue tax inspectors are very much concerned with consistency in the way like items are dealt with from one year to the next. Any alteration in methods used should be noted, and the effect on the profit/loss then judged.

7.4.2 Disclosure

All material facts which affect accounts should be made known to the users of those accounts. Directors can now be fined and even sent to gaol for deliberately withholding information from auditors, and consequently the shareholders.

A good example of information that must be shown and could have an effect on the interpretation of the figures are contingent liabilities. These are liabilities that could arise given certain circumstances (e.g. an impending law suit).

7.4.3 Matching

As stated previously, the preparation of annual accounts is somewhat artificial. Business does not cease on the evening of a particular day and recommence the next morning: it is an ongoing process.

It is vital that the revenues and expenditures for a particular period, usually a year for external purposes, are 'matched' with each other. Accounts are not prepared on a 'cash received' and 'cash paid' basis; revenues earned, even though the money has still to be received, and expenses incurred, but still to be paid in the future, must be interpreted correctly.

This is an appropriate time to remember the procedure of accounts preparation, when stocks, depreciation, accruals, and prepayments are taken into account in order to isolate those revenues and expenses to a given period.

7.4.4 Objectivity

Opinions regarding possible future events should be excluded from accounts.

Valuations in accounts should be made on the basis of facts as they exist at present.

Thus, historical cost (or possibly current cost) should be applied to valuing stocks, in preference to anticipated future costs.

Example of objectivity

A confectionery firm purchased £15,000 worth of cocoa in August, on the basis of a rumour that world prices of the commodity were to rise. The directors believed that by the end of December the price will rise to £25,000 and suggest valuing it at that figure in anticipation. Correctly, the valuation should remain at £15,000: what would happen, for instance, if the price of cocoa actually fell by December?

Links with other topics

Concepts and conventions link implicitly with many other areas of study, and underpin the ideas and ideals by which accountants operate.

All public limited companies include information in their published accounts, concerning the accounting policies which have been adopted, and also concerning the treatment of such items as stock valuation, depreciation, research and development etc. This information relates to concepts such as consistency, prudence and conservatism, as well as linking with Statements of Standard Accounting Practice.

When preparing company accounts, the matching concept is well to the fore, while entity is inherent in the preparation of sole proprietor accounts, for example. Going concern is uppermost in the minds of auditors when reporting to shareholders.

It is important to be consistent in the preparation of figures, treating them in the same way from one year to the next, in order that comparisons are meaningful.

Sample questions

1 Explain clearly, in terms which a non-accountant would understand, the following accounting terms:

(a) historic cost;

(b) historic cost accounting;

(c) objectivity;

(d) prudence.

To what extent is historic cost accounting objective and prudent?

ACCA Level 1

Answer plan

This question tests the ability to give simple but clear explanations of accounting concepts and to relate several concepts together.

A basic understanding of the theory of concepts will lead to the following points:

Historic cost is the actual amount of money (or money's worth) that was paid out in obtaining some item or service, while historic cost accounting records items in the recording system at historic cost, and retains that figure unless and until some specific reason for an alteration arises.

Objectivity implies precision and a lack of personal opinion. It implies that the answer will not be influenced by the personality of the person giving the answer. It follows that different people, working independently, would give the same answer.

Prudence implies that where there is uncertainty we should err on the side of caution. We should tend to risk an understatement of assets rather than an overstatement, and to risk an understatement of profits, rather than an overstatement.

The answer to the second part of the question requires a more fundamental understanding of accounting and accounting principles.

Points which could be made include:

(a) Historic cost accounting is not by any means totally objective. There can be problems with determining cost and expense allocation.

(b) With rising prices, historic cost will tend to lead to asset figures which are lower than alternative methods and to this extent it can be regarded as prudent.

(c) However, since today's asset is tomorrow's expense, this will often lead to an understatement of expenses, and therefore to an overstatement of profits.

2 One of the well-known accounting concepts is that of materiality.

Required:

(a) Explain what is meant by this concept.

(b) State and explain three types of situation to which the concept might be applicable.

(c) State and explain two specific difficulties in applying this concept.

ACCA Level 1

Answer plan

This is a question testing theoretical knowledge and its applications.

Part (a) requires knowledge, which can be memorized, of what materiality concerns and mentioning items of insufficient importance and subjective judgment will show that some understanding is apparent. However, note that a business must always admit and discharge a liability however small.

Parts (b) and (c) require a much more in-depth reasoning, giving examples of how materiality might work in practice rather than theory.

Examples which could be mentioned in answering (b) might include capital and revenue expenditure, apportionment of expenses over departments, and disclosure. Accounts are published usually to the nearest thousand pounds, and small sums of expense are too trivial to analyse separately.

Part (c) is capable of being approached by mentioning:

(i) that accuracy sometimes has to be sacrificed for the benefit of information produced at a lower cost;

(ii) lack of consistency in the treatment of items is due to subjective judgments being applied in deciding their materiality.

3 The normal accounting approach with credit sales is to recognize revenue on the sale when it is made and then allow for the possibility of some bad debts.

Required:

Outline, by reference to appropriate accounting conventions, the justification for this approach.

ACCA Level 1

Answer plan

There is a critical event in all sales transactions when the revenue is capable of objective measurement. This is when legal ownership of the goods is transferred to the purchaser and the asset value receivable in the exchange is reasonably certain.

This probably seems inconsistent with the prudence convention, but it is normal practice to provide for doubtful debts at the year end in the accounts to give a more prudent estimate of the eventual cash outcome, i.e. to 'reorganize all possible losses and not to overstate assets'.

Although not strictly required in this answer, do you remember the circumstances when revenue **cannot** be recognized at point of sale?

4 On 20 December 1987, your client paid £10,000 for an advertising campaign. The advertisements will be heard on local radio stations between 1 January and 31 January 1988. Your client believes that as a result sales will increase by 60 per cent in 1988 (over 1987 levels), and by 40 per cent in 1989 (over 1987 levels). There will be no further benefits.

Required:

Write a memorandum to your client explaining your views on how this item should be treated in the accounts for the three years 1987 to 1989. Your answer should include explicit reference to at least THREE relevant traditional accounting conventions and to the requirements of TWO classes of user of published financial accounts.

ACCA Level 1

Answer plan

The answer should revolve around the following conventions:

1 prudence;

2 matching;

3 consistency;

4 materiality.

For example, a possible treatment in the accounts would be to write the sum off in 1987 (prudence). Any return could be considered highly speculative. How were similar items treated previously needs to be considered (consistency), and so on. A valid argument could be put up for following any of the four suggested conventions.

Refer to shareholders and trade creditors as two classes of users of published financial accounts. Both groups will be concerned with future trends of profits and it can be argued that application of the matching convention is an essential requirement for showing a fair indication of present profit and current and future trends.

5 In which ways are the accounts of businesses affected by the operation of:

  (i) the 'going concern' concept, and

  (ii) the 'prudence' concept?

ACCA Level 1

Answer plan

An outline of accounting concepts and conventions mentioned will suffice in answer to this question.

The 'going concern' concept concerns the usual assumption that a business is a continuing entity and not on the brink of cessation. Consider the effect and the value of stocks, for example, if not valued on a 'going concern' basis and the implications for balance sheets and profit and loss accounts.

The implication of 'prudence' (or 'conservation') concept is that revenue and profits are not anticipated, but only recognized when realized in cash or other assets whereby eventual cash realization can be assessed with reasonable certainty. Also that when an estimate must be made, the lower, rather than the higher, of a range of likely values is used.

6 What do you understand by the 'accruals' concept in accounting?

CIMA Level 1

Answer plan

The 'accruals' concept is also known as the 'matching' principle. The answer should outline that when a profit statement is compiled, the cost of the goods sold should be set against the revenue for their sale. Expense and revenue must be 'matched up' so that they concern the same goods and time period, if a true profit is to be computed. Costs concerning a future period must be carried forward as a prepayment of that period and not charged in the current profit and loss account. Expenses of the current period not yet entered in the books must be estimated and inserted as accruals.

Further reading

M. W. E. Glautier and B. Underdown *Accounting Theory and Practice* (Pitman), chapter 1.
A. Pizzey *Accounting and Finance – a Firm Foundation* (Holt Rinehart & Winston), second edition, chapter 2.
F. Wood *Business Accounting 1* (Pitman), fifth edition, chapter 7.

8 Accounting for depreciation

Depreciation of fixed assets is a major expense for most businesses. For example, in 1987, ICI's annual depreciation of fixed assets totalled £464 million. Without this expense ICI's trading profit would have been almost 36 per cent greater. ICI's financial results for 1987 are shown in appendix 1.

The main points that will be covered in this chapter are as follows:

1 The main reasons for providing for depreciation.

2 The major methods of providing for depreciation.

3 Accounting entries for depreciation in the ledger, income statement and balance sheet.

Depreciation is defined in Statement of Standard Accounting Practice No. 12 (*Accounting for Depreciation*, issued December 1977, amended November 1981, revised in January 1987) as:

> . . . the measure of the wearing out, consumption or other reduction, in the useful economic life of a fixed asset, whether arising from use, effluxion of time or obsolescence through technological and market changes.

Questions may be asked on any of the three main points that will be covered, namely:

1 Questions on the main purposes for providing for depreciation, particularly on the replacement aspect and its associated problems.

2 Questions on the different methods of providing for depreciation, their advantages and disadvantages, and on comparing and contrasting these methods.

3 Questions involving the entry of depreciation transactions into the ledger, income statement, and balance sheet, including adjustments for the disposal of assets.

8.1 The main purposes of providing for depreciation

8.1.1 To allocate the cost of the asset over its estimated useful life

A fixed asset provides a benefit over each year of its useful life; therefore, the cost of the asset is allocated over the same period. To satisfy the accruals/matching concept, the reduction in the asset's cost must be charged against the goods or services produced.

Depreciation is an essential cost component, as is rent and rates, and must be entered in the income statement.

8.1.2 To account for the loss in value of the asset

By charging depreciation in the income statement, the loss of value, or 'expired' cost, will have been accounted for. The balance of the cost of the asset, the 'unexpired' cost, will be carried forward and shown in the balance sheet at the end of the accounting period. In ICI's case, in 1987 this figure was £3,750m.

The unexpired cost is not meant to represent a market or realizable value, but simply the cost not yet written off. **Depreciation is a method of allocating the cost of an asset and is not a method of valuation.** A business may, however, revalue its assets from time to time, particularly land and buildings, or show its assets at current replacement cost, or some other value. In these instances, the balance will not represent the unexpired cost, but whatever valuation method the company is using.

8.1.3 To provide a fund for the replacement of the asset at the end of its useful life

The charging of depreciation, a non-cash expense, in the income statement reduces the profit for withdrawal purposes, and thereby retains an equivalent amount of funds in the business. These funds are represented by an increase in the general assets of the business, unless they are withdrawn in the mean time. This increase could, therefore, be in any of the assets of the business, such as stock, debtors or another fixed asset, and not necessarily in cash. When the business has to replace the fixed asset there is therefore no guarantee that the funds required will be in a readily realizable form. An additional problem is that a business may have retained insufficient funds, because the replacement cost of the fixed asset in question may have increased. Many businesses charge depreciation on a replacement cost basis, rather than historic cost, to overcome this particular problem. It is important for the management of a business to ensure that sufficient funds are retained to replace assets and that either those funds or new capital are available.

If a business did not provide for depreciation, profits would be overstated, and if these profits were withdrawn, the funds of the business would eventually be run down and capital depletion would occur. In addition the balance sheet would show a false position. Charging depreciation, therefore, helps to conserve and retain the proprietor's investment, although it does not automatically provide a fund, or savings scheme, out of which replacement assets can be acquired.

8.2 The major methods of providing for depreciation

8.2.1 Straight line method

This is the most widely used method of depreciation. It is simple to use and easy to understand. Any scrap value is subtracted from the historic cost of an asset, and the resultant balance is charged in equal instalments over the estimated useful life of the asset. The formula is:

$$\frac{\text{Annual}}{\text{Charge}} = \frac{\text{Cost} - \text{Scrap value}}{\text{Life of asset}}$$

Example: A second-hand car cost £3,995, and had an estimated life of five years, when it was expected to have a scrap value of £495. The annual charge to the income statement for the next five years would be £700:

$$\frac{£3,995 - £495}{5 \text{ years}} = £700 \text{ p.a.}$$

In this method, depreciation is regarded as a function of time, and not of use. There is an underlying assumption that the efficiency of the asset being depreciated remains constant throughout its life and produces an equal amount of goods or services. This method is illustrated in Fig. 8.1.

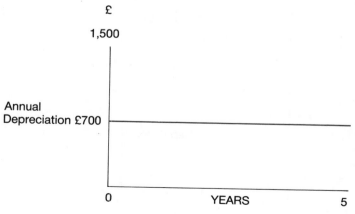

Fig. 8.1 Straight line method

8.2.2 Reducing balance method

This involves writing off a fixed percentage of the cost of the asset in the first year and then applying the same percentage to the written down value at the end of the second year, and so on until the asset is fully written off. To find the appropriate percentage, the following formula can be used:

$$r = \left(1 - \sqrt[n]{\tfrac{s}{c}}\right) \times 100\%$$

where $r \simeq$ the depreciation rate.

n = the number of useful years of the asset.

s = the scrap value of the asset.

c = the cost of the asset.

Using the example of the car, the depreciation rate would be:

$$\left(1 - \sqrt[5]{\tfrac{£495}{£3,995}}\right) \times 100\% \simeq 34\%$$

With a depreciation rate of 34 per cent, the following table shows the depreciation charge each year and the written down value:

	£	
Cost	3,995	
Year 1 Charge at 34%	1,358	Written down
	2,637	values at end
Year 2 Charge at 34%	897	of each year
	1,740	
Year 3 Charge at 34%	592	
	1,148	
Year 4 Charge at 34%	390	
	758	
Year 5 Charge at 34%	258	
	500	

(Because of rounding down the percentage, the final written down value of £500 does not quite match the estimated scrap value of £495.)

This method is illustrated in Fig. 8.2.

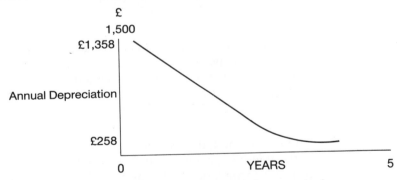

Fig. 8.2 Reducing balance method

8.2.3 Sum of digits

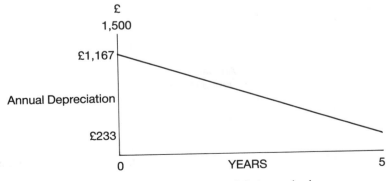

Fig. 8.3 Sum of digits method

The digits of the number of years are added up for the useful life, and the depreciation is charged in a descending order. In the example of the car, the digits would be 15 (5 + 4 + 3 + 2 + 1), and 5/15ths of £3,500 (£1,167) would be charged in the income statement in the first year, 4/15ths of £3,500 (£933) in the second year, and so on until the value of the car is written off. This method is illustrated in Fig. 8.3.

The following table shows a comparison of the three methods of providing for depreciation:

	Straight line	Reducing balance	Sum of digits
	£	£	£
Cost	3,995	3,995	3,995
Year 1 Charge	700	1,358	1,167
	3,295	2,637	2,828
Year 2 Charge	700	897	933
	2,595	1,740	1,895
Year 3 Charge	700	592	700
	1,895	1,148	1,195
Year 4 Charge	700	390	467
	1,195	758	728
Year 5 Charge	700	258	233
	£ 495	£ 500	£ 495

In both the latter methods, larger amounts are written off in the earlier years, and this may be matched by a corresponding short-fall in the revenues that the assets may be able to generate during these years. Certain assets may also decline fairly rapidly in value in the early stages of their life, and these methods of providing for depreciation reflect this. It is also quite possible that the repairs and maintenance on an asset may increase over its life, and that the sum of the depreciation charge, repairs and maintenance may represent a reasonable and fair charge against revenue for the relevant period. If there is uncertainty about the estimated life of an asset, and/or its obsolescence, a conservative approach to depreciation with larger amounts written off in the early years might make good accounting sense.

8.2.4   Other methods

There are various other methods of providing for depreciation, including the revaluation of assets, and methods based on the units of output or the number of hours that machinery is operating. In addition to providing for depreciation, some businesses invest an equivalent amount of funds in investments outside the business, in what are called sinking funds. When an asset needs replacing, the sinking fund investments are realized and the funds are used to purchase the replacement fixed asset. The management of the business must decide which are the most appropriate methods for their own particular circumstances, having regard to the type of asset, its use in the business and the impact they have on the profits.

8.3   Actual practice

Once a method of depreciation has been chosen, this should be used consistently, and changes should only be made on the grounds that a new method will give a fairer presentation of the results and of the financial position. ICI's accounting policy on depreciation is to write off each tangible fixed asset evenly over its estimated remaining life.

Financial Reporting 1983/84: A Survey of UK Published Accounts, published by the Institute of Chartered Accountants in England and Wales, which is a report based on the financial statements of 300 industrial and commercial companies, showed that 259 of these companies adopted the straight line method of depreciation.

8.4 Accounting entries for depreciation in the ledger, income statements and balance sheet

Businesses must keep accounts to record the cost and depreciation of their assets. ICI, for example, has asset accounts for 1987 which total £7,665m, being land and buildings £1,358m, plant and equipment £5,692m, and assets in the course of construction £615m. ICI also has provision for depreciation accounts for land and buildings £517m, and for plant and equipment £3,398m.

Using the previous example for the car, assuming it to have been purchased on 1 January 1988 and using the straight line method of depreciation, the car account and provision for depreciation on car account would appear as follows:

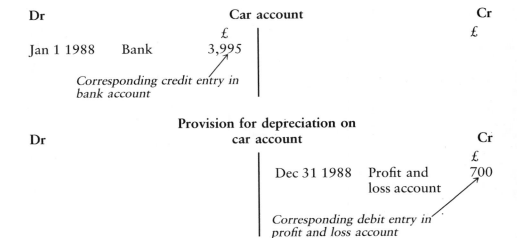

Extracts from the income statement for the year ending 31 December 1988 and the balance sheet on the same date would show the following:

Income statement for year ending 31 December 1988

	£	£
Gross profit		—
Less Expenses	—	
Rent	—	
Depreciation on car	700	
Rates	—	
Etc. Etc.	—	—
Net profit		—

Balance sheet as at 31 December 1988

Fixed assets	Cost	Depreciation to date	Written down value
£	£	£	£
Car	3,995	700	3,295

One year later, on 31 December 1989, the entries in the ledger would appear as follows:

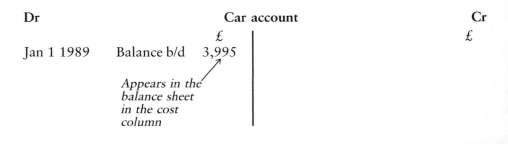

Provision for depreciation on car account

Dr			£			Cr £
Dec 31 1989	Balance c/d	1,400		Jan 1 1989	Balance b/d	700
				Dec 31 1989	Profit and loss account	700
		1,400				1,400
				Jan 1 1990	Balance b/d	1,400

Appears in balance sheet as depreciation to date

The income statement for 1989 would be charged with £700 depreciation on the car again, and an extract from the balance sheet at 31 December 1989 would appear as follows:

Balance sheet as at 31 December 1989

Fixed assets	Cost	Depreciation to date	Written down value
	£	£	£
Car	3,995	1,400	2,595

8.5 Disposal of assets

If the car is sold it will be necessary to open another ledger account, called the disposal of car account (*Step 1*). The cost and depreciation provided to the date of the sale will be transferred to this account (*Step 2*), and any scrap value or sale proceeds will be credited to the account (*Step 3*).

The balance on this account is a profit or loss, and is transferred to the income statement (*Step 4*). This amount represents an under- or over-charge for depreciation in the past.

If, for example, the car was sold on 31 December 1989 for £1,500, the entries in the ledger would be as follows:

Car account

		£			£
Jan 1 1989	Balance b/d	3,995	Dec 31 1989	Trans. to disposal account	3,995
		3,995			3,995

Provision for depreciation on car account

		£			£
Dec 31 1989	Trans. to disposal account	2,100	Jan 1 1989	b/d	1,400
			Dec 31 1989	Profit and loss account	700
		2,100			2,100

Disposal of car account

		£			£	
Step 1 Dec 31 1989	Car account *Step 2*	3,995	Dec 31 1989	Provision for depreciation on car acct.	2,100	*Step 2*
			Dec 31 1989	Bank (proceeds)	1,500	*Step 3*
			Dec 31 1989	Loss to profit & loss acct.	395	*Step 4*
		3,995			3,995	

In the above example, a full year's depreciation has been charged in the year of sale, but some businesses do not charge depreciation on assets sold during the year, or alternatively may only charge for a proportion of the year, dependent upon the date of sale.

Links with other topics

Depreciation is a very important area of study in financial accounting, and has links with topics in many of the other chapters, including chapter 2, on balance sheets, chapter 3, on income statements, chapter 4, on recording business transactions, and chapter 7, on concepts and conventions.

The latest standard accounting practice for depreciation is referred to in chapter 9, on accounting standards. Depreciation's importance as a non-cash expense and its role in the retention of funds is highlighted in chapter 16, on funds flow. Finally, its significance when preparing accounts for changing prices will be developed in chapter 18, on accounting for changing prices.

Sample questions

1 At the beginning of Year 1, College Road Products Ltd bought a new piece of equipment, which cost £48,000 and was expected to last for about eight years. What would be wrong with treating the whole cost as an expense, in calculating the profit for the year in which the equipment was purchased? Alternatively, what would be the effect of treating it as a fixed asset, and leaving it in the books at the original cost during its life?

Explain both aspects, having regard to the measurement of profit and to the balance sheet figures. What important accounting concept is involved?

First year business studies degree course level

Understanding the question

Depreciation of fixed assets accounts for a very significant proportion of the operating expense of most businesses, but it is also one of the most difficult aspects to measure. It is important, therefore, to have a clear understanding of the functions and problems of depreciation accounting, and its effect on profit calculations and balance sheets.

Answer plan

(a) Explain the need to treat cost as an expense in proportion to amount of use each year.

(b) The principle of matching revenue with expenses should be discussed.

(c) Resources could be over/under-stated, as could profit. Truth and fairness of accounts should be highlighted and the effect on future cash availability for the replacement of fixed assets is worthy of comment.

2 College Road Products Ltd decide to charge depreciation on the equipment on a straight-line basis, and it is assumed that there will be no scrap value at the end of its eight years' expected life.

(a) What is the percentage rate of depreciation to be charged, and what is the annual charge against profits?

(b) Assuming that this is the only item of equipment, show the balance sheet entry at the end of year 1.

(c) Explain what the net figure in the balance sheet(s) represents.

(d) If the equipment had been specially designed for College Road Products Ltd, and would be no value to anyone else, even when relatively new, would this make any difference to your answers? Explain why and say what assumption is implied in your answer.

(e) If it was uncertain how long the equipment would last, but the probability was somewhere between 8 and 12 years, would this affect the amount of annual depreciation to be charged in the first year or two? What accounting convention is involved?

(f) If it was originally thought that the equipment would have an eight-year life, but during the seventh year it was realized that it would continue to be of use for at lea

12 years, would you change the annual rate for the seventh year and onwards, or would this be contrary to the convention of consistency?

First year business studies degree course level

Understanding the question

The accounting principles and concepts play an important role in this question. The actual calculation of figures is straightforward where the straight line method of providing for depreciation is understood.

Answer plan

(a) Calculate the amount of depreciation to be charged annually, which is 12½ per cent, or £6,000.

(b) The balance sheet entry will be cost (£48,000), less depreciation (£6,000) — £42,000 net value.

(c) The £42,000 is the proportion of cost representing expected future use.

(d) This equipment is not intended for resale, therefore its value is that expected from future use. Explain the concept of going concern.

(e) The concept of prudence would need to be emphasized, so probably no change in depreciation charge.

(f) Charge £2,000 per annum. Matching principle, in this instance, overrides consistency.

3 A firm buys a fixed asset for £10,000. The firm estimates that the asset will be used for 5 years, and will have a scrap value of about £100, less removal expenses. After exactly 2½ years, however, the asset is suddenly sold for £5,000. The firm always provides a full year's depreciation in the year of purchase and no depreciation in the year of disposal.

Required:

(a) Write up the relevant accounts (including disposal account but not profit and loss account) for each of years 1, 2 and 3:
 (i) Using the straight line method (assume 20 per cent p.a.);
(ii) Using the reducing balance depreciation method (assume 40 per cent p.a.).

(b) (i) What is the purpose of depreciation? In what circumstances would each of the two methods you have used be preferable?
(ii) What is the meaning of the net figure for the fixed asset in the balance sheet at the end of year 2?

(c) If the asset was bought at the beginning of year 1, but was not used at all until year 2 (and it is confidently anticipated to last until year 6), state under each method the appropriate depreciation charge in year 1, and briefly justify your answer.

ACCA Level 1

Understanding the question

The answer to (a) is fairly simple and straightforward, requiring you to make a few depreciation entries for three years into the ledger, for two different methods of providing for depreciation; (b) and (c) require you to outline the purpose of depreciation and link it with two of the basic concepts listed in SSAP 2.

Answer plan

(a) (i)

Straight line method
Fixed asset account

	£		£
Year 1 Cash	10,000		
Year 2 Balance b/d	10,000		
Year 3 Balance b/d	10,000	Year 3 Transfer to disposal account	10,000
	10,000		10,000

**Provision for depreciation
on fixed asset account**

	£		£
		Year 1 Profit and	
		loss account	2,000
Year 2 Balance c/d 4,000		Year 2 Balance b/d	2,000
		Year 2 Profit and	
		loss account	2,000
	4,000		4,000
Year 3 Transfer 4,000		Year 3 Balance b/d	4,000
to disposal			
account			
	4,000		4,000

Disposal of fixed asset account

	£		£
Year 3 Transfer		Year 3 Transfer	
from fixed		from depreciation	
asset account 10,000		account	4,000
		Year 3 Cash	
		proceeds	5,000
		Year 3 Loss to	
		profit and	
		loss account	1,000
	10,000		10,000

(a) (ii)   **Reducing balance method**

The fixed asset account will be identical to the one shown in (a) (i) above.

**Provision for depreciation
on fixed asset account**

	£		£
		Year 1 Profit and	
		loss account	4,000
Year 2 Balance c/d 6,400		Year 2 Balance b/d	4,000
		Year 2 Profit and	
		loss account	2,400
	6,400		6,400
Year 3 Transfer		Year 3 Balance b/d	6,400
to disposal			
account	6,400		
	6,400		6,400

Disposal of fixed asset account

	£		£
Year 3 Transfer		Year 3 Transfer	
from fixed		from depreciation	
asset account 10,000		account	6,400
Year 3 Profit to		Year 3 Cash	
profit and		proceeds	5,000
loss account	1,400		
	11,400		11,400

(b) (i) The main purpose(s) of providing for depreciation, as shown under sectio
8.1 in this chapter, are:

1 To allocate the cost of the asset over its estimated useful life.

2 To account for the loss in value of the asset.

3 To provide a fund for the replacement of the asset at the end of its useful life.

The method that most 'fairly' charges the depreciation against the profits in the relevant accounting period would be a sensible choice. The company determines which method(s) to use. The reducing balance method charges a greater amount in the earlier years. The nature of the particular fixed asset would be important in determining which method was preferable.

(b) (ii) The net figure for the fixed asset in the balance sheet at the end of year 2 is the net book value not yet written off. This will be written off against future accounting periods when it is 'matched' against income/benefits accruing.

(c) As shown in (b) above, depreciation is a charge each year against the profits/benefits arising from the use or service provided by the particular fixed asset in question. If the fixed asset is not used in year 1, then there will be no charge, for either method of depreciation. This is the matching concept. There could, of course, be a loss of 'value' during the period and then the company will have to decide whether it is prudent to charge depreciation, or not.

4 A selection of objective test questions:

(a) Which of the following assets is most likely to appreciate rather than depreciate?
    (i) plant and machinery;
    (ii) land and buildings;
    (iii) motor vehicles;
    (iv) fixtures and fittings.

(b) A firm keeps its asset accounts at cost. The entries for depreciation at the end of the year should be:

	Debit	**Credit**
(i)	Profit and loss account	Provision for depreciation account
(ii)	Provision for depreciation account	Asset account
(iii)	Profit and loss account	Bank account
(iv)	Profit and loss account	Asset account

(c) Depreciation is caused by:
    (i) obsolescence;
    (ii) wear and tear;
    (iii) passage of time.
Answer A if (i), (ii), and (iii) are correct
     B if (i) and (ii) only are correct
     C if only (i) is correct
     D if only (iii) is correct

(d) The cost of a firm's assets three years ago was £24,000. Depreciation was charged at the rate of 10 per cent per annum by the straight-line method. It decided to change its method to diminishing balance, at 10 per cent per annum, with retrospective effect. The total difference in the profits over the three years would be:
    (i) £669
    (ii) £696
    (iii) £966
    (iv) £969

First-year business studies degree course level

Understanding the questions

A thorough knowledge of the subject matter is usually required to answer well-constructed objective test questions. Consider the alternatives carefully – do not make wild guesses!

The answers are (ii), (i), A, and (ii) respectively.

5 A company keeps its plant and machinery account in its ledger at net book value (cost minus depreciation), and the balance on this account at 31 October 1984 was £38,125. This was made up of plant purchased at cost on the dates given over:

		£
30 April 1984		10,000
31 January 1983		5,000
31 July 1982		20,000
31 October 1979		15,000
30 April 1975		30,000
31 October 1974		40,000

Depreciation is calculated at the rate of 10 per cent per annum on cost commencing on the date of purchase and continuing to the date of sale or disposal, except that depreciation must not exceed 100 per cent of cost. Any profit or loss on sale or disposal is shown as a separate item from depreciation in the profit and loss account.

The following transactions occurred during the year ended 31 October 1985:

(i) 31 January 1985 – sold plant which originally cost £10,000 on 30 April 1975 for £400 in cash;

(ii) 30 April 1985 – purchased plant costing £8,000;

(iii) 31 July 1985 – scrapped plant which orginally cost £5,000 on 31 October 1979;

(iv) 31 October 1985 – scrapped plant which originally cost £10,000 on 31 October 1974.

You are required to:

(a) write up the plant and machinery account (at net book value) in the company's ledger for the year ended 31 October 1985 carrying down a balance on that date and showing clearly the depreciation charge and any profit or loss on sale or disposal for the year;

(b) give the entries in the balance sheet at 31 October 1985 for plant and machinery, showing cost, depreciation and net book value.

CIMA Foundation Stage

Understanding the question

You are required to write up the plant and machinery account for one year only, 1984/85. The account is kept at net book value (N.B.V.) whereas, in practice, the cost, depreciation to date and disposals are frequently recorded in separate accounts. It will, therefore, be necessary to show your workings clearly.

Part (b) requires you to show the entries in the balance sheet at the end of the accounting year. This will necessitate calculating cost and depreciation to date figures, and the workings in your answer to part (a) will enable you to do this.

Answer plan

Part (a)

Plant and machinery account (N.B.V.)

1984		£	1985		£
Nov 1	Balance b/d	38,125	Jan 31	Sale proceeds – Bank	400
1985			July 31	Loss on plant scrapped [2]	2,125
Jan 31	Profit on sale to profit and loss a/c [1]	150	Oct 31	Depreciation for 1984/5 to profit and loss a/c [3]	6,52?
Apr 30	Purchases	8,000	Oct 31	Balance c/d	37,22?
		46,275			46,27?
Nov 1	Balance b/d	37,225			

Notes:

£

1 Plant sold on 31/1/85

	£
cost 30/4/75	10,000
Depreciation from 30/4/75 to 31/1/85 ($9\frac{3}{4}$ yrs)	
($10\% \times 10,000 \times 9\frac{3}{4}$)	9,750
N.B.V.	250
Sale	400
Profit	150

2 Plant scrapped 31/7/85

	£
Cost 31/10/79	5,000
Depreciation from 31/10/79 to 31/7/85 ($5\frac{3}{4}$ yrs)	
($10\% \times 5,000 \times 5\frac{3}{4}$)	2,875
N.B.V.	2,125

3 Depreciation charge for 1984/85:

	£
Cost at start of year	120,000
Less sold or scrapped in the year	25,000
	95,000
Less remaining fully-depreciated plant	30,000
*Less fully-depreciated plant (halfway through the year)	20,000
	45,000
$10\% \times 45,000 =$	4,500
Depreciation on plant sold/scrapped during 1984/85	625
*Depreciation on plant fully-depreciated halfway through the year	1,000
Depreciation on new assets	400
Total charge	6,525

Part (b)   **Balance Sheet as at 31 October 1985**

Fixed assets	Cost	Depreciation to date	N.B.V.
	£	£	£
Plant and machinery (i)	103,000	65,775 (ii)	37,225

Workings

(i) (£10,000 + £5,000 + £20,000 + £15,000 + £30,000 + £40,000 − £10,000 + £8,000 − £5,000 − £10,000)

(ii) You can check the depreciation to date figure by calculating 10 per cent depreciation on each of the individual assets still held at the end of the year.

6 (a) Identify the four factors which cause fixed assets to depreciate.

(b) Which one of these factors is the most important for each of the following assets?

 (i) a gold mine.

(ii) a motor lorry.

(iii) a 50 year lease on a building.

(iv) land.

 (v) a ship used to ferry passengers and vehicles across a river following the building of a bridge across the river.

(iv) a franchise to market a new computer software package in a certain country.

(c) The financial year of Ochre Ltd will end on the 31 December 1986. At 1 January 1986 the company had in use equipment with a total accumulated cost of £135,620 which had been depreciated by a total of £81,374. During the year ended 31 December 1986, Ochre Ltd purchased new equipment costing £47,800 and sold off equipment which had originally cost £36,000 and which had been depreciated by £28,224 for £5,700. No further purchases or sales of equipment are planned for December. The policy of the company is to depreciate equipment at 40 per cent using the diminishing balance method. A full year's depreciation is provided for on all equipment in use by the company at the end of each year.

Required:
Show the following ledger accounts for the year ended 31 December 1986:

 (i) the equipment account,
 (ii) the provision for depreciation – equipment account,
 (iii) the assets disposals account.

AAT

Understanding the question

The question is a fairly simple and straightforward one requiring you to identify the important factors which cause assets to depreciate and state which are the most important ones for certain assets. Part (c) requires you to open ledger accounts to record depreciation on equipment and its acquisition and sale.

Answer plan

Part (a) The definition of depreciation given in SSAP 12 covers the four factors involved, namely: wearing out, consumption/depletion, economic factors and effluxion of time.

Part (b)
(i) Gold mine – depletion   (ii) Motor lorry – wearing out   (iii) Lease – time
(iv) Land – quite often land appreciates in value   (v) Ship – economic factors – obsolescence through technological changes   (vi) Franchise – time

Part (c)

Ochre Limited Equipment account

1986		£	1986		£
Jan 1	Balance b/d	135,620	Jan to Dec	Equipment	
Jan to Dec	Purchases	47,800		disposal a/c	36,000
			Dec 31	Balance c/d	147,420
		183,420			183,420
1987					
Jan 1	Balance b/d	147,420			

Depreciation on equipment account

1986		£	1986		£
Jan to Dec	Equipment		Jan 1	Balance b/d	81,374
	disposal a/c	28,224	Dec 31	Profit and loss a/c	*37,708
Dec 31	Balance c/d	90,858			
		119,082			119,082
			1987		
			Jan 1	Balance b/d	90,858

*40% × (£135,620 + £47,800 − £36,000 − £53,150)

Equipment disposal account

1986		£	1986		£
Jan to Dec	Equipment a/c	36,000	Jan to Dec	Provision for	
				depreciation on	
				equipment a/c	28,224
				Sales proceeds	5,700
				Loss to profit and	
				loss a/c	2,076
		36,000			36,000

7 In November 1986, John Brown and Partners, building contractors, decided to build a new workshop for the manufacture of window frames. The workshop, built on freehold land already owned by the partnership, was constructed mainly by the firm's own workforce. The building was completed and came into use on 1 May 1987.

During the year ended 31 October 1987, the following expenditure was incurred in connection with the new workshop:

1987		£
January–April	Construction costs:	
	Direct materials	15,000
	Direct labour	9,000
	Variable overheads	3,000
February	Central Electrics Limited –	
	supply of electric installation	2,400
March	Central Electrics Limited – repair of electric	
	installation following vandalism	1,000
August	Redecoration costs following fire:	
	Direct materials	2,000
	Direct labour	1,600
	Variable overheads	300

The firm's policy is to apportion budgeted fixed overheads to contracts or jobs done in proportion to the cost of direct labour. The firm's budgeted fixed overheads and budgeted total direct labour costs for the year ended 31 October 1987 were £450,000 and £225,000, respectively.

The firm's insurers paid the following amounts in full and complete settlement of insurance claims made during the year ended 31 October 1987:

		£
June 1987	March 1987 vandalism claim	800
October 1987	August 1987 fire claim	4,000

Depreciation is provided on the straight line basis on the firm's buildings at the rate of 5 per cent per annum assuming nil residual values.

Required:

(a) Prepare the following accounts for the year ended 31 October 1987 in the books of John Brown and Partners:

New workshop at cost;
New workshop provision for depreciation;
Workshop repair.

(b) Explain why it is necessary to distinguish in accounting between revenue expenditure and capital expenditure.

AAT

Understanding the question

You are required to prepare three separate accounts from certain accountancy data and your study of this chapter and chapters 3 and 4 should help you to do this.

In Part (b), you are required to distinguish between revenue and capital expenditure which is important for depreciation purposes.

Answer Plan

Part (a)

John Brown and Partners
New workshop account

1987		£	1987		£
Jan/Apr	Construction costs:		October 31	Balance c/d	47,400
	Direct materials	15,000			
	Direct labour	9,000			
	Variable overheads	3,000			
	Fixed overheads				
	(2 × £9,000)[1]	18,000			*(cont'd.)*

(cont'd.)

		£			£
February	Central Electrics Ltd	2,400			
		47,400			47,400
November 1	Balance b/d	47,400			

Workshop repair account

1987		£	1987		£
March	Central Electrics Ltd	1,000	June	Insurers re vandalism	800
August	Redecoration costs:		October	Insurers re fire claim	4,000
	Direct materials	2,000			
	Direct labour	1,600	October	Manufacturing account	3,300
	Variable overheads	300			
	Fixed overheads[1] (2 × £1,600)	3,200			
		8,100			8,100

New workshop provision for depreciation account

		1987		£
		Oct 31	Profit and loss a/c[2]	1,185

[1]Fixed overheads are allocated at £2 $\left(\dfrac{£450,000}{£225,000}\right)$ for every £1 of direct labour.

[2]Depreciation from 1/5/87: $6/12 \times 5\% \times £47,400 = £1,185$

Part (b)
Revenue expenditure is concerned with day-to-day expenditure – such as wages, salaries, rent, depreciation, etc. – and is 'used up' in a particular accounting period. Revenue expenditure is 'charged' in the manufacturing, trading or profit and loss accounts.

Capital expenditure is concerned with the improvement or acquisition of new assets and will require depreciating in subsequent years. Capital expenditure will be added to the fixed assets in the balance sheet.

If these two types of expenditure are entered incorrectly, the profit and loss account and balance sheet will show incorrect profits/losses and financial position.

Further reading

M. Harvey and F. Keer *Financial Accounting Theory and Standards* (Prentice Hall International), second edition, chapter 5: the depreciation problem.
G. A. Lee *Modern Financial Accounting* (Nelson), fourth edition, Part 1, chapter 6: asset valuation and income measurement: historical cost accounting.

9 Accounting standards

In the past, businesses have used a wide variety of different accounting policies and practices when preparing financial statements. This has resulted in variable income and financial position statements, and account users found this situation increasingly difficult to understand.

From the early 1940s onwards, the major accountancy bodies issued various recommendations on accountancy principles, in an attempt to resolve the difficulties that had arisen as a result of different accounting practices. These recommendations were non-mandatory, however, and the discrepancies and weaknesses in accountancy practices continued, becoming increasingly apparent, in the United Kingdom and in the United States of America, during the 1950s and 1960s, mainly as a result of a number of well-publicized takeovers and mergers.

As a result of increasing controversy, an **Accounting Standards Steering Committee** (ASSC) was formed by the Institute of Chartered Accountants in England and Wales (ICAEW) in 1969. The Institute published a Statement of Intent, which declared that it was their intention to advance accounting standards, and in particular to lessen the areas of difference and variety in accounting practice.

The other five major accountancy bodies joined the ASSC later, and it then became the Accounting Standards Committee (ASC). The ASSC issued the first mandatory standard in 1970, and the ASC has continued to issue standards to supplement the legal framework of accountancy. The main points which will be covered in this chapter are as follows:

1 the nature of accounting standards;

2 the supervision and enforcement of accounting standards;

3 the scope of statements of standard accounting practice (SSAPs);

4 the standard-setting process;

5 the international dimension;

6 accounting standards in practice;

7 SSAPs and conceptual framework;

8 future developments;

9 definitive list of UK SSAPs and International Accounting Standards (IASs) (as at 1 June 1988).

Questions may be asked on any of the main points that will be discussed in this chapter. The questions range from those of a general nature concerning supervision, scope of standards, etc., to more specific ones concerned with the detailed content of any of the existing UK or international accounting standards. The specific questions quite often require you to relate the standards to financial accounting theory and/or practice.

9.1 The nature of accounting standards

Standardization of accounting practice is particularly important to a wide range of users, who want as much consistency as possible in accounting policies and practices. This consistency enables users to make realistic comparisons between the financial statements of different enterprises.

Accounting standards have been developed to reduce the choices of practice available, and yet at the same time not to impose too much uniformity. They are not intended to be a comprehensive code of rigid rules, because it would be impracticable for such a code to cater for all business situations and circumstances. Any significant departures in financial statements from applicable accounting standards must be disclosed and explained (see section 9.7).

9.2 The supervision and enforcement of accounting standards

Accounting standards continue to be formulated and issued by the accountancy profession, although there have been discussions on the possibility of alternative authorizing bodies. The six major professional accounting bodies set up the Consultative Committee of Accountancy Bodies (CCAB), and its members are expected to observe the standards and also to draw the attention of non-member directors and other officers of businesses to the existence and purpose of the standards, and ensure their full understanding of them. Where members of the CCAB act as auditors, the onus will be on them to ensure disclosure of any significant departures from the standards, and the extent to which the auditor's concurrence is stated or implied. The auditor will qualify his report if the standards are not complied with and the departure procedures not followed; a qualified report is the principal sanction against a business. Despite the lack of very effective enforcement and sanctions, compliance with standards has been reasonable.

9.3 The scope of SSAPs

All SSAPs apply to the financial statements of every enterprise which give a **true and fair view** of the state of affairs, irrespective of the size of enterprise. Certain standards have been issued, however, which have a 'restricted' nature and apply only to some businesses. An example of this is SSAP 3 (*Earnings per share*), which applies only to listed companies.

The Companies Act (1985) gave legislative effect to the provisions of various SSAPs. Schedule 4 of the Act enacts certain fundamental accounting principles to be followed in arriving at the amounts to be included in a company's financial statements. These follow closely the fundamental accounting concepts in SSAP 2; namely the going concern, consistency, prudence, and the accruals concepts. In certain instances, conflicts can arise between the Companies Act and certain of the SSAPs. It is important to note that Section 228 of the Companies Act lays down the requirement that every balance sheet and profit and loss account shall give a true and fair view, and this overrides all other requirements of the Act relating to company accounts.

9.4 The standard-setting process

The standard-setting process involves a wide-ranging active consultation process at each stage, with a consultative group comprised of nominees of organizations concerned with financial accounting and reporting. The process has been continually reviewed and amended, in the light of changing circumstances. The main stages in the process are the identification of topics, research, issue of consultative documents, the finalization and issue of standards, and the issue of guidance notes, appendices to the standards, and technical releases.

The consultative documents include a **discussion paper**, which is exploratory in nature and sets out a discussion of the issues involved as a means of seeking public comment. A subsequent consultative document, called a **statement of intent** (SOI) sets out a brief summary of how the Accounting Standards Committee intends to deal with a particular accounting matter, but in much less detail than in an exposure draft. The third main consultative document is an **exposure draft** (ED), which is the full text of a proposed standard, and normally has an exposure period of six months, during which any interested parties can submit comments on it.

Guidance notes and **appendices** to the standards do not form part of the standards, but amplify and assist their understanding, by giving non-mandatory guidance. A **technical release** is normally issued along with a standard, giving background information including a note of the comments received during the exposure period and the reasons why the main suggestions in the proposed standard were, or were not, taken up.

The ASC also publish **statements of recommended practice** (SORPs) on issues which, although of sufficient importance to require an authorative pronouncement, do not meet all the criteria for an accounting standard. They are developed in the public interest, and set out the current best accounting practice. The primary aim of a SORP is the same as that of standards, to reduce the areas of difference and variety in accounting treatment, in order to enhance the usefulness of published accounting information. Where an accounting subject is of specialized application, it may be considered preferable for the development of the statement to be the responsibility of the industry concerned. The ASC will review these SORPs and, when they have been approved, will **frank** them accordingly. The processes by which a SORP is prepared is similar to that of standards, with a comprehensive programme of consultation, even though a SORP is non-mandatory.

9.5 The international dimension

The International Accounting Standards Committee (IASC) came into existence in 1973 as a result of an agreement by the accountancy bodies of a number of countries, including the United Kingdom. The principal objectives of the IASC are:

1 to formulate and publish accounting standards in the public interest;
2 to promote the standards and gain world-wide acceptance and observance;
3 to work generally for the improvement and harmonization of regulations, accounting standards and procedures to the presentation of financial statements.

International Accounting Standards (IASs) promulgated by the IASC do not override the local regulations governing the issue of financial statements in a particular country. The obligations undertaken by the members of the IASC provide that where IASs are not complied with in all material respects, this fact should be disclosed. Where local regulations require deviation from IASs, the local members of the IASC endeavour to persuade the relevant authorities of the benefits of harmonization with IASs. A list of IASs is shown in section 9.10.

9.6 Accounting standards in practice

The vast majority of companies comply with SSAPs, but there are a few companies, including some prominent ones, which depart from them. As indicated in section 9.3, an auditor will qualify his report if the standards are not complied with and the departure procedures not followed. SSAP 9 was revised in November 1988 and should eliminate the conflict with the requirements of Schedule 4 of the CA 1985.

Some companies may be reluctant to comply with the standards because they have no statutory basis. The degree of flexibility of some standards, and the situations in which a modified or alternative treatment must be adopted, also cause problems. At the time of writing, the ASC is considering a formalized system to monitor published accounts and to discipline those responsible for non-compliance.

9.7 SSAPs and the conceptual framework

Over the years, the accounting profession has developed a number of rules of accounting practice, variously referred to as concepts, conventions etc., as discussed in chapter 7.

The prime objective of these practices is to enhance comparability and increase users' understanding of, and confidence in financial statements. There has been a fairly pragmatic approach to the conceptual framework of accounting, which has allowed a reasonable degree of freedom to accountants to prepare statements.

An alternative approach is to develop a more 'complete' conceptual framework, with a common body of accounting theory, from which solutions to any important questions on accounting practice can be provided. A framework of this nature would spell out the objectives of financial reporting and accounting, and how alternative practices would help to achieve these objectives.

The development of accounting standards from 1970 would appear to have presented the accountancy profession with an opportunity to develop such a conceptual framework, in which the objectives of accounting, accounting practice and concepts would all be linked together. Instead a pragmatic approach has been adopted, however, and the standards have been developed in a piecemeal way, with no single undisputed reference model. SSAP 2 (*Disclosure of accounting policies*) was issued in 1971, but did not attempt to identify and explain all the concepts of accounting. A more comprehensive theoretical approach would have included more than the four fundamental concepts.

Other accounting standards have continued to be issued, using a similar approach. The lack of a conceptual framework has caused difficulties with a number of standards, as evidenced by the attempts to produce a mandatory standard on inflation accounting.

A lot of research has been carried out over the years in the United States by the Financial Accounting Standards Board (FASB), to develop a conceptual framework for accounting. In 1981 the ASC commissioned a report to look into the possibilities of developing such a framework for setting accounting standards in the UK, but considerable difficulties have arisen from trying to develop this framework, including the problem of agreeing on the definition of such terms as 'income' and 'value', which have important implications for the measurement of profits and net assets. There have also been problems on agreeing on the objectives of financial reporting and the means of achieving them. It is difficult to give precise answers to all accounting problems from a body of accounting theory, and there is still a need for individual users of financial statements to exercise subjective judgment.

In the mean time, research continues in this area, and it is particularly important that discussion should continue with the users of accounting information, about their needs and how these can be satisfied in ever-changing circumstances.

9.8 Future developments

Although views differ as to the success, or otherwise, of accounting standards, there is a large measure of agreement on the need for them to continue to be issued in the foreseeable future. The task of reducing uncertainty and confusion in annual reports and accounts, to aid comparison, has not been completed. The existing standards need to be reviewed for deficiencies, and also because business objectives change over time. In addition to this process, which has led to many amendments, revisions and additions to existing standards, many new projects are under consideration.

The ASC intends to continue to issue standards which deal only with those matters which are of major and fundamental importance, and will apply to all accounts giving a true and fair view. These standards will state broad principles, and enforcement may come through a system of compliance monitoring. Standard-setting will continue to involve as broad and open a consultation process as possible, and the consultative documents already discussed in section 9.5.

In November 1988 a major report dealing with the need for enforcement of accounting standards was issued by the CCAB. It will be considered by the ASC in 1989 although changes are not likely before 1990.

9.9 List of UK SSAPs (as at 1 June 1988)

SSAP	Title	Date of issue	
1	*Accounting for associated companies*	January 1971	Amended August 1974, revised April 1982
2	*Disclosure of accounting policies*	November 1971	
3	*Earnings per share*	February 1972	Revised August 197
4	*The accounting treatment of government grants*	April 1974	
5	*Accounting for value added tax*	April 1974	
6	*Extraordinary items and prior year adjustments*	April 1974	Revised June 1975
7	*Accounting for changes in the purchasing power of money*	May 1974	Provisional. Withdrawn January 1978
8	*The treatment of taxation under the imputation system of accounts*	August 1974	Appendix 3 added December 1977
9	*Stocks and work in progress*	May 1975	Part 4 added August 1980, revised November 1988
10	*Statements of source and application of funds*	July 1975	

11	*Accounting for deferred tax*	August 1975	Amended October 1976 – subsequently replaced by SSAP 15
12	*Accounting for depreciation*	December 1977	Revised January 1987
13	*Accounting for research and development*	October 1977	
14	*Group accounts*	September 1978	
15	*Accounting for deferred taxation*	October 1978	Revised May 1985
16	*Current cost accounting*	March 1980	Mandatory status suspended June 1985
17	*Accounting for post-balance sheet events*	August 1980	
18	*Accounting for contingencies*	August 1980	
19	*Accounting for investment properties*	November 1981	
20	*Foreign currency translation*	April 1983	
21	*Accounting for leases and hire-purchase contracts*	August 1984	
22	*Accounting for goodwill*	December 1984	
23	*Accounting for acquisitions and mergers*	April 1985	
24	*Accounting for pension costs*	May 1988	

9.10 List of international accounting standards (as at 1 June 1988)

IAS	Title	Date of issue	
1	*Disclosure of accounting policies*	January 1975	
2	*Valuation and presentation of inventories in the context of the historical cost system*	October 1975	
3	*Consolidated financial statements*	June 1976	
4	*Depreciation accounting*	October 1976	
5	*Information to be disclosed in financial statements*	October 1976	
6	*Accounting responses to changing prices*	June 1977	Withdrawn and superceded by IAS 15
7	*Statement of changes in financial position*	October 1977	
8	*Unusual and prior period items and changes in accounting policies*	February 1978	
9	*Accounting for research and development activities*	July 1978	
10	*Contingencies and events occurring after the balance sheet date*	October 1978	
11	*Accounting for construction contracts*	March 1979	
12	*Accounting for taxes on income*	July 1979	
13	*Presentation of current assets and current liabilities*	November 1979	

14	*Reporting financial information by segment*	August 1981
15	*Information reflecting effects of changing prices*	November 1981
16	*Accounting for property, plant and equipment*	March 1982
17	*Accounting for leases*	September 1982
18	*Revenue recognition*	December 1982
19	*Accounting for retirement benefits in the financial statements of employers*	January 1983
20	*Accounting for government grants and disclosure of government assistance*	November 1984
21	*Accounting for the effects of changes in foreign exchange rates*	November 1984
22	*Accounting for business combinations*	November 1984
23	*Capitalization of borrowing costs*	November 1984
24	*Related party disclosures*	November 1984
25	*Accounting for investments*	January 1987
26	*Accounting and reporting by retirement benefit plans*	January 1987

Links with other topics

Accounting standards have become an increasingly important area of study, and link closely with both the theory and practice of financial accounting in many of the other chapters. The 'foundation' standard, SSAP 2 (*Disclosure of accounting policies*) links with chapter 7, Concepts and conventions.

A number of other standards are studied in more depth, both from a theoretical and practical point of view, in the relevant chapters. For example, SSAP 12 (*Accounting for depreciation*) in chapter 8, Accounting for depreciation; SSAP 10 (*Statements of source and application of funds*) in chapter 16, Funds flow; SSAP 9 (*Stocks and work in progress*) in chapter 17, Working capital control; and SSAP 16 (*Current cost accounting*) in chapter 18, Accounting for changing prices.

In addition to this, a large number of the standards are relevant to published accounts, and will be highlighted in chapter 10, Company annual reports and accounts.

Sample questions

1 Discuss the areas in which you think it would be beneficial for financial accounting and reporting users to have new accounting standards issued.

First-year Accounting degree level

Understanding the question

The student will need to be aware of contemporary issues in financial accounting theory and practice, to be able to suggest possible areas for new accounting standards.

Answer plan

The ASC publish a work programme periodically and invite comments on it. The present programme includes:

(a) Segmental reporting

This is concerned with the analysis of general company information between separate divisions or classes of business. This is a particular problem for the user when the organization is large and/or a multinational. The Stock Exchange and CA (1985) already have some disclosure requirements in this area, and an accounting standard would supplement these requirements. An exposure draft, ED45, Segmental Reporting, was published in November 1988.

(b) Interim reporting

Draft guidance notes were published in 1982 on CCA interim reporting, but the topic has not been fully dealt with. An accounting standard in this area would lead to greater uniformity in content and presentation and would help both preparers and users. The Stock Exchange has certain requirements in this area already.

(c) Materiality

This is a controversial area, and an accounting standard would assist in overcoming some of the income measurement problems.

(d) Review of existing SSAPs

The ASC continues to review the existing standards to meet the changing circumstances. The first standard, SSAP 1, was published in 1971, and has subsequently been amended, in August 1974, and revised in April 1982. SSAP 3, SSAP 6, SSAP 9 and SSAP 12 have also been revised, and there is a continuing programme of revision and amendment for the remaining standards.

(e) Other franked SORPs

The franking of SORPs is a relatively new development and there is continuing scope for new SORPs in specialized areas.

2 'Fundamental accounting concepts are here defined as broad basic assumptions which underlie the periodic financial accounts of business enterprise. It is expedient to single out for special mention four in particular . . .' (SSAP 2).

(a) You are required to explain what the four concepts are, and how their relative importance can vary.

(b) SSAP 2 distinguishes between the fundamental concepts and accounting bases and accounting policies. You are required to distinguish clearly these three terms in the context of understanding and interpreting financial accounts.

First-year Accounting degree level

Understanding the question

The student will have to be able to identify the four fundamental accounting concepts contained in SSAP 2, and how they complement and conflict with each other in practice. The standard defines concepts, bases and policies, and the student will have to distinguish carefully between each one and endeavour to give a practical example of their application.

Answer plan

(a) An explanation is required of each of the four concepts, which are:
 (i) the going concern;
 (ii) the accruals concept;
 (iii) the consistency concept;
 (iv) the prudence concept.

These concepts have general acceptances in the preparation and reporting of published financial data, and their observance is presumed, unless stated otherwise. They are practical rules rather than theoretical ideas, and are capable of variations. The concepts are the broad basic assumptions underlying the periodic financial accounts and their relative importance may vary according to the circumstances of the particular case.

There are particular problems in the application of the fundamental concepts and the main difficulties arise from the fact that many business transactions have financial effects spreading over a number of years. Specific examples are those concerning the future benefits to be derived from stocks and work in progress at the end of the year, the future benefits to be derived from fixed assets, and the extent to which expenditure on research and development can be expected to produce future benefits.

(b) As noted above, the fundamental concepts are the broad basic assumptions which underly the periodic financial accounts. Accounting bases are the methods developed for applying these concepts to financial transactions, and items for the purpose of financial accounts. Accounting policies are the specific accounting bases selected and consistently followed by the business.

3 The valuation of stocks and work in progress, and long-term contract work in progress, has caused considerable problems over the years for financial reporters.

(a) Outline how stocks and work in progress and long-term contract work in progress should be valued for year end financial statements, as stated in SSAP 9.

(b) Discuss the problems that have arisen over the valuations of these items over the last 10/15 years.

First-year Accounting degree level

Understanding the question

SSAP 9 details how stocks and work in progress should be valued for financial statements, and knowledge of this will be required. Students should be aware of what companies have done, and are doing, in practice in terms of valuation of stocks and work in progress vis-à-vis SSAP 9, from textbooks, articles etc.

Answer plan

(a) Stocks and work in progress other than long-term contract work should be stated, in the periodic financial statements, as the total of the lower of cost and net realizable value of the separate items of stock and work in progress or of groups of similar items. Long-term contract work in progress is stated in periodic financial statements as cost plus any progress payments received and receivable. If, however, anticipated losses on individual contracts exceed cost incurred to date less progress payments received and receivable, such excess should be shown separately as provisions.

(b) Many of the problems involved in arriving at the valuation to be shown are of a practical nature, rather than resulting from matters of principle.

These areas of difficulty include the allocation of overheads, the methods of costing (including the determination and application of net realizable value) and ascertaining the cost of long-term contract work in progress.

4 'The accounting policies to be followed in respect of research and development expenditure must have regard to the fundamental accounting concepts . . .' (SSAP 13).

Discuss the application of the fundamental accounting concepts to the accounting treatment of research and development expenditure, as outlined in SSAP 13.

First-year Business Studies degree level

Understanding the question

A knowledge of the fundamental accounting concepts contained in SSAP 13 will be required, and how these are applied in the accounting treatment of research and development.

Answer plan

The fundamental accounting concepts include the accruals concept, by which revenue and costs are accrued, matched and dealt with in the period to which they relate, and the prudence concept, by which revenue and profits are not anticipated, but are recognized only when realized in the form of either cash or other assets, the ultimate cash realization of which can be established with reasonable certainty.

It is a corollary of the prudence concept that expenditure should be written off in the period in which it arises, unless its relationship to the revenue of a future period can be established with reasonable certainty.

The application of the concepts should be related to the recommended standard accounting practice for research and development, namely:

(a) The cost of fixed assets acquired or constructed in order to provide facilities for research and development activities over a number of accounting periods should be capitalized and written off over their useful life.

(b) Expenditure on pure and applied research should be written off in the year of expenditure.

(c) Development expenditure should be written off in the year of expenditure except in certain circumstances when it may be deferred to future periods. These circumstances are spelt out in the standard.

5 Statements of Standard Accounting Practice (SSAPs) are very much a part of the accountant's day-to-day world.

You are required to state the advantages and disadvantages of such Statements, giving examples where you can.

CIMA Professional Stage

Understanding the question

This is a fairly 'practical' type of question requiring you to state the advantages and disadvantages of Statements of Standard Accounting Practice. You should relate your practical working experience of accounting standards with the background knowledge in this chapter and your other readings of this topic.

Answer plan

Advantages include:

(a) areas of difference in accounting practice are narrowed;

(b) financial reporting of a business is carried out according to whatever the accounting profession consider to be the best accounting practice(s);

(c) significant departures from best accounting practice are disclosed;

(d) inter- and intra-group comparisons are facilitated;

(e) aids other users of financial report, e.g. other directors/managerial staff and shareholders of a business;

(f) expertise and transferability of accounting staff are improved;

(g) consistency in preparation should lead to reduced time and cost, etc.

A number of these advantages, particularly the first three, could have many wide-ranging benefits including an impact on the market capitalization of a business.

Disadvantages include:

(a) a degree of flexibility in some standards, leading to several alternative accounting practices being allowed:

(b) rigidity in some standards;

(c) some standards (e.g. SSAP 16), or sections of them (e.g. SSAP 9) not being generally accepted;

(d) audit 'qualification' in certain circumstances;

(e) expense-in terms of knowledge, training, communication, etc.;

(f) they may lead to false confidence in the results by financial users in some situations;

(g) the lack of a coherent theoretical framework;

(h) a business or industry, private or public, may have special accounting requirements such that the accounting practice required by the SSAPs is not the most suitable for that enterprise;

(i) lack of enforcement – there is no compliance monitoring and no provision for penalties for non-compliance (to date – the ASC is considering some form of compliance monitoring).

Wherever possible you need to give examples for the advantages and disadvantages listed above, from your practical or theoretical knowledge.

Further reading

M. Harvey and F. Keer *Financial Accounting Theory and Standards* (Prentice Hall International), second edition, chapter 3: concepts in accounting, and chapter 8: towards accounting standards.

Sir Ronald Leach and Professor Edward Stamp *British Accounting Standards* (Woodhead Faulkner):

Part one:

chapter 1, the birth of British accounting standards;

Part three:

chapter 7, British standards in a world setting,

chapter 12, standards, objectives and the corporate report;

Part four:

chapter 14, are accounting standards necessary?

chapter 17, a view from academie.

R. Macve *A Conceptual Framework for Financial Accounting and Reporting* (The Institute of Chartered Accountants in England and Wales).

10 Company annual reports and accounts

In chapter 2, Balance sheets, and chapter 3, Incomes statements, we examined the preparation of 'final' accounts for sole traders and partnerships. This chapter is concerned with the preparation of final accounts for limited liability companies.

Limited liability companies are subject to the requirements of the Companies Act, 1985 (CA 1985), and other constraints, and have many formalities to observe when preparing and presenting their accounts.

The initial part of this chapter will look at some of the background aspects of limited liability companies, and will then examine the preparation of their accounts for 'internal' purposes. The main differences between limited liability company accounts and those prepared for unincorporated businesses as shown in chapters 2 and 3 will be outlined.

Almost the whole of the remaining, and most important, part of this chapter will cover the preparation of company accounts for publication purposes, and will look in outline at the requirements and formats of the CA 1985. The other constraints that limited liability companies are subject to in the preparation of their published accounts, namely the requirements of the Stock Exchange and the Accounting Standards Committee, will also be covered briefly.

The structure of the chapter will be as follows:

1 background aspects of limited liability companies;
2 final accounts for internal presentation;
3 final accounts for publication purposes;
4 Stock Exchange requirements;
5 accounting standards.

Questions on company annual reports and accounts are usually fairly predictable: you are generally required to prepare an income statement and balance sheet from a list of balances, or from a trial balance. Preparation of final accounts for internal purposes could include the manufacturing accounts as well as the trading and profit and loss accounts. To prepare final accounts for publication purposes it is necessary to know, or have reference to, the detailed disclosure requirements and alternative formats of the CA 1985. The questions become more difficult when a large number of adjustments are involved.

10.1 Background aspects of limited liability companies

10.1.1 Limited liability

A limited liability company has a separate legal identity from that of its owners, and its creditors can only sue the company for outstanding debts. Once the shareholders of a limited liability company have paid any amounts outstanding on their shares, they have no further liability for the company's debts.

Formation

Limited liability companies are formed by a minimum of two persons, who may register a company by lodging certain documents with the Registrar of Companies. The most important of these documents are the Memorandum and Articles of Association. The Memorandum is concerned with the relationship between the company and outsiders, and contains six clauses (CA 1985, Section 2), namely:

1 the name of the company;
2 that the company is a public one, if that is the case;
3 the country of domicile;
4 the objects of the company;
5 a statement to the effect that the liability of members is limited;
6 the amount of the share capital divided into shares of fixed amounts.

The Articles contain rules which govern the internal regulations of the company.

10.1.2 Public and private companies

A company which states that it is a public company in its memorandum must have a minimum allotted share capital of £50,000, of which at least one quarter of the nominal value of the allotted shares, and the whole of any premium, are paid up. A minimum of two directors is necessary, and the company must use the words 'public limited company', or the abbreviations 'plc' or 'PLC' after its name.

A private company, on the other hand, is one which is restricted from offering its shares and debentures to the public (CA 1985, Section 81). Prior to the Companies Act, 1980, companies were public companies unless they complied with certain requirements. The position has since been reversed, however, and registered companies are now assumed to be private unless they satisfy certain requirements, of which the main ones have been outlined above. The vast majority of companies are private ones. There are now just over one million companies in the UK and above 99.5 per cent of these are private.

10.1.3 Shares

There are two main types of shares, preference shares and ordinary shares.

Preference shares

Preference shares have a fixed rate of dividend, and the dividends are paid out of profits before any other kind of shareholder. Some types of preference shares are cumulative, which allows for any unpaid dividends to accumulate, and to be paid when the company makes profits. If a company is liquidated, then the preference shareholders will normally be repaid their capital prior to any other type of shareholder, but after all other liabilities have been paid.

Ordinary shares

Ordinary shareholders do not receive a fixed rate of dividend but are allocated a dividend after any preference dividend has been paid, so what they receive will depend on the size of profits. If a company does not make any profits, then there will be no ordinary dividend, unless distributable reserves are available from previous years. If a company is liquidated, then its ordinary shareholders will rank last for repayment of capital. Ordinary shareholders are the risk-bearers of companies, the entrepreneurs, and are often called the equity shareholders.

Both kinds of share have nominal values, e.g. 10p, 25p, £1, and dividends are based on these values. If ordinary shares are issued by a company for more than the nominal value, this 'extra' amount is called a share premium, and is part of the reserves of the company.

Shares are issued at a premium when their market value is above the nominal value. If, for example, a company's shares have a nominal value of 25p, and the market price of its existing shares is £1.50, it would be a nonsense to issue new shares at 25p. Such an issue would be heavily over-subscribed, with almost everyone wanting shares at such a bargain. The company would fail to raise the maximum funds, and the existing shareholders would suffer.

Shares are normally issued to existing shareholders (as a rights issue) at a discount on the market price of somewhere between 15 per cent and 25 per cent, depending on circumstances at the time. If, in the above example, the shares were issued at 125p, 25p would be added to the ordinary share capital and 100p to the share premium account, for every share issued.

10.2   Final accounts for internal presentation

Limited liability companies must keep accounts, like any other business and will prepare final accounts for management purposes at suitable time intervals, to enable company performance to be judged. These accounts will include a manufacturing account (where relevant), trading account, a profit and loss account, and a balance sheet, and these will be prepared following the concepts and conventions examined in earlier chapters.

The manufacturing and trading accounts will be prepared in a similar way to those shown in chapter 3 for sole traders. The profit and loss account will also follow a similar pattern, except that certain expenses will appear which are unique to limited liability companies. These include directors' remuneration and debenture interest, which would not arise in sole traders' accounts. An example of a profit and loss account would be as follows:

Profit and loss account
for period ended 31 December 1989

	£	£
Gross profit		500,000
Less:		
Rent and rates	110,000	
Directors' remuneration	25,000	
Salaries	95,000	
Selling and distribution expenses	100,000	
Debentures interest	10,000	340,000
Profit before taxation		160,000
Taxation		75,000
Profit after taxation		85,000

10.2.1   Appropriation account

A company's profit and loss account is different in one other way from those of sole traders, because there is an 'extension' to it, called an appropriation account. In a sole trader's accounts, the whole of the net profit (or losses) belongs to the proprietor, whereas with a limited liability company, it is necessary to divide, or 'appropriate', the profit amongst the shareholders.

The company's appropriation account commences with the profit after tax from the current year's trading activities; any balance remaining from the previous year's appropriation account, the unappropriated balance, will be added to it. From this figure, any dividend (paid and proposed) will be deducted.

Dividends are expressed as a percentage of the nominal value of each share or at so many pence per share. If, for example, a limited company had one million ordinary shares of 25p each, and the company were to declare a dividend of 16 per cent, the proposed dividend to be entered in the appropriation account would be £40,000, equivalent to a dividend of 4p per share.

Any proposed dividends will also be shown as a current liability in the balance sheet. Companies frequently pay interim dividends during the accounting year, and these will also be entered in the appropriation account. The amount of dividend paid to ordinary shareholders will depend mainly upon the level of profits, and the amount of capital that the directors wish to retain within the company. Most companies try to achieve a stable dividend policy, with small increases in dividends each year, if possible. An erratic payout of dividends could have serious implications for the market price of existing shares, and could prejudice the possibility of raising funds again from the existing shareholders.

In addition to dividends, any amounts that the directors decide to transfer to reserves, to plough back into the company, are deducted as well. Retained funds are the single most important source of finance for companies. Such transfers might be to general reserves, which are then available for subsequent dividend distribution purposes, if required, or to specific reserves, such as reserves to replace fixed assets. These transfers to reserves will be added to any existing reserves, and listed in the balance sheet. The final unappropriated balance on the appropriation account will also be shown in the balance sheet under the section for reserves.

An example of an appropriation account would be as follows:

Appropriation account for year ended 31 December 1989

		£	£
Profit after tax			85,000
Add unappropriated balance brought			
forward from last year			15,000
			100,000
Less dividends:			
Preference shareholders	paid	10,000	
	proposed	10,000	
Ordinary shareholders	paid	10,000	
	proposed	40,000	
		70,000	
Transfers to general reserves		10,000	80,000
Unappropriated balance carried forward			20,000

10.2.2 Balance sheet

The balance sheet is prepared on similar lines to that of a sole trader, shown in chapter 2, but in place of the proprietor's capital, there will be share capital and reserves.

Reserves arise from trading activities, and will include the balance on the appropriation account, together with any general (or revenue) reserves. These reserves will be available for dividend distribution purposes. There are also specially created, reserves, such as plant replacement reserves, which are for specific purposes only and are not, therefore, available for distribution. These reserves are also transferred from profits made by the company, via the appropriation account as shown earlier.

Reserves can also arise from non-trading activities. Such reserves (still sometimes known as capital reserves) are not available for distribution. Examples of these are revaluation reserves, where some of a company's assets, such as land and buildings, are revalued upwards, and a reserve created to match this increase. These reserves would only be available for distribution if the assets in question were sold. Another example of a non-trading activity reserve would be share premium, which has very restricted uses (CA 1985, Section 130).

All these reserves, both distributable and non-distributable, and the share capital, are represented in the balance sheet by net assets, such as buildings, plant, stock, bank etc., less current liabilities; they should not be thought of as a vault full of money, kept in the company office.

The next section of the balance sheet will often comprise debentures or loans, which are an important source of funds to companies, as well as share capital and retained profits. Debentures are secured loans to a company, which will have to be repaid at some future date. In the mean time, the debenture holders will be paid a fixed rate of interest, which must be paid whether or not the company makes any profits. The interest is an expense which will be charged in the profit and loss account as shown previously, and the debentures will appear in the balance sheet as a liability. Debentures are essentially creditors of the company, with no voting rights. The debentures will be secured on one or more of the company's assets, in the form of a fixed or floating charge.

The layout and presentation of the income statement and balance sheet for internal purposes is a matter for the internal management of a company. This is in contrast to the detailed disclosure and format requirements of the Companies Act, which are covered later in this chapter.

10.2.3 Illustration of company accounts preparation for internal presentation

The following is an illustration of the preparation of a set of company final accounts for internal purposes, from a list of balances extracted from the books of a limited company, as at 31 December 1989. Note particularly the format of the appropriation section of the profit and loss account, and the layout of the balance sheet.

	£
10% preference shares of £1 each	300,000
Ordinary shares of 50p each	600,000
(All the above authorized shares have been issued and fully paid)	
Share premium	280,000
Creditors	150,000
Reserves for replacement of equipment	135,000
12% debentures	180,000
Unappropriated profits brought forward	52,500
Cash in hand	4,500
Sales	3,000,000
Debtors	165,000
Stock 1 January 1989	75,000
Cash at bank	54,000
Purchases	1,560,000
Deposit account in the bank	158,000
Directors fees and salaries	51,000
Rent, rates and telephone	375,000
Salaries	216,000
General overhead expenses	450,000
Plant (cost £225,000)	150,000
Discounts allowed	4,500
Equipment (cost £765,000)	540,000
General reserves	370,000
Buildings (cost £1,290,000)	1,185,000
Stationery	79,500

The following information is to be taken into account:

1 Stock on hand at 31 December 1989 has been valued at £66,000.

2 Rates of £15,000 have been prepaid.

3 Depreciation on cost of 10 per cent for plant and equipment and 5 per cent for buildings must be provided for.

4 Salaries of £9,000 are outstanding.

5 There is a liability for corporation tax of £30,000, payable on 1 October 1990.

6 The interest on the debenture and the dividend on the preference shares have to be provided for.

7 The directors have recommended a dividend of 6 per cent on the ordinary shares, and the transfer of £15,000 to general reserves.

Trading and profit and loss account for the year ended 31 December 1989

	£	£
Sales		3,000,000
Less Cost of sales		
Opening stock	75,000	
Add Purchases	1,560,000	
	1,635,000	
Less Closing stock	66,000	1,569,000
Gross profit		1,431,000
Less Directors fees and salaries	51,000	
Rent, rates, telephone [1]	360,000	
Salaries [3]	225,000	
General overhead expenses	450,000	
Discounts allowed	4,500	
Stationery	79,500	
Debenture interest [4]	21,600	

(cont'd.)

(cont'd.)		£	£
Depreciation[2]			
Buildings		64,500	
Equipment		76,500	
Plant		22,500	1,355,100
Profit before tax			75,900
Corporation tax			30,000
Profit after tax			45,900
Add Unappropriated balance brought forward			52,500
			98,400
Less:			
Preference Dividends outstanding[5]		30,000	
Ordinary dividends proposed[6]		36,000	
		66,000	
Transfer to general reserves		15,000	81,000
Unappropriated balance carried forward			17,400

Balance sheet as at 31 December 1989

Assets employed

Fixed assets	Cost	Depreciation to date	Net value	
	£	£	£	£
Buildings	1,290,000	169,500	1,120,500	
Plant	225,000	97,500	127,500	
Equipment	765,000	301,500	463,500	
	2,280,000	568,500	1,711,500	1,711,500
Current assets				
Stock		66,000		
Debtors		165,000		
Bank deposits		158,000		
Cash at bank		54,000		
Cash		4,500		
Prepayment		15,000		
		462,500		
Less Current liabilities				
Creditors	150,000			
Proposed dividends	66,000			
Taxation	30,000			
Accruals	30,600	276,600		
Net current assets				185,900
Net assets				1,897,400

Financed by:

Authorized issued and fully-paid

10% preference shares, 300,000 of £1 each			300,000
Ordinary shares 1,200,000 of 50p each			600,000
			900,000

Reserves

Share premium		280,000	
Reserves for replacement of equipment		135,000	
		415,000	
General reserves	385,000		
Profit and loss account	17,400	402,400	817,400
Shareholders' funds			1,717,400
Loan capital 12% debentures			180,000
			1,897,400

Workings:

1. Rent, rates and telephone £375,000 − £15,000 prepayment = £360,000
2. Depreciation – buildings   5% × £1,290,000   = £64,500
   Depreciation – plant   10% × £225,000   = £22,500
   Depreciation – equipment 10% × £765,000   = £76,500
3. Salaries £216,000 + £9,000   = £225,000
4. Interest on debentures – 12% × £180,000   = £21,600
5. Preference dividend – 10% × £300,000   = £30,000
6. Ordinary dividend   – 6% × £600,000   = £36,000

10.3 Final accounts for publication purposes

This part of the chapter is concerned with the preparation of 'final' accounts for limited liability companies, in published form.

The CA 1985 lays down the form and content for these accounts. As well as observing these legal requirements, a company's directors will have to satisfy other sources of authority and guidance when preparing accounts, namely the Stock Exchange and the professional accounting bodies. The Stock Exchange requirements and statements of standard accounting practice will be looked at briefly later in this chapter.

Accounts and audit requirements applying to companies generally are contained in Part VII chapter 1 of the CA 1985, Sections 221 to 256 and Schedules 4 to 8. The most important sections, for this chapter's purpose, are summarized on the following pages. Group accounts are ignored at this stage because they will be looked at later in your studies of accounting and finance.

10.3.1 Accounting records (Section 221)

Every company has to keep accounting records, to show and explain their transactions. The records must show the day-to-day entries of monies received and paid, and a record of the assets and liabilities of the company. The Companies Act also details what the accounting records should contain when a company's business involves dealing in goods. The records must be sufficient to enable the financial position to be determined with reasonable accuracy at any time, and to allow the preparation of a profit and loss account and balance sheet in the form and content required by the Act.

10.3.2 Directors' duty to prepare accounts (Section 227)

The directors of a company are required to prepare for each accounting reference period a profit and loss account for the financial year, and a balance sheet as at the last day of that year.

10.3.3 Form and content of individual company accounts (Section 228)

The balance sheet has to give a true and fair view of the state of affairs of the company as at the end of the financial year, and the profit and loss account must give a true and fair view of the profit or loss of the company for the financial year. The true and fair view is an over-riding requirement, which may mean departing from the requirements of the Act as to matters to be included in the accounts or notes.

Schedule 4 of the Act specifies the required form and content of the balance sheet and profit and loss account, and any additional information to be provided by way of notes to the accounts.

10.3.4 The required formats for accounts (Schedule 4, Part I Section B)

Four alternative formats are permitted for company profit and loss accounts. Formats 1 and 2 have a vertical presentation, while formats 3 and 4 have a horizontal presentation. Formats 1 and 3 classify income and operating expenses by function, whereas formats 2 and 4 classify information by the type of income and expense.

Two alternative formats are permitted for company balance sheets – the first format shows the balance sheet items arranged vertically, whilst the second one has the items arranged horizontally.

Formats 1 and 2 for the profit and loss account, and format 1 for the balance sheet, are those most likely to be found in practice in the UK, and are the ones illustrated below:

Profit and loss account format 1

1 Turnover.
2 Cost of sales.
3 Gross profit or loss.
4 Distribution costs.
5 Administrative expenses.
6 Other operating income.
7 Income from shares in group companies.
8 Income from shares in related companies.
9 Income from other fixed asset investments.
10 Other interest receivable and similar income.
11 Amounts written off investments.
12 Interest payable and similar charges.
13 Tax on profit, or loss on ordinary activities.
14 Profit or loss on ordinary activities after taxation.
15 Extraordinary income.
16 Extraordinary charges.
17 Extraordinary profit or loss.
18 Tax on extraordinary profit or loss.
19 Other taxes not shown under the above items.
20 Profit or loss for the financial year.

Profit and loss account format 2

1 Turnover.
2 Change in stocks of finished goods and in work in progress.
3 Own work capitalized.
4 Other operating income.
5 (a) Raw materials and consumables.
  (b) Other external charges.
6 Staff costs:
  (a) wages and salaries;
  (b) social security costs;
  (c) other pension costs.
7 (a) Depreciation and other amounts written off tangible and intangible fixed assets;
  (b) Exceptional amounts written off current assets.
8 Other operating charges.
9 Income from shares in group companies.
10 Income from shares in related companies.
11 Income from other fixed asset investments.
12 Other interest receivable and similar income.
13 Amounts written off investments.
14 Interest payable and similar charges.
15 Tax on profit or loss on ordinary activities.
16 Profit or loss on ordinary activities after taxation.
17 Extraordinary income.
18 Extraordinary charges.
19 Extraordinary profit or loss.

20 Tax on extraordinary profit or loss.

21 Other taxes not shown under the above items.

22 Profit or loss for the financial year.

Balance sheet format 1

1 Called up share capital not paid.

2 Fixed Assets.

  (a) Intangible assets:

    (i) development costs;

    (ii) concessions, patents, licences, trade marks and similar rights and assets;

    (iii) goodwill;

    (iv) payments on account.

  (b) Tangible assets:

    (i) land and buildings;

    (ii) plant and machinery;

    (iii) fixtures, fittings, tools and equipment;

    (iv) payments on account, and assets in course of construction.

  (c) Investments:

    (i) shares in group companies;

    (ii) loans to group companies;

    (iii) shares in related companies;

    (iv) loans to related companies;

    (v) investments other than loans;

    (vi) other loans;

    (vii) own shares.

3 Current assets:

  (a) Stocks:

    (i) raw materials and consumables;

    (ii) work in progress;

    (iii) finished goods and goods for resale;

    (iv) payments on account.

  (b) Debtors:

    (i) trade debtors;

    (ii) amounts owed by group companies;

    (iii) amounts owed by related companies;

    (iv) other debtors;

    (v) called up share capital not paid;

    (vi) prepayments and accrued income.

  (c) Investments:

    (i) shares in group companies;

    (ii) own shares;

    (iii) other investments.

  (d) Cash at bank and in hand.

4 Prepayments and accrued income.

5 Creditors: amounts falling due within one year.

  (a) Debenture loans.

  (b) Bank loans and overdrafts.

  (c) Payments received on account.

  (d) Trade creditors.

  (e) Bills of exchange payable.

  (f) Amounts owed to group companies.

  (g) Amounts owed to related companies.

  (h) Other creditors, including taxation and social security.

  (i) Accruals and deferred income.

6 Net current assets (liabilities).

7 Total assets less current liabilities.

8 Creditors: amounts falling due after more than one year.
   (a) Debenture loans.
   (b) Bank loans and overdrafts.
   (c) Payments received on account.
   (d) Trade creditors.
   (e) Bills of exchange payable.
   (f) Amounts owed to group companies.
   (g) Amounts owed to related companies.
   (h) Other creditors, including taxation and social security.
   (i) Accruals and deferred income.

9 Provision for liabilities and charges.
   (a) Pensions and similar obligations.
   (b) Taxation, including deferred taxation.
   (c) Other provisions.

10 Accruals and deferred income.

11 Capital and reserves.
   (a) Called up share capital.
   (b) Share premium account.
   (c) Revaluation reserve.
   (d) Other reserves:
        (i) capital redemption reserve;
        (ii) reserve for own shares;
        (iii) reserves provided for by the articles of association;
        (iv) other reserves.
   (e) Profit and loss account.

10.3.5 Accounting principles (Schedule 4, Part II Section A)

The accounting principles which a company must use when preparing their accounts are detailed in Schedule 4. They can be summarized as follows:

1 The company shall be presumed to be carrying on business as a going concern.

2 Accounting policies should be applied consistently from one financial year to the next.

3 The amount of any item shall be determined on a prudent basis.

4 All income and charges relating to the financial year of the accounts shall be included, without regard to the dates of receipt or payment.

5 In determining the aggregate amount of any item, the amount of each individual asset or liability that falls to be taken into account shall be determined separately.

If there are special reasons for departing from any of the above principles, then these reasons, and the effects of the departure should be set out in a note to the accounts. The principles follow closely the fundamental accounting concepts which are given special mention in SSAP 2 (*Disclosure of accounting policies*), namely, **going concern, accruals, consistency,** and **prudence**.

10.3.6 Historical cost accounting rules (Schedule 4, Part II Sections B and C)

The Act specifies two sets of accounting rules in Schedule 4. Section B contains the historical cost accounting rules which are based on the historical cost convention, and Section C contains alternative accounting rules, whereby companies can prepare accounts based on current cost accounting principles, or a blend of historic cost and current cost principles.

10.3.7 Notes to the accounts (Schedule 4, Part III)

Schedule 4, Part III details the information which must be given by way of notes to the accounts. Information, in the form of notes, is required to supplement the balance sheet on the following items: share capital and debentures; fixed assets; investments; reserves and provisions; provision for taxation; details of indebtedness; guarantees and other financial commitments and certain miscellaneous matters. Notes are also required to supplement the profit and loss account on the following items: separate statement of certain items of income and expenditure (for example, the amount charged to revenue in respect of sums payable for the hire of plant and machinery and the amount of rent from land); particulars of taxation; particulars of turnover; particulars of staff; certain miscellaneous matters, and general notes concerning foreign currencies and corresponding figures.

The accounting policies adopted by the company in determining the amounts to be included in respect of items shown in the balance sheet and in determining the profit or loss of the company must be stated.

Additional disclosure required in notes to accounts (Section 231)

In addition to the notes supplementing the balance sheet and profit and loss account required by Schedule 4, certain information is required under Schedule 5.

Part V of Schedule 5 is concerned with the emoluments of directors (including emoluments waived), pensions of directors and past directors, and compensation for loss of office to directors and past directors.

Part VI of Schedule 5 is concerned with disclosure of the number of company employees who are remunerated at higher rates.

10.3.8 Directors' reports (Section 235)

The directors of a company must prepare a report every financial year, which contains:

1 A fair review of the development of the business of the company (and its subsidiaries) and their position at the end of the year.

2 The amount (if any) which the directors recommend should be paid as dividend and the amount (if any) transferred to reserves.

3 A list of the names of all persons who were directors at any time during the year.

4 A statement concerning the principal activities of the company (and its subsidiaries) in the course of the year and any significant changes in those activities in the year.

Schedule 7, Part I contains the matters of a general nature to be dealt with in the directors' report, which include changes in asset values, directors' shareholdings and other interests, political and charitable gifts, and miscellaneous matters. Part II covers matters concerning the disclosure required by a company acquiring its own shares, Parts III, IV and V apply to disclosure concerning employment etc. of disabled persons, health, safety and welfare at work of company employees, and employee involvement in the affairs, policy and performance of the company.

10.3.9 Auditors' reports (Section 236)

A company's auditors have to make a report to its members on the balance sheet and profit and loss account.
The auditors' report must state:

1 Whether, in the auditors' opinion, the balance sheet and profit and loss account have been properly prepared in accordance with the Act.

2 Whether in their opinion a true and fair view is given:
(a) in the balance sheet of the state of the company's affairs at the end of the financial year;
(b) in the profit and loss account of the company's profit or loss for the financial year.

The auditors' duties and powers are contained in Section 237.

10.3.10 Signing of balance sheet: documents to be annexed (Section 238)

Company balance sheets must be signed on behalf of the board of directors by two of the directors of the company (but only one if the company has only one director).

10.3.11 Documents to be included in company accounts (Section 239)

The following are the documents that must be included:

1 profit and loss account and balance sheet;

2 directors' report;

3 auditors' report.

10.3.12 Persons entitled to receive accounts as of right (Section 240)

A copy of a company's accounts for the financial year must be sent not less than 21 days before the meeting which considers the accounts, to every member of the company and every debenture holder.

10.3.13 Directors' duty to lay and deliver accounts (Section 241)

The directors have a duty to present a copy of the accounts before a general meeting for every financial year. The auditors' report has to be read and open for inspection by any member. The directors have also to deliver a copy of the accounts to the Registrar of Companies.

Period allowed for laying and delivery (Section 242)

The period allowed for laying and delivering accounts is determined by reference to the end of the relevant accounting period. The period allowed for a private company is 10 months after the end of the relevant accounting reference period, and for a public company it is seven months.

10.3.14 Modified accounts (Sections 247, 248 and 249)

In accordance with Part 1 of Schedule 8, company directors may deliver modified accounts, where the company is small or medium-sized. A company qualifies as 'small' in a financial year if two or more of the following conditions are satisfied:

1 The amount of its turnover for the year is not more than £1.4m.

2 Its balance sheet total is not more than £700,000.

3 The average number of persons employed by the company in the year does not exceed 50.

A company qualifies as 'medium-sized' in a financial year if two or more of the following conditions are satisfied:

1 The amount of its turnover for the year is not more than £5.75m.

2 Its balance sheet total is not more than £2.8m.

3 The average number of persons employed by the company in the year does not exceed 250.

The details of the modified accounts are contained in Schedule 8, Part I. Small companies are not required to deliver either a profit and loss account, or a directors' report, and the balance sheet need only be in an abbreviated form.

Medium-sized companies have to deliver a full balance sheet and directors' report but the profit and loss account need only be in an abbreviated form.

10.4 The Stock Exchange requirements

All companies that are listed on the London Stock Exchange must comply with certain disclosure requirements, which are additional to those imposed by legislation and accounting standards. The following are some of the more important items of information that must be disclosed in the directors' report to satisfy these requirements:

1 If the company fails to comply with any SSAP, the reasons for this must be stated.

2 An analysis of turnover and trading results for operations outside the UK, on a geographical basis.

3 Details of directors' interests in the company's share capital, information on the company's contracts in which its directors have a material interest, and any waivers of dividends by shareholders and/or emoluments by directors.

4 Explanations of material differences between actual trading results and forecasts.

5 In respect of each company in which an equity holding of at least 20 per cent is held:

(a) principal country of operation;

(b) particulars of issued shares and loan capital;

(c) percentage of categories of loan capital in which an interest is held.

Other information has also to be disclosed in the half-yearly interim reports, including:

1 taxation;

2 extraordinary items;

3 dividend rates;

4 earnings per share;

5 comparative figures;

6 any supplementary information the directors consider necessary for a reasonable appreciation of the results.

10.5 Statements of standard accounting practice

Statements of standard accounting practice, SSAPs, have already been covered in chapter 9, Accounting standards. Most of the SSAPs contain some disclosure requirements, and companies must take these into account, as well as the Companies Act and Stock Exchange requirements, when preparing published final accounts.

SSAP 2, *Disclosure of accounting policies*, is particularly important. It makes it clear that there will be a presumption that the four fundamental accounting concepts (see earlier in this chapter) have been followed, in the preparation of the accounts and the accounting policies disclosed.

The following are the more important SSAPs which have to be taken into account when preparing the published accounts:

SSAP 3 *Earnings per share*
SSAP 6 *Extraordinary items and prior year adjustments*
SSAP 9 *Stocks and work in progress*
SSAP 10 *Statements of source and application of funds*
SSAP 12 *Accounting for depreciation*
SSAP 13 *Accounting for research and development*
SSAP 15 *Accounting for deferred taxation*
SSAP 17 *Accounting for post-balance sheet events*
SSAP 18 *Accounting for contingencies*
SSAP 20 *Foreign currency translation*
SSAP 21 *Accounting for leases and hire-purchase contracts*
SSAP 21 *Accounting for goodwill*

10.6 Illustration of the preparation of a published profit and loss account and balance sheet

Company accounts for publication will be prepared on similar lines to the internal company final accounts already shown earlier in this chapter, and incorporating the main points included in chapter 2, chapter 3, and chapter 7. The main area of difference is that the formats and disclosure requirements of the CA 1985 must be adhered to.

An illustration of the preparation of a published profit and loss account and balance sheet follows, in which it is assumed that the company will disclose only the minimum information, and format 1 is used for both the profit and loss account and balance sheet.

List of balances extracted from company books
as at 31 December 1989

	£
8% Preference share capital: 50p shares	500,000
10% Debentures (redeemable in 5 years)	800,000
Ordinary share capital: 25p shares	600,000
Revenue reserves	455,000
Bank overdraft	50,000
Revaluation reserves	137,250
Trade creditors	520,500
Profit and loss account balance 1 January 1989	192,000
Trade debtors	745,000
Stock in trade at 1 January 1989	1,071,000
Trademarks	161,500
Sales	4,500,000
Shares in associated companies	175,000
Goodwill	424,000
Sales returns	115,000
Motor vehicles at cost	325,000
Accumulated depreciation on motor vehicles at 1 January 1989	145,000
Purchases	2,187,500
Plant and equipment at cost	1,775,000
Accumulated depreciation on plant and equipment at 1 January 1989	588,000
Discounts received	127,000
Wages and salaries – sales staff	625,000
Discounts allowed	51,000
Wages and salaries – administrative staff	341,500
Bad debts	31,000
Motor vehicles expenses	166,250
Directors' remuneration	185,500
Distribution expenses	82,000
Administration expenses	80,000
Debenture interest	40,000
Income from shares in associated companies	51,500
Costs arising on closure of a factory	85,000

The following additional information has to be taken into account:

1 Stock in trade at 31 December 1989 was valued at £1,460,000.

2 Depreciation is to be provided on the plant and equipment at 15 per cent of cost. and for the motor vehicles at 20 per cent on the written down value.

3 Motor vehicles expenses and depreciation on motor vehicles are to be allocated 75 per cent to distribution and 25 per cent to administration.

4 Administration expenses of £5,500 have accrued due and distribution expenses o £1,000 have been paid in advance.

5 There is a liability for corporation tax on the profits amounting to £110,000. Thi is payable in nine months' time.

6 The outstanding preference dividend and the interest on the debentures must b provided for.

7 The directors have recommended an ordinary share dividend of 10 per cent, an the transfer of £100,000 to revenue reserves.

Profit and loss account
for the year ended 31 December 1989

	£	£
Sales		4,385,000
Cost of sales [1]		1,798,500
Gross profit		2,586,500
Distribution costs [2]	857,688	
Administrative expenses [3]	884,312	1,742,000
		844,500
Other operating income:		
income from shares in associated companies	51,500	51,500
		896,000
Interest payable		80,000
Profit on ordinary activities before taxation		816,000
Tax on profit on ordinary activities		110,000
Profit on ordinary activities after taxation		706,000
Extraordinary charge		85,000
Profit for the financial year		621,000
Undistributed profits from last year		192,000
		813,000
Preference dividend accrued	40,000	
Ordinary dividend proposed	60,000	
	100,000	
Transfer to revenue reserves	100,000	200,000
Undistributed profits carried forward		613,000

Earnings per share [4]: 29.42p

Balance sheet as at 31 December 1989

	£	£	£
Fixed assets			
Intangible assets:			
Trademarks	161,500		
Goodwill	424,000	585,500	
Tangible assets:			
Plant and equipment [5]	920,750		
Motor vehicles [6]	144,000	1,064,750	
Investments:			
Shares in associated companies		175,000	1,825,250
Current assets			
Stock in trade		1,460,000	
Trade debtors		745,000	
Prepayment		1,000	
		2,206,000	
Creditors: amount falling due within one year			
Bank overdraft	50,000		
Trade creditors	520,500		
Other creditors [7]	250,000		
Accruals	5,500	826,000	
Net current assets			1,380,000
Total assets less current liabilities			3,205,250
Creditors: amounts falling due after more than one year			
10% Debentures			800,000
			2,405,250

(cont'd.)

(*cont'd.*)

	£
Capital and reserves	
Called up share capital	1,100,000
Revaluation reserves	137,250
Revenue reserves	555,000
Profit and loss account	613,000
	2,405,250

In addition to stating the accounting policies adopted by the company, information in the form of notes would then be given supplementing the profit and loss account and balance sheet, as required by Schedules 4 to 8.

Workings

£

1 **Cost of sales**

	£
Opening stock	1,071,000
Add purchases	2,187,500
	3,258,500
Less Closing stock	1,460,000
	1,798,500

2 **Distribution costs**

	£
Wages and salaries—	
Sales staff	625,000
Distribution expenses (less prepaid £1,000)	81,000
Motor vehicle expenses	
(75/100 × 166,250)	124,688
Motor vehicle depreciation	
(20/100 × 180,000 × 75/100)	27,000
	857,688

3 **Administrative expenses**

	£
Wages and salaries	341,500
Bad debts	31,000
Motor Vehicle Expenses	
(25/100 × 166,250)	41,562
Directors' remuneration	185,500
Administration expenses	80,000
Add accrual	5,500
Depreciation on motor vehicles	
(20/100 × 180,000 × 25/100)	9,000
Depreciation on plant and equipment	
(15/100 × 1,775,000)	266,250
Discounts allowed	51,000
	1,011,312
Less Discounts received	127,000
	884,312

4 **EPS**

$$\frac{\text{Profit on ordinary activities after taxation}}{\text{Number of ordinary shares}} = \frac{£706,000}{2,400,000} = 29.42\text{p}$$

5 **Plant and equipment**

	£
Cost	1,775,000
Less accumulated depreciation at 1.1.1989	588,000
This year's charge	266,250
Written down value	920,750

6 **Motor vehicles**

	£
Cost	325,000
Less accumulated depreciation at 1.1.1989	145,000
This year's charge	36,000
Written down value	144,000

7 Other creditors	£
Corporation tax	110,000
Interest on debentures	40,000
Preference dividend	40,000
Ordinary dividend	60,000
	250,000

It would be useful to examine ICI's annual report and accounts, which can be found in the appendix. Please note the formats adopted, the statement of accounting policies and the detailed disclosure requirements contained in the accounts and notes as required by the CA 1985, the Stock Exchange, and the ASC.

Links with other topics

Company annual reports and accounts link with many of the other chapters in the book. The first seven chapters, in particular, provide a sound foundation upon which company annual reports can be prepared. Chapter 8, Accounting for depreciation, chapter 9, Accounting standards and chapter 11, Taxation, also include information which is closely linked. Most of the remaining chapters, 12 to 18, are concerned with analysing and interpreting the prepared and presented annual report and accounts, like those prepared in this chapter. Sources and application of funds statements are an important part of the published financial reporting package and they are covered in chapter 16, Funds flow.

Sample questions

1 The summarized trial balance of Helen Ltd at 31 December after the calculation of the net operating profit was as follows:

	Dr £	Cr £
Ordinary shares of 50p each		10,000
10% Preference shares of £1 each		9,000
10% Debentures		8,000
Fixed assets at net book value	35,000	
Current assets	30,100	
Creditors		20,000
Capital redemption reserve		5,000
Share premium		4,000
Profit and loss balance 1 January		3,000
Debenture interest	400	
Preference dividend	450	
Net operating profit for year		8,450
Interim ordinary dividend	2,000	
Corporation tax		500
	67,950	67,950

The following is to be taken into account:
 (i) A building, net book value currently £5,000, is to be revalued to £9,000.
 (ii) Preference dividends of £450 and a final ordinary dividend of 10p per share are to be proposed.
(iii) The balance on the corporation tax account represents an overprovision of tax for the previous year. Corporation tax for the current year is estimated at £3,000.

Required:
(a) Prepare completed final accounts for internal use, within the limits of the information available. Ignore taxation except as specifically stated in the question.
(b) What are reserves in the context of limited companies, and what essential features distinguish reserves from debentures and share capital? Explain briefly the differences between capital and revenue reserves, using the reserves in the balance sheet of Helen Ltd for the purpose of illustration.

ACCA Level 1

Understanding the question

This is a relatively straightforward question requiring the preparation of a condensed profit and loss account and balance sheet for a company for **internal purposes** for part (a).

It is necessary to understand clearly the difference(s) between share capital, reserves and debentures to answer part (b) and use the items in the trial balance to illustrate your answer.

Answer plan

(a)

Helen Ltd
Profit and loss account for year ending 31 December 19—

	£	£	£
Net operating profits for year			8,450
Less Debenture interest			
(includes outstanding interest)			800
			7,650
Less Taxation (£3,000 less overprovision)			2,500
Profit for year after taxation			5,150
ADD Profit and loss account			
balance b/fwd			3,000
			8,150
Less Appropriations			
Dividends:			
Preference: paid	450		
proposed	450	900	
Ordinary: paid	2,000		
proposed	2,000	4,000	4,900
Profit and loss account balance c/fwd			3,250

Balance sheet as at 31 December 19—

	£	£	£
Fixed assets			39,000
Current assets		30,100	
Less current liabilities			
Creditors	20,000		
Corporation tax	3,000		
Debenture interest	400		
Dividends proposed	2,450	25,850	
Working capital			4,250
Net assets			43,250
Share capital			
10% Preference shares – £1 each			9,000
Ordinary shares – 50p each			10,000
			19,000
Reserves			
Share premium		4,000	
Capital redemption		5,000	
Revaluation		4,000	
Profit and loss account		3,250	16,250
Shareholders' funds			35,250
Loan capital 10% debentures			8,000
			43,250

(b) It is necessary to define share capital, reserves and debentures and clearly distinguish the important differences between them. Reserves can be divided int' capital and revenue reserves and you are required to explain the differences between them. The question includes examples of both, i.e. capital reserves include the share premium, capital redemption reserve and revaluation reserve, whilst revenue reserves comprise the balance on the profit and loss account. One of the most important differences concerns their availability for distribution purposes.

2 You are given the following trial balance of Grace Ltd as at 31 December 1987, as prepared by the firm's bookkeeper. All figures are in £000s:

	Dr £000	Cr £000
Share capital (200,000 50p shares)		100
Share premium		50
Profit and loss balance 1 January 1987		100
Debentures (10% interest p.a.) issued in 1974		100
Stock	200	
Motor vehicles	100	
Motor vehicles depreciation 1 January 1987		60
Machinery	120	
Machinery depreciation 1 January 1987		50
Buildings at cost 1 January 1987	230	
Sales		750
Purchases	350	
Discounts	2	
Returns	2	
Carriage	2	
General expenses	200	
Advertising	10	
Creditors		200
Debtors	200	
Provision for doubtful debts		6
Debenture interest	5	
Bank balance		5
	1,421	1,421

You are also given the following information:

(a) The bookkeeper, in an attempt at simplification, has posted both discounts received and discounts allowed to the discounts account. He has also posted both returns inwards and returns outwards to the returns account, and both carriage inwards and carriage outwards to the carriage account.

Discounts received were actually £1,000
Returns outwards were actually £1,000
Carriage outwards was actually £1,000

(b) The following items are already included in general expenses:

 (i) Rates for the 12 months to 31 March 1988, £4,000;

(ii) Insurance for the 12 months to 31 December 1988, £2,000. Half of this amount relates to the managing director's private yacht.

(c) Your own charges of £1,000 for accountancy services need to be included.

(d) A debtor of £20,000 has gone bankrupt. The provision for doubtful debts is required to be 5% of debtors.

(e) A dividend of 5p per share is proposed.

(f) Closing stock is £180,000.

(g) Depreciation of £20,000 is to be provided on the motor vehicles and of £10,000 on the machinery. The buildings are to be revalued by £30,000.

Required:
Prepare a profit and loss account and balance sheet for Grace Ltd for the year (for internal purposes).

ACCA Level 1

Understanding the question

You are required to prepare from a trial balance a profit and loss account and balance sheet for a limited company for internal purposes. There are a number of adjustments to take into account. One approach to this type of question is to decide which 'statement' each item is to be entered into and make a note of this on the question paper or your working notes. The same approach is required for the adjustments, remembering that each adjustment must be shown twice in the statements.

Answer plan

Grace Ltd
Profit and loss account
for the year ending 31 December 1987

	£000	£000	£000	£000
Sales			750	
Less returns			3	747
Less cost of sales:				
Opening stock		200		
Plus net purchases	349			
Plus carriage	1	350		
		550		
Less closing stock		180		370
Gross profit				377
Plus discounts received				1
				378
Less expenses:				
Discounts allowed		3		
Carriage		1		
General expenses (200 − 3)		197		
Advertising		10		
Bad debts		20		
Increase in provision for doubtful debts		3		
Debenture interest (5+5)		10		
Accountancy services		1		
Depreciation		30		275
Net profit				103
Add Balance b/f				100
				203
Less dividends proposed				10
Balance c/f				193

Balance Sheet as at 31 December 1987

	Cost/valuation	Depreciation	W.D.V. to date
	£000	£000	£000
Fixed assets			
Buildings	260	—	260
Machinery	120	60	60
Motor vehicles	100	80	20
	480	140	340
Current assets			
Stock		180	
Debtors less			
provision (180 − 9)		171	
Prepayments		3	
		354	

(cont'd.

	(cont'd.)	£000	£000	£000
	Less current liabilities			
	Creditors	200		
	Accruals (5 + 1)	6		
	Bank	5		
	Dividends	10	221	133
	Net current assets			473
	Financed by:			
	Share capital –			
	200,000 50p shares		100	
	Reserves			
	Share premium	50		
	Revaluation reserve	30		
	P & L a/c	193	273	373
	Shareholders' funds			
	10% debentures			100
				473

3 The following information has been extracted from the books of account of Rufford plc for the year to 31 March 1986:

	Dr	Cr
	£000	**£000**
ACT (paid on 14 October 1985)	3	
Administration expenses	97	
Deferred taxation		24
Depreciation on office machinery		
(for the year to 31 March 1986)	8	
Depreciation on delivery vans		
(for the year to 31 March 1986)	19	
Distribution costs	33	
Dividends received		
(from a UK listed company on 31 July 1985)		14
Factory closure expenses (net of tax)	12	
Interest payable on bank overdraft		
(repayable within five years)	6	
Interim dividend (paid on 30 September 1985)	21	
Interest receivable		25
Purchases	401	
Retained profit at 31 March 1985		160
Sales (net of VAT)		642
Stock at 1 April 1985	60	

Additional information:

1 Administrative expenses include the following items:

	£000
Auditors' remuneration	20
Directors' emoluments	45
Travelling expenses	1
Research expenditure	11
Hire of plant and machinery	12

2 It is assumed that the following tax rates are applicable for the year to 31 March 1986:

	%
Corporation tax	50
Income tax	30

3 There was an overprovision for corporation tax of £3,000 relating to the year to 31 March 1985.

4 Corporation tax payable for the year to 31 March 1986 (based on the profits for that year) is estimated to be £38,000. The company, in addition, intends to transfer a further £9,000 to its deferred taxation account.

5 A final dividend of £42,000 for the year to 31 March 1986 is expected to be paid on 2 June 1986.

6 Stock at 31 March 1986 was valued at £71,000.

7 As a result of a change in accounting policy, a prior year charge of £15,000 (net of tax) is to be made.

8 The company's share capital consists of 420,000 ordinary shares of £1 each. There are no preference shares and no change had been made to the company's issued share capital for some years.

Required:
(a) Insofar as the information permits, prepare the company's published profit and loss account for the year to 31 March 1986 in the vertical format in accordance with the Companies Act 1985 and with related statements of standard accounting practice. (N.B. A statement of the company's accounting policies is NOT required.)

(b) Prepare balance sheet extracts in order to illustrate the balances still remaining in the following accounts at 31 March 1986:

   (i) corporation tax;
  (ii) advanced corporation tax;
 (iii) proposed dividend; and
  (iv) deferred taxation.

(N.B. a detailed balance sheet is NOT required.)

AAT Final membership examination

Understanding the question

Part (a) of the question requires you to prepare the published profit and loss account only (not the balance sheet). In the following answer plan all items have to be entered into format 1 as shown in this chapter. Part (b) requires you to prepare balance sheet extracts; the workings carried out for part (a) will help you to arrive at the necessary figures.

Answer plan

Part (a)

Rufford plc
Profit and loss account
for the year ending 31 March 1986

	£000	£000
Sales		642
Cost of sales		390
Gross profit		252
Distribution costs	52	
Administrative expenses	105	(157)
		95
Other income[1]		45
		140
Interest payable		(6)
Profit on ordinary activities before taxation		134
Tax on profit on ordinary activities[2]		(50)
Profit on ordinary activities after taxation		84
Extraordinary charge		(12)
Profit for the financial year		72

(cont'd

(*cont'd.*)

	£000	£000
Dividends		63
Undistributed profits		9
Balance of retained profits brought forward	160	
Less prior year adjustment	(15)	145
Undistributed profits carried forward		154
Earnings per share 20p		

Notes

Notes would be required for turnover, items requiring disclosure in the profit and loss account (e.g. auditors remunerations), taxation, extraordinary items, dividends and earnings per share.

Workings
[1]Other income

	£000
Dividends received (grossed up at the standard rate of tax (30%): (14 × 100/70)	20
Interest receivable	25
	45

[2]Tax

Corporation tax (see note **4**)	38
Overprovision (see note **3**)	(3)
Tax on dividends received[1]	6
Transfer to deferred tax account (see note **4**)	9
	50

Part (b)

Extracts from balance sheets as at 31 March 1986

	£000
Creditors: amounts falling due within one year	
Other creditors[1]	95
Provision for liabilities and charges	
Deferred taxation[2]	15

Workings
[1]Other creditors

	£000
Corporation tax (see note **4**)	38
Proposed dividends (see note **5**)	42
ACT paid (see trial balance)	(3)
ACT deduct from proposed dividends at 30% (3/7 × 42,000)	18
	95

[2]Deferred taxation

	£000
Trial balance figure	24
Transfer (see note **4**)	9
ACT on proposed dividend[1]	(18)
	15

4 The following trial balance has been extracted from the books of Arran plc as at 31 March 1987:

	£000	£000
Administrative expenses	95	
Advance corporation tax paid	6	

(*cont'd.*)

(cont'd.)	£000	£000
Called up share capital (all ordinary shares of £1 each)		210
Cash at bank and in hand	30	
Debtors	230	
Deferred taxation (at 1 April 1986)		60
Distribution costs	500	
Fixed asset investments	280	
Franked investment income		7
Interim dividend paid	21	
Overprovision of last year's corporation tax		5
Land and buildings at cost	200	
Land and buildings: accumulated depreciation at 1 April 1986		30
Plant and machinery at cost	400	
Plant and machinery: accumulated depreciation at 1 April 1986		170
Profit and loss account (at 1 April 1986)		235
Profit on extraordinary item (before taxation)		50
Purchases	1,210	
Sales		2,215
Stocks at 1 April 1986	140	
Trade creditors		130
	3,112	3,112

Additional information:

1 Stocks at 31 March 1987 were valued at £150,000.

2 Depreciation for the year to 31 March 1987 is to be charged against administrative expenses as follows:

	£000
Land and buildings	5
Plant and machinery	40

3 Assume that the basic rate of income tax is 30 per cent.

4 Corporation tax of £165,000 is to be charged against profits on ordinary activities for the year to 31 March 1987.

5 £4,000 is to be transferred to the deferred taxation account.

6 Corporation tax of £15,000 is payable on the extraordinary profit.

7 The company proposes to pay a final ordinary dividend of 30p per share.

Required:
Insofar as the information permits, prepare the company's profit and loss account for the year to 31 March 1987 and a balance sheet as at that date in accordance with the Companies Act 1985 and related statements of standard accounting practice.

(**NOTE:** Profit and loss account and balance sheet notes are NOT REQUIRED, but you should show the basis and computation of earnings per share at the foot of the profit and loss account, and your workings should be submitted.)

AAT Final membership examination

Understanding the question

This question requires you to prepare a profit and loss account and balance sheet for publication purposes. The first step is to decide into which of the two statements each item in the trial balance is to be entered, taking into account the seven 'adjustments'. The statements must then be prepared in a prescribed format (format 1 is used here), bearing in mind the Companies Act 1985 and SSAP disclosure requirements. Publication notes are not required, but you are specifically asked to show your workings and should do so clearly.

Answer plan

Arran plc
Profit and loss account
for the year ending 31 March 1987

	£000	£000
Sales		2,215
Cost of sales[1]		(1,200)
Gross profit		1,015
Distribution costs	500	
Administrative expenses[2]	140	(640)
		375
Income from investments[3]		10
Profit on ordinary activities before taxation		385
Tax on profit on ordinary activities[4]		(167)
Profit on ordinary activities after taxation		218
Extraordinary income	50	
Less taxation (see note 6)	(15)	35
Profit for the financial year		253
Dividends		(84)
Undistributed profit carried forward		169
Earnings per share 103.8p		

Balance sheet as at 31 March 1987

	£000	£000	£000
Fixed assets			
Intangible assets	—	—	—
Tangible assets[5]			
Land and buildings		165	
Plant and machinery		190	355
Investments			280
			635
Current assets			
Stocks		150	
Debtors		230	
Cash		30	
		410	
Less creditors: amounts falling due within one year			
Trade creditors	130		
Other creditors[6]	264	(394)	
Net current assets			16
Total assets less current liabilities			651
Less provisions for liabilities and charges: deferred taxation[7]			(37)
			614
Capital and reserves:			
Called up share capital			210
Profit and loss account			404
			614

(cont'd.)

(cont'd.)
Workings   £000

¹**Cost of sales**
Opening stock   140
Purchases   1,210
                                                        1,350
Less closing stock   150
                                                        1,200

²**Administrative expenses**
As per trial balance   95
Depreciation   45
                                                          140

³**Franked investment income**
This income has to be grossed up to take
 account of tax paid at standard rate,
 i.e. 7 × 100/70   10

⁴**Taxation**
Corporation tax (see note **4**)   165
Over-provision (see trial balance)   (5)
Tax on income³   3
To deferred tax account (see note **5**)   4
                                                          167

⁵**Tangible assets**

	Cost	Depreciation to date	W.D.V.
	£000	£000	£000
Land and buildings	200	35	165
Plant and machinery	400	210	190
	600	245	355

⁶**Other creditors**
Corporation tax (see note **4**)   165
ACT paid (see trial balance)   (6)
Corporation tax on extraordinary item   15
Proposed dividend (see trial balance)   63
ACT deducted from proposed dividend
 (3/7 × 63)   27
                                                          264

⁷**Provision for liabilities and charges**
Deferred tax (see trial balance)   60
Transfer (see note **5**)   4
ACT on proposed dividend⁶   (27)
                                                           37

5 The following information has been extracted from the books of account of
Billinge public limited company as at 30 June 1986:

	Dr £000	Cr £000
Administration expenses	242	
Cash at bank and in hand	107	
Cash received on sale of fittings		3
Corporation tax (over-provision for the previous year)		10
Deferred taxation		60

(cont'd.

(*cont'd.*)	£000	£000
Depreciation on fixtures, fittings, tools and equipment (at 1 July 1985)		132
Distribution costs	55	
Factory closure costs	30	
Fixtures, fittings, tools and equipment at cost	340	
Profit and loss account (at July 1985)		40
Purchase of equipment	60	
Purchase of goods for resale	855	
Sales (net of VAT)		1,500
Share capital (450,000 authorized, issued and fully paid ordinary shares of £1 each)		450
Stock (at 1 July 1985)	70	
Trade creditors		64
Trade debtors	500	
	2,259	2,259

Additional information:

1 The company was incorporated in 1970.

2 The stock at 30 June 1986 (valued at the lower of cost or net realizable value) was estimated to be worth £100,000.

3 Fixtures, fittings, tools and equipment all relate to administrative expenses. Depreciation is charged on them at a rate of 20 per cent per annum on cost. A full year's depreciation is charged in the year of acquisition, but no depreciation is charged in the year of disposal.

4 During the year to 30 June 1986, the company purchased £60,000 of equipment. It also sold some fittings (which had originally cost £20,000) for £3,000 and for which depreciation of £15,000 had been set aside.

5 The corporation tax based on the profits for the year at a rate of 35 per cent is estimated to be £85,000. A transfer of £40,000 is to be made to the deferred taxation account. Tax relief of £15,000 is available against the factory closure costs.

6 The company proposes to pay a dividend of 20p per ordinary share.

7 The standard rate of income tax is 30 per cent.

Required:

Insofar as the information permits, prepare Billinge public limited company's profit and loss account for the year to 30 June 1986, and a balance sheet as at that date in accordance with the Companies Act 1985 and appropriate statements of standard accounting practice.

AAT Final membership examination

Answer plan

Billinge plc
Profit and loss account for the year ending 30 June 1986

	£000	£000
Sales		1,500
Less cost of sales		(825)
Gross profit		675
Less: Distribution costs	55	
Administrative expenses[1]	320	(375)
Profit on ordinary activities before taxation		300
Tax on profit on ordinary activities[2]		(115)
Profit on ordinary activities after taxation		185
Extraordinary item[3]		(15)
Profit for the financial year		170
Dividends		(90)
Undistributed profits carried forward		80
Earnings per share 41.1p		

Balance sheet at 30 June 1986

	£000	£000	£000
Fixed assets			
Intangible assets	—	—	—
Tangible assets			
Fixtures, fittings, tools and equipment[4]			187
Current assets			
Stocks		100	
Debtors		500	
Cash		107	
		707	
Creditors: amounts falling due within			
one year			
Trade creditors	64		
Other creditors[5]	199	(263)	
Net current assets			444
Total assets less current liabilities			631
Provisions for liabilities and charges			
deferred taxation[6]			(61)
			570
Capital and reserves			
Called up share capital			450
Profit and loss account			120
			570

Notes to the accounts:

Notes to the financial statements should include details of:

> accounting policies;
>
> administration expenses;
>
> taxation;
>
> extraordinary items;
>
> dividends;
>
> tangible fixed assets;
>
> share capital; and
>
> earnings per share.

You are recommended to study the accounting policies and notes for ICI plc which can be found in the appendix, and then attempt to make similar suitable notes for Billinge plc.

Workings

[1]**Administrative expenses**	£000	£000
As per trial balance		242
Depreciation of fixtures, fittings, tools and		
equipment (see notes **3** and **4**):		
Cost of start	340	
Less sales	(20)	
	320	
Plus additions	60	
	380	
At 20% on cost		76
Adjustment for sale of fittings: under		
depreciated		
(£20,000 − £15,000 − £3,000)		2
		320

[2] Taxation

Corporation tax for year (see note 5)	85
Over-provision (see trial balance)	(10)
Transfer to deferred tax account (see note 5)	40
	115

[3] Extraordinary item

The factory closure costs of £30,000 shown in the trial balance are costs outside the ordinary activities of the business and must be included in this section, less £15,000 tax relief shown in note 5.

[4] Fixed assets

	Cost	Depreciation to date	W.D.V.
	£000	£000	£000
At start of year	340	132	208
Additions (note 4)	60	—	60
Sales (note 4)	(20)	(15)	(5)
Charge for the year (note 3)	—	76	(76)
	380	193	187

[5] Other creditors

Corporation tax for year (note 5)	85
Tax (relief) on extraordinary item	(15)
Proposed dividends	90
ACT on above proposed dividends (3/7 × 90)	39
	199

[6] Deferred taxation

Per trial balance	60
Transfer (see note 5)	40
ACT on proposed dividend[5]	(39)
	61

6 The following trial balance has been extracted from the books of Baganza plc as at 30 September 1987:

	£000	£000
Advance corporation tax (paid on interim dividend)	87	
Administrative expenses	400	
Called up share capital (1,200,000 ordinary shares of £1 each)		1,200
Cash at bank and in hand	60	
Corporation tax (overpayment for the year to 30 September 1986)		20
Deferred taxation (at 1 October 1986)		460
Distribution costs	600	
Dividends received (on 31 March 1987)		249
Extraordinary item (net of tax)	1,500	
Freehold property:		
at cost	2,700	
accumulated depreciation (at 1 October 1986)		260
Interim dividend (paid on 30 June 1987)	36	
Investments in United Kingdom companies	2,000	
Plant and machinery:		
at cost	5,200	
accumulated depreciation (at 1 October 1986)		3,600
Profit and loss account (at 1 October 1986)		2,109
Purchases	16,000	

(cont'd.)

	£000	£000
(cont'd.)		
Research expenditure	75	
Stock (at 1 October 1986)	2,300	
Tax on extraordinary item		360
Trade creditors		2,900
Trade debtors	2,700	
Turnover		19,500
	32,158	32,158

Additional information:

1 The stock at 30 September 1987 was valued at £3,600,000.

2 Depreciation for the year to 30 September 1987 is to be charged on the historic cost of the fixed assets as follows:
Freehold property: 5%
Plant and machinery: 15%

3 The basic rate of income tax is assumed to be 27 per cent.

4 The directors propose a final dividend of 60p per share.

5 The company was incorporated in 1970.

6 Corporation tax based on the profits for the year at a rate of 35 per cent is estimated to be £850,000.

7 A transfer of £40,000 is to be made to the deferred taxation account.

Required:
Insofar as the information permits, prepare Baganza plc's profit and loss account for the year to 30 September 1987, and a balance sheet as at that date in accordance with the Companies Act 1985 and appropriate statements of standard accounting practice.

However, formal notes to the accounts are NOT required, although detailed workings should be submitted with your answer, which should include your calculation of earnings per share.

AAT Final membership examination

Understanding the question
You are required to prepare a profit and loss account and balance sheet for publication purposes for a limited company. You should enter the items into a format 1 layout for both statements and show your workings clearly.

Answer plan

Baganza plc
Profit and loss account
for the year ending 30 September 1987

	£000
Sales	19,500
Cost of sales	14,700
Gross profit	4,800
Distribution costs[1]	(600)
Administrative expenses	(1,390)
	2,810
Other operating income[2]	341
Profit on ordinary activities before taxation	3,151
Tax on profit on ordinary activities[3]	(962)
Profit on ordinary activities after taxation	2,189
Extraordinary income	1,500
Profit for the financial year	3,689
Dividends	(756)
Transfer to reserves	2,933

Earnings per share 182.4p

Balance sheet as at 30 September 1987

	£000	£000	£000
Fixed assets			
Intangible assets	—	—	—
Tangible assets[4]			
Freehold property	2,305		
Plant and machinery	820	3,125	
Investments		2,000	5,125
Current assets			
Stocks		3,600	
Debtors		2,700	
Cash		60	
		6,360	
Creditors: amounts falling due within			
one year			
Trade creditors	2,900		
Other creditors[5]	2,109	(5,009)	
Net current assets			1,351
Total assets less current liabilities			6,476
Provision for liabilities and charges[6]			(234)
			6,242
Capital and reserves			
Called up share capital			1,200
Profit and loss account			5,042
			6,242

Workings

[1]Administrative expenses

	£000
As per trial balance	400
Research expenditure	75
Depreciation	
property	135
plant and machinery	780
	1,390

[2]Other operating income

Dividends received (£249) need to be grossed up
for publication purposes using the income tax
rate of 27% (see note 3)

tax: 249 × 27/73	92
Dividend (before tax)	249
	341

[3]Taxation

Corporation tax (see note 6)	850
Overpayment of tax (see trial balance)	(20)
Tax on dividends[2]	92
Transfer to deferred tax account (see note 7)	40
	962

[4]**Tangible assets**

	Cost	Depreciation to date	W.D.V.
	£000	£000	£000
Freehold property	2,700	395	2,305
Plant and machinery	5,200	4,380	820
	7,900	4,775	3,125

[5]**Other creditors**

Corporation tax: (see note 6)	850	
(see trial balance)	360	
(see trial balance)	(87)	
	1,123	1,123
ACT payable on dividends (27/73 × 720)		266
Proposed dividends		720
		2,109

[6]**Provisions for liabilities and charges**

Deferred tax (see trial balance)	460
Plus transfer to this account (see note 7)	40
Less ACT on proposed dividends	(266)
	234

7 When preparing the profit and loss account of a public limited company in accordance with the requirements of the Companies Act 1985 and with statements of standard accounting practice, it is necessary to disclose a minimum amount of information about certain matters.

Required:
State what details should be disclosed in dealing with each of the following items:

(a) turnover;

(b) directors' emoluments;

(c) employees; and

(d) extraordinary items.

AAT Final membership examination

Understanding the question

You are required to state the disclosure requirements for four different accounting items that appear in published annual reports and accounts. The information is contained in the Companies' Act 1985 and the accounting standards, and both areas have been covered in this chapter and chapter 9.

Answer plan

Part (a)
Turnover – Briefly the details required are the amount, the method of computation used, a geographical analysis in each market and the amount attributable to each class of business.

Part (b)
Directors' emoluments – Briefly the details required include the aggregate emoluments, fees, benefits in kind and pension contributions, aggregate directors' and past directors' pensions, aggregate amounts paid as compensation for loss of office to directors and past directors and, if the aggregate emoluments exceed £60,000, further details including the number of directors within brackets of a scale of £5,000, chairman's emoluments, the number of directors who have waived their emoluments, if any, and the emoluments paid to the highest paid director. There are certain limitations to these requirements detailed in the Act.

Part (c)

Employees – Briefly, the requirements include aggregate remuneration, split into categories, average weekly number of employees, again analysed into categories, and the number of employees whose aggregate emoluments are over £30,000 per annum.

Part (d)

Extraordinary items – Extraordinary items are those transactions outside the ordinary activities of the business which are material and not expected to recur frequently (SSAP 6). They should be disclosed in the profit and loss account after profit from ordinary activities. The total profit/loss should be analysed for each extraordinary item, detailing gains and losses and the item's size and nature.

Further reading

J. B. Lake *Company Reports and Accounts* (Pitman), chapters 1, 3, 4, 6 and 8.
F. Wood *Business Accounting 2* (Pitman), fifth edition, chapters 11 to 19.

11 Taxation

This chapter will concentrate on how tax is levied on the profits made by companies and individuals. Taxes such as corporation tax, which is paid by companies, and capital gains tax and income tax, which are paid by individuals, are known as **direct taxes**. If income is sufficient, tax is either deducted at source, as with 'pay as you earn', or payable on demand to the Inland Revenue.

Taxes such as value added tax, duty on tobacco and petrol, for example, are known as **indirect taxes**, and are paid when we purchase certain categories of goods. The study of indirect taxes is outside the scope of this chapter. However, outstanding VAT, either payable to the Customs and Excise or refundable by them, will appear in balance sheets as creditors/debtors, and sales revenue does not include VAT charged to customers, when preparing the profit and loss account.

During the spring of each year, the Chancellor of the Exchequer traditionally delivers his **budget**, outlining any proposals which he may have for amending the system of both direct and indirect taxation. Any study of taxation must take account of such changes in legislation.

The main points that will be covered in this chapter are as follows:

1 A brief insight into the tax system as affecting employees.

2 How profits from business are assessed for tax.

3 Allowances for capital expenditure.

It need not be expected that detailed aspects of business taxation are likely to be examined, at least on first-year accountancy courses, but one should be prepared for questions of a computational nature in the following two main areas:

1 Adjusting profits as shown by the profit and loss accounts of companies and sole traders for corporation tax and income tax (Schedule D).

2 Calculating capital allowances due on fixed assets purchased in the current and previous years.

Essay-type questions could be set on the use of taxation as an instrument of economic policy, and perhaps explaining the difference between **progressive** and **regressive** taxes.

11.1 Income tax

Students at many colleges embark on courses involving a sandwich element of work experience, usually one period of a year, or two periods of six months. As a consequence, direct experience of the workings of the tax system as affecting employees is quickly obtained.

Employers deduct tax from wages and salaries in accordance with **code numbers** issued by the Inland Revenue, which are based on **personal allowances** available to individual employees. Responsibility for the correctness of these code numbers rests with individual employees, who should ensure that they are obtaining all the allowances to which they are legally entitled. Personal circumstances such as marriage, separation, the death of a husband, being a single parent, or being a registered blind person, are examples of how a person's tax situation can be affected.

An example of income tax for a married man earning a salary of £15,000 per annum is as follows:

His code number will be 1/10th of his personal allowances. In this case, the tax allowance is £4,095 for a married man in the year ended 5 April 1989.

	£
Salary	15,000
Married man's personal allowance	4,095
Taxable income	10,905
Tax payable (@ 25%)	2,726

His code number of 409 will allocate the allowance of £4,095 equally over the year, in either weeks (52) or months (12), so that the correct amount of tax, £2,726, is deducted from his income.

11.2 Taxation of businesses

The following example illustrates how tax is levied on business profits:

		£
The **Net profit** from the **profit and loss account** is taken:	say	500,000
Certain adjustments, some added and some subtracted, are made to this figure (see later)	say	50,000
		550,000
Allowances given for expenditure on fixed assets (see later) can then be deducted	say	60,000
Amount charged to either corporation tax or income tax		490,000

Whether employed or self-employed, individuals are entitled to the same range of personal allowances, such as single and married personal allowances, and pay income tax at the same rates. Companies are assessed to tax on income as are individuals, but pay what is known as **corporation tax** instead of income tax. The basis of assessing both individuals and companies on profits from trading is very similar, therefore the comments that follow apply equally to both.

Accurate accounts are essential if business profits are to be charged correctly to either income tax or corporation tax. Because companies must produce audited accounts, Inspectors of Taxes can usually rely on such figures as being reasonably accurate (however, the question of whether 'small' companies should continue to be obliged by law to have an annual audit is constantly being discussed).

What should not be overlooked is that accounts of **all** self-employed persons are submitted to the Inland Revenue for assessment. The system used for recording daily business transactions will come under scrutiny by the Inspector of Taxes, who will also use analytical methods (as described elsewhere in this book) to decide whether the figures seem fair and reasonable. No one likes paying tax, but for anyone caught deliberately evading their correct liability, the penalties can be severe, and in some cases will mean prison sentences.

Business profits assessable to tax are usually not simply the profits shown by the profit and loss account. For tax purposes, certain items which appear as expenses in the account are not allowed, and have to be added to the profits shown. On the other hand, there are certain types of receipt which are not taxed, or are chargeable under some other heading. These must be deducted from the profits shown.

11.2.1 Expenditure not allowed

Some of the following apply only to individuals, but most are applicable to both companies and persons:

1 Expenses **not wholly and exclusively** laid out for the purpose of the business.

2 Expenses for **domestic** or **private** purposes.

3 The cost of **business entertaining**.

4 The proportion of rent, rates, insurance and heating and lighting applicable to private living quarters of premises used also for business (e.g. a flat above a ground floor shop).

5 Any **capital sums** used in, or withdrawn from the business.

6 The cost of **improvements and alterations** to an asset, as distinct from **repairs**. (A 'repair' for this purpose being the cost of restoring an asset to no more than its original state).

7 Debts, other than bad debts arising from trading or those estimated to be doubtful. In this context, loans to customers or employees which are no longer recoverable are not allowed.

8 **Depreciation**. (However, **capital allowances** may be available. See later in this chapter.)

9 **Penalties** for breaking the law, and legal and accounting charges in connection therewith.

10 **Reserves** (except for discounts and specific doubtful debts). Therefore transfers to reserves of a general nature are not allowed.

11 Income tax, corporation tax, or any other direct taxes paid.

12 Certain **legal expenses**, but those involved in defending an asset are usually allowable. For example, legal charges in connection with the purchase of land and buildings are not allowed, but costs in connection with debt collecting are allowable.

This list is not exhaustive, but readers should be aware that 'paper' profits and taxable profits are rarely the same figure. Reference to the latest budget proposals is essential, as amendments to what is allowable and non-allowable have been made in recent budgets.

11.2.2 Expenditure which is allowed

It follows that the majority of business expenditure is allowed for tax purposes, including the following:

1 Any sums expended wholly and exclusively for the business may usually be deducted in the computation of profits, unless the outlay is of a capital nature.

2 Advertising expenditure (but not the original cost of permanent signs).

3 Bad and doubtful debts.

4 Costs of raising business loans finance.

5 **Interest** incurred for business purposes.

6 Insurance for business purposes (not life assurance). Note that recoveries under insurance policies must usually be included in assessable profits, e.g. claims for stock damaged by fire.

7 **Legal expenses** for recovering debts, or incurred in connection with other non-capital business matters.

8 **Redundancy payments** made to former employees.

9 **Rent** of business premises (some restriction may be necessary if premises are used also for private accommodation).

10 **Repairs** to fixed assets (excluding improvements and alterations).

11 Wages, salaries and pensions paid to employees and past employees or their dependants.

12 National insurance contributions paid in respect of employees (not self-employed person's own national insurance).

The above list is not intended to be comprehensive, but is indicative of the type of expenditure which may be charged against business profits to arrive at the figure on which tax will be imposed.

11.2.3 Adjusting accounts

The following example shows how the adjustments mentioned above are made.

A retail tradesman, using a van for delivery of goods, and living over his shop premises, submits the following profit and loss account. Certain items appearing in the accounts are not allowable deductions for tax purposes, and have to be added back to arrive at the assessable profit, while adjustments have to be made in respect of the trader's living accommodation.

Profit and loss account

		£	£
Gross profit on trading			38,939
Less: Wages and salaries		12,210	
National insurance		1,050	
Rent and rates		4,117	
Heating and lighting		710	
Repairs to premises		515	
Postages and telephone		517	
Printing, stationery and advertising		424	
Van running costs		1,027	
Depreciation of van		1,000	
Electric name sign		460	
General expenses		492	
Insurances		218	
Bank interest and charges		83	
Extension to garage and storeshed		2,700	25,523
Net profit			13,416

Adjustment for tax purposes

	£
Net profit as per profit and loss account	13,416
Add: Items not allowable:	
Electric name sign	460
Extension to garage and storeshed	2,700
Depreciation of van	1,000
For living accommodation (say ⅓):	
Rent and rates	1,372
Heating and lighting	237
Repairs to premises	172
Profit for tax purposes	19,357
Less: Capital allowances (say)	1,500
Taxable income	17,857

One difference between self-employed persons and limited companies relates to the way in which the tax is paid. Individuals pay their liability in two equal instalments, on 1 January and 1 July. Companies pay corporation tax in one instalment, usually nine months after the end of the accounting year.

11.3 Allowances for capital expenditure

Capital expenditure incurred by an individual or a company carrying on a trade cannot usually be subtracted when calculating business profits. However, expenditure on acquiring certain assets may enable them to obtain capital allowances, which are set against business profits.

Changes in these allowances are liable to be made in the annual budget; indeed, major changes took place for expenditure incurred after 13 March 1984, and the following examples reflect those changes.

11.3.1 Plant and machinery

An annual allowance of 25 per cent per annum on the reduced balance of unrelieved expenditure remaining after subtracting allowances for earlier years is available for many items commonly used in business, including industrial equipment, shop fittings, tractors, motor cars, typewriters, desks, chairs, and canteen equipment, among others.

Example

A manufacturer has been carrying on business for many years, preparing accounts to 31 March annually. On 4 September 1987 he incurred expenditure of £52,000 on the purchase of machinery.

	£
Cost during year to 31 March 1988	52,000
Writing down allowance of 25%	13,000
	39,000
Writing down allowance of 25% for 1989	9,750
	29,250
Writing down allowance of 25% for 1990	7,312
Available for future writing down allowances	21,938

See previous example for how these allowances can be deducted from taxable profit.

11.3.2   Motor cars

Taxation allowances on the purchase of motor cars have never enjoyed the same advantages as plant and machinery, fixtures and fittings, tractors, etc. Buying an expensive car does not give particularly generous tax allowances ('expensive' at present means any vehicle costing more than £8,000). The 25 per cent writing down allowance is restricted to £2,000 per annum on any one car.

Example

A veterinary surgeon purchased a motor car for use in his practice on 17 June 1987 at a cost of £16,500. Assuming the vehicle is used entirely for the business, the calculation of capital allowances will proceed as follows (accounts made up to 31 March):

	£
Cost June 1987	16,200
Writing down allowance year ended 5 April 1988	
25%, but restricted to £2,000	2,000
	14,500
Writing down allowance year ended 5 April 1989	
25%, but restricted to £2,000	2,000
	12,500
Writing down allowance year ended 5 April 1990	
1991, and 1992, again restricted to £2,000 per annum	6,000
	6,500
Writing down allowance year ended 5 April 1993	1,625
available for future writing down allowances	4,875

11.3.3   Industrial buildings

The cost of buildings used for the purpose of a trade carried on in a mill, factory or similar premises qualifies for a tax allowance, called industrial buildings allowance.

This allowance is not available for retail shops, offices, and other non-industrial buildings. Note the effect on companies such as Marks & Spencer, the major clearing banks and insurance companies.

Example

On 1 February 1987, a manufacturer incurred expenditure of £200,000 on the construction of an industrial building. Accounts are prepared to 31 March annually. The allowances available are as follows:

	£
Cost during year to 31 March 1987	200,000
Allowances year to 31 March 1987:	
Writing down allowance 4% of £200,000	8,000
Available for future writing down allowances	192,000

Thereafter 4% per annum on cost of building
(note difference to plant and motor cars).

11.3.4 Other capital allowances

Capital allowances are also available on agricultural buildings expenditure, ships, oil wells, patents, research, and working mines. Special allowances are also available for expenditure in enterprise zones.

Links with other topics

Taxation links with topics in chapters that have already been covered as well as some yet to be covered.

Chapters 2 and 3 concern the amount of tax outstanding at the accounting year end. In company accounts in particular, profit for the year is shown before and after tax (see ICI accounts in appendix). See chapter 4 concerning recording in the ledgers of taxation paid and charged. Chapter 9 deals with accounting for deferred taxation. The accounting consequences of the deviation between accounting profit and taxable profit may be noted, and SSAP 8 covers the treatment of corporation tax in company accounts. Chapters 15 and 17 are concerned with profit before and after tax.

Sample questions

1 The firm of Gordon's Taxis has been in existence for a number of years. The proprietor lives on the premises. The income statement for the 12 months to 31 March this year was:

	£	£
Gross profit (after charging all taxi running expenses)		17,420
Add: profit on sale of old vehicle		250
		17,670
Less: office salaries (part-time)	2,800	
Rent and rates (25% private)	1,252	
Heating and lighting (30% private)	450	
Postage and stationery	170	
Advertising	720	
Telephone (20% private)	800	
Repairs to premises (25% private)	256	
Accountancy charges	150	
Depreciation	1,900	
General expenses	870	9,368
Net profit		8,302

Note: General expenses include:

	£
Taxi Proprietors' Association subscription	40
Fines for speeding and illegal parking	200
Employees' Christmas gifts	40
Donations to Oxfam	15
Bowling club subscription	30

First year Business Studies degree, Staffordshire Polytechnic

Understanding the question

This question is typical of many whereby students are required to adjust profits/losses as per profit and loss accounts for taxation purposes. A thorough understanding of which expenditure is allowable and which is non-allowable is essential.

Answer plan

Always commence with the net profit/loss for the year. Decide which items contained in the accounts are not allowable deductions, and add those to the net profit.

The following items come under this category:

25% of rent and rates; 30% of heating and lighting; 20% of telephones; 25% of repairs to premises; depreciation; fines, Oxfam and bowling club subscription.

Then look for any items that have increased the profit, but are not liable to tax. The profit on sale of vehicle must be deducted in arriving at assessable profit. Always work to the nearest £ in all tax questions.

Your answer should be £10,869.

2 Describe the difference between regressive and progressive taxes, giving examples of each.

First year Business Studies degree, Staffordshire Polytechnic

Understanding the question

It is necessary to understand that the effect of taxation is not felt to the same extent by all taxpayers. Those with higher income can probably afford to pay more than those who earn less.

Answer plan

Examples on which to base your answer could centre around Road Fund Licences for cars, VAT and income tax. Income tax meets the basic definition of a progressive tax, in that the taxpayer's **average** tax rate rises as his/her income rises.

3 A manufacturing company's financial year end was 31 March each year.

During the year ended 31 March 1988, the following purchases of fixed assets took place.

	£
9 May 1987 2 machines at a cost of:	10,000
2 July 1987 motor car	12,500
22 August 1987 lorry	32,000
7 December 1987 completion of factory extension (additional manufacturing capacity)	150,000
27 March 1988 office equipment	5,000

The residue of capital expenditure (written-down values for tax purposes) coming forward at 31 March 1987 was as follows:

	£
Plant and machinery	80,000
Office equipment	12,000
Motor cars	4,000

You are required to calculate the amount of capital allowances due to the company for the year ended 31 March 1988.

Answer plan

Capital allowances are far simpler to calculate, since March 1984, than hitherto, and once it is recognized that different percentages are in force for plant and machinery and industrial buildings, and that motor cars are a special case, no real problem should ensue.

The total allowances due for the year to 31 March 1988 are £43,750. Do you agree?

4 Sims commenced business on 1 January 1987. He earned an adjusted profit of £2,400 in 1987, £1,800 in 1988 and £2,000 in 1989. Set out the original and final assessments for the first four years.

Answer plan

There are special arrangements for the assessment of profits to Schedule D tax for sole traders and partnerships in the early years of trading. These arrangements do not apply to companies. The workings are mechanical and revolve around whether the taxpayer chooses to be assessed under Section 62 of the Taxes Act 1988. All opening assessments on new businesses require the figures to be calculated twice, once by the normal method and once under Section 62 to see if this is beneficial or not.

The assessment will be as follows:

Original assessments

Year	Basis period	£	£
1986/87	Actual 1.1.87–5.4.87	600	
1987/88	1st 12 months to 31.12.87	2,400 ⎫	
1988/89	Preceding year	2,400 ⎬	4,800
1989/90	Preceding year	1,800	

Section 62 election

Year	Basis period	£	£
1986/87	As above	600	
1987/88	Actual 6.4.87–5.4.88	2,250 ⎫	
1988/89	Actual 6.4.88–5.4.89	1,850 ⎬	4,100
1989/90	Preceding year (as above)	1,800	

Thus, Sims would choose to pay tax on the lower assessments under Section 62 for 1987/88 and 1988/89. The election must cover both years.

5 Omega Electronics prepare accounts to 31 July annually. On 1 August 1973 they erected a factory block in the UK for use in their manufacturing business. The factory block was completed on 31 December 1973. The total cost of £65,000 was made up as follows:

	£
Land – freehold	5,000
Tunnelling	800
Factory	49,600
Canteen	3,200
Drawing office	3,400
General office	3,000
	65,000

On 1 January 1989 the building was sold to Pickard & Co Ltd for £100,000 exclusive of the land.

Compute the industrial buildings allowances available to Omega Electronics for the period of their ownership.

Answer plan

Computing IBA is straightforward, providing some golden rules are observed. Firstly IBA can **never** be given on the cost of land, although preparation of the land for building is allowable (tunnelling comes into this category). Initial allowances could only be claimed up to the date of the 1984 Finance Act. The rate of initial allowance in 1973 was 40 per cent. Since 1962, the annual writing down allowance has been 4 per cent per annum on cost. Office buildings can be claimed provided they do not exceed 25 per cent of the total cost.

The Industrial Buildings Allowance for Omega Electronics will be as follows:

		£	£
1975/76	(Basis year to 31.7.74)		
	Qualifying expenditure		
	(£65,000 less land)		60,000
	Initial allowance (40%)	24,000	
	Writing down allowance (4%)	2,400	
		26,400	
1976/77 to 1989/90 (Basis years 1.8.74–31.7.88)			
	W.D.A. 14 years @ 4% (14 × £2,400)	33,600	60,000
	Written down value prior to sale		Nil
1990/91	(Basis year to 31.7.89) Sale proceeds		100,000

There will be a **balancing charge** restricted to the allowances given of £60,000. The excess (£40,000) will be liable to capital gains tax.

6 A trader's adjusted profits are as follows:

Years ending 31 January	£
1985	9,000
1986	15,000
1987	12,000
1988	18,000
6 months to 31.7.88 (when trading ceased)	6,000

Set out the original and final assessments for the final four years.

Answer plan

As with opening assessments for sole traders and partnerships, special provisions also apply when a business ceases trading. The Inland Revenue have options for the penultimate and ante-penultimate years under Section 63 of the 1988 Taxes Act. The choice is the Inland Revenue's, i.e. the higher assessment will be the amount due.

In this case, the assessments would be as follows:

Original assessment

Year	Basis period	£	£
1988/89	Actual 6.4.88 to 31.7.88		
	(4/6 × £6,000)	4,000	
1987/88	PYB – Y/E 31.1.87	12,000 ⎱	27,000
1986/87	PYB – Y/E 31.1.86	15,000 ⎰	
1985/86	PYB – Y/E 31.1.85	9,000	

Section 63 revision

Year	Basis period	£	£
1988/89	Actual (as before)	4,000	
1987/88	Actual	16,000 ⎱	29,000
1986/87	Actual	13,000 ⎰	
1985/86	PYB – (as before) Y/E 31.1.85	9,000	

The Revenue will assess the 1986/87 and 1987/88 assessments under the Section 63 rules as the aggregate obtained is higher than under the normal basis.

7 (a) Why is it important to distinguish between a capital gain and a revenue gain? Describe the so-called 'badges of trade' that are used to try to achieve this.

(b) Discuss very briefly the extent to which the following expenses are allowed to a trader for taxation purposes:

(i) bad debts
(ii) National Insurance contributions
(iii) salaries paid to a member of the trader's family
(iv) entertaining customers.

AAT

Answer plan

Part (a)

The 1988 Finance Act make the ratio of income tax and capital gains tax the same for individuals – 25 per cent basic rate and 40 per cent for higher earners. Nevertheless, the annual exemption, whereby the first £5,000 of capital gains is tax free, means that it is still important to distinguish between capital and revenue gains. Future Finance Acts may well change the rates of income tax and capital gains tax, making the distinction more important again.

There are six 'badges' or 'indicators' of trade which assist in determining whether the disposal of a particular item is considered a trading transaction. They are:

1 the subject matter of the disposal;

2 the length of the period of ownership;

3 the frequency of a number of similar transactions;

4 supplementary work;

5 motive;

6 the reasons for the realization.

Part (b)

(i) Bad debts are allowed provided they are incurred wholly and exclusively for the purpose of the trade. (Note that a loan to an employee no longer recoverable would not be allowed.) A case for deduction may be made in respect of a specific bad debts reserve against named debtors.

(ii) Currently, a trader can obtain a deduction from total income of 50 per cent of his final Class 4 National Insurance contributions.

(iii) Salaries paid to a member of the trader's family are allowed provided they do not exceed a reasonable commercial rate.

(iii) Since 15 March 1988, no entertaining expenses are allowable, whether the customer is a UK resident or not.

Further reading

There are many excellent tax guides published each year following the Budget. Any of these would be quite sufficient for the needs of first-year accountancy students, rather than extensive manuals or textbooks, which are both expensive and technical.

12 The interpretation of accounts

Assuming that the accounts have been prepared, all the accounting postulates concepts and principles have been applied, and that, in the case of company accounts the requirements of the Companies Act 1985, Statements of Standard Accounting Practice, and of the Stock Exchange, have been enacted, there is then the question of what the figures reveal about the business, both in the past and as a guide to the future.

A careful study of accounting figures can provide lots of useful information to users of accounting information. This is probably where an accountant can be of most service, particularly to non-accountants, using a blend of skill and experience to explain the relative importance of the figures and their relationships with one another.

The accountant may be interpreting results to management, for example comparing the performance of the company in a group with another. He may even be called upon to comment on the business to potential investors, such as a City institution or the client of a stockbroker, or to his own managers, perhaps when consideration is being given to a takeover or merger. Therefore, we must bear in mind the recipient of the analysis, when drawing out the meaning of a set of accounts, a what is significant to one user may be less so to another. The profit record, dividend cover and growth potential will be important to an investor, whereas the asset base and profit earnings ratio will usually be of greater interest in a takeover bid.

Auditors will use analysis to determine whether the accounts under review give 'true and fair view', and inspectors of taxes will use profitability ratios in order to determine the correctness of figures for assessment purposes. However, whilst published accounts are employed by many users in decision making, the information represents only one of the information inputs to the user's decision-making process.

Interpretation of accounts questions are usually certain to be set in financial accounting examinations. Most ask for calculations to be made on profitability liquidity and performance, very often leaving the student to choose which calculation seem most appropriate.

The majority of questions require a summary to be given of the findings disclosed by the ratios/percentages calculated, culminating with a final appraisal of the well being, or otherwise, of the company under consideration.

12.1 Essential knowledge

To comment on a set of accounts, some standards against which they can be judged are needed. The three areas to be concerned with are as follows:

1 The company's previous results (usually those of the preceeding year).

2 The company's expected results (a budget will almost certainly have been prepared for the year now under review). These are normally available only to internal users

3 Inter-firm comparisons. Performance of one or more comparable companies. With greater detail being disclosed in company accounts since 1981, together with rigid formats, this is somewhat less difficult than hitherto.

There is a set of basic questions to which the interpreter will seek answers. Each question answered will lead to further questions. Gradually a picture will emerge of what has happened and what is likely to happen to the company.

12.1.1 Profitability

Probably the first question that springs to mind with most people concerns profitability. The accountant will look at both gross profit and net profit. The gross profit is considered to be very important to accountants. It is computed by setting the gross profit against sales and it is expressed as a percentage, i.e. gross profit/sales × 100. Clearly it can be used as a control device, since it brings together all the elements of the trading account. The gross profit is computed by adding opening stock to purchases, and subtracting closing stock to give the cost of goods sold. This figure is then subtracted from sales, leaving the gross profit. The mark-up of profit percentage added to cost when selling price is determined should be reflected by the gross profit percentage, and if there is a difference, the accountant knows that some figure in the trading account contains an error. A word of warning, however: a percentage mark-up on purchases of, say, 50 per cent will not show a like figure when the gross profit on sales is calculated. Let us see this explained in an example.

An article is purchased for £1 and sold for £1.50, a 50 per cent increase on cost. The profit made on the sale is 50p. On the selling price of £1.50, the gross profit on sales is 33⅓ per cent. Some further examples of how this works are as follows:

Mark-up on cost	Gross profit on sales
100%	50%
33⅓%	25%
25%	20%

Try some figures for yourself to prove this point.

It is not only the accountant who takes a close interest in gross profit percentages. As we have seen elsewhere, all accounts of companies and self-employed persons are submitted to the Inland Revenue, where inspectors of taxes closely examine the figures to see if possible 'fiddles' have been attempted, and a good place to start is with the gross profit, to see how it compares in percentage terms with similar businesses, both locally and nationally.

12.1.2 Differences in profit margins

Many factors can contribute to differences in margins between what is expected and what materializes. Suppose, for example, that the closing stock figure is wrong. An error in the closing stock can be caused by miscounting the number of items in stock, by extending them at the wrong cost on the stock sheet, or by miscalculating when the amounts are multiplied and added up on the stock sheet. Error may also arise by going against convention, calculating the stock by a method inconsistent with that of the previous year. If left unrectified, not only is the current year's trading account, and therefore gross profit, incorrect, but so is next year's as well. This year's closing stock is next year's opening stock, so accurate and worthwhile comparison between years is not attainable until a third year has passed.

Alternatively, the sales figure may be wrong; perhaps, by mistake, some sales have not been recorded, (e.g. cut-off procedures not adhered to); or this may have been done on purpose if cash received has been stolen. If stock has been pilfered by customers or staff, the cost of the goods sold will increase, and the gross profit percentage will not agree with the mark-up. Good internal control, both in the recording of transactions and over assets such as stock, is essential.

It is now time to look at the level of indirect expenses, being usually divided into three main categories: administration, selling and distribution and financial. The total indirect expenses deducted from gross profit gives the net profit before tax. The net profit ratio expresses the amount of net profit per hundred pounds of sales. This may not be very stable, due to the great variety and discretionary nature of so many of the expenses and charged against profits. One should be careful before drawing conclusions about apparent increases and decreases in indirect expenses, without satisfactory explanations being sought.

12.1.3 Return on capital employed

The final net profit must be considered in terms of a return on capital at the company's disposal. The return on capital employed (ROCE) should show whether profits are sufficient to warrant the amount of funds invested in a business, the risk taken by investing those funds, and whether a better return for the same degree of risk might be earned by an alternative employment of the funds. This approach leads to questions to determine whether assets are employed in the right way or in the best combination, and whether a company may be on the threshold of a profit break-through after some lean years when reorganization may have taken place.

One should be aware of the limitations of return on capital employed:

1 Definitions of capital employed vary, and confusion may arise when return on capital is discussed, unless terms are rationalized. Some authorities prefer to set net profit against gross capital employed (fixed and current assets) to show what the management have really produced from all the assets at their disposal. The ratio of net profit to shareholders' funds (share capital and reserves) expresses the return on capital contributed by the legal owners of the business, but cannot indicate managerial efficiency. The net capital employed, defined as fixed assets plus working capital, is often used for ROCE. There is some difference of opinion among accountants about whether net profit before or after tax should be used for this ratio, because the ratio of tax to profit is not consistent (see chapter 11 on taxation).

2 The return on capital is a misleading guide to efficiency, unless assets are valued at current prices.

3 Comparison between firms by means of return on capital employed is difficult. Are we really comparing like with like?

4 The return on capital employed does not take risk into account. High returns may equal high risks.

5 Capital investment is long-term, and early years may well see a low return.

To sum up profitability analysis, let us look at a typical profit and loss account and examine the questions one can ask to back the various percentages calculated.

Profit and loss account

Set your standard: the previous year 19X4 £			19X5 £
800,000	Sales	Compare sales levels. Sales have increased. Is this due to more units being sold, or merely price increases? Has mix of sales varied? Rationalization may have led to unprofitable lines being eliminated, and concentration on the more profitable areas of activity.	1,000,000
600,000	Direct expenses		700,000
200,000 (25%)	Gross profits (rate)	Calculate gross profit ratio. Has this increased? This is a good sign, as it means profit on production of each unit sold has increased. Does this, however, hide falling margins in some areas, and higher margins in others?	300,000 (30%)
150,000	Indirect expenses	Compare totals of indirect expenses. Why have these increased? Some are fixed, others variable. Compare each individual expense to see where increase has occurred.	200,000
50,000	Profit before taxation		100,000
			Use profit before taxation as a basis to compute return on capital employed.

12.2 Solvency

The second area of concern is solvency. The following questions spring to mind:

1 Assets. What are these worth today?

2 Liquidity. Has the company got enough cash to meet expected demands within the next few months? Is the company strong enough to remain a going concern in the foreseeable future?

3 Contingent liabilities. These should be evaluated.

A chapter on the methods of finance available to a company is contained elsewhere in the book, but in discussing solvency it will assist to keep in mind the following:

1 Issuing shares (share capital).

2 Taking out long-term loans, including debentures (loan capital).

3 Retaining profits within the company (reserves).

4 Current liabilities, i.e. short-term loans, current overdrafts, increased creditors.

Broadly speaking, solvency or liquidity is the ability of a company to meet its debts as and when they fall due. Note that it is important for a company to maintain sufficient cash balances, as well as to make profits.

12.2.1 Measuring liquidity

In reviewing the balance sheet, one must distinguish between:

1 Immediate liquidity – enough to pay the weekly wages bill, for example.

2 Short-term liquidity – enough to pay creditors for next few months.

3 Medium-term liquidity – enough to repay loans and debentures which fall due in the next few years.

4 Long-term liquidity – is the company's financial structure strong enough to make it a viable going concern?

There are two ratios which can be used to measure liquidity, namely the current assets ratio and the quick assets ratio (sometimes referred to as the acid-test ratio).

To measure short-term liquidity, the current assets ratio is used:

$$\frac{\text{Current assets}}{\text{Current liabilities}}$$

This ratio must be greater than one, since although current liabilities and assets should all fall due or be realized over the next year, they may not do so in a convenient order.

To measure immediate liquidity, use the quick assets ratio:

$$\frac{\text{Quick assets}}{\text{Immediate liabilities}}$$

This ratio should normally be about one. It includes current assets which will become cash within six weeks (which probably excludes most of the stock, particularly in manufacturing) and current liabilities which are due in the next six weeks.

As will be realized, it is quite possible to have a healthy current assets ratio but a poor quick assets ratio, due to a preponderance of stock in the current assets.

If these ratios show an unsatisfactory position, or a marked deterioration from the previous year, one should consider the possible reasons for this, always bearing in mind that if a firm owns valuable freehold property, banks will normally be willing to loan to such businesses because of the security.

1 Does the company not collect its debts quickly enough?

2 How does the amount of debtors outstanding at the balance sheet date relate to sales and credit period given to customers? (Cash sales obviously ignored in this calculation.)

3 Does the company pay its debts too quickly?

4 Does the company hold more stock than it needs to? Here one can look at the stock ratio:

$$\frac{\text{Stock as per balance sheet}}{\text{Cost of sales in year}}$$

Respectively, these ratios will show, on average, how many days' credit are allowed to debtors and taken to pay suppliers, and how many days' stock is held.

What the norm is will vary from industry to industry, and statistics are readily available to enable inter-firm comparisons to be made within a particular industry.

12.2.2 Investigating liquidity

Ratios help to pin-point areas requiring explanations, a process which can be likened perhaps to a medical examination. But remember, ratios are only as good as the figures from which they are calculated.

If ratios move unfavourably, or even apparently favourably, further examination may be required as to whether this is a result of deliberate management policy, e.g. allowing customers more credit as an advertising boost on sales, stockpiling to meet an expected peak in sales, or paying more promptly to obtain discounts. Alternatively, it may reflect poorer control by management, which could be improved by temporarily reducing production, so that stock falls to acceptable levels, or by less prompt payment to creditors, taking care not to lose the good will of suppliers, or by tightening up on credit control, to get in cash more quickly.

With medium and long-term liquidity, one should look for specific items of expenditure falling due over the next few years, and take steps to ensure that finance will be available to meet them. This could take the form of issuing further shares, holding investments which could be encashed at an appropriate time, or perhaps the negotiation of a bank loan to repay debentures.

To sum up steps to be taken when commenting on a company's current position, let us examine a typical balance sheet.

Balance sheet

	19X4	19X5
	£000s	£000s

Set your standard:
The previous year.

Fixed assets:	Are depreciation methods adequate? Consider replacement cost.
Land and buildings:	What is land worth today compared with original cost? Leaseholds: how many years to run?
Plant and machinery:	Age of plant? Obsolescence? Will some have to be replaced to compete with other firms?
Investments:	Quoted and trade. What is their present value?
Current assets *Stocks:*	Raw materials, work-in-process, finished goods. Is basis of valuation consistent with previous years? Have allowances been made for old stock? Look at stock turnover ratio.
Debtors:	Is collection period satisfactory? Has adequate provision been made for doubtful debts?
Cash *Current liabilities* *Creditors:*	Are full credit terms being taken?

> Taxation
> Dividends
> *Net current assets:* Is current assets ratio satisfactory?
>   Is acid test satisfactory?
>
> *Borrowed capital* Is company low or high geared?
> *Reserves*   Will company have resources available to repay loans when due?

12.3 Key ratios

A summary of the key ratios and percentages which are commonly used in questions is as follows:

Liquidity	1 Current	$\dfrac{\text{Current assets}}{\text{Current liabilities}}$
	2 'Quick' or acid test	$\dfrac{\text{CA} - \text{Stock}}{\text{Immediate current liabilities}}$
Activity	3 Stock turnover	$\dfrac{\text{Cost of goods sold}}{\text{Average stock}}$
	4 Collection period for debtors	$\dfrac{\text{Debtors}}{\text{Sales per day}}$
	5 Fixed assets to turnover	$\dfrac{\text{Sales}}{\text{Fixed assets}}$
Profitability	(All ratios are percentages)	
	6 Gross profit	$\dfrac{\text{Gross profit}}{\text{Sales}}$
	7 Net profit	$\dfrac{\text{Net profit}}{\text{Sales}}$
	8 Return on shareholders' funds employed	$\dfrac{\text{Net profit}}{\text{Funds employed}}$

1 The current ratio is a measure of the short-term solvency, but is perhaps not a valid measure of ability to meet immediate payments due. This is because of the rather longer time which certain current assets, and in particular stock, take before ultimate conversion into cash.

2 The 'acid-test'. This ratio attempts to overcome the shortcomings of the current assets.

3 The number of times that stock turns over in any accounting period is an important measure which will aid in accurate forecasts of cash requirements. Ideally, the figures should include average stock, statistically determined, and cost of sales. Because of the difficulties that have arisen in compilation of tables of comparison, sales is often used as the numerator, instead of cost of sales.

4 Collection period for debtors. This gives an indication of the rigidity with which the credit terms are being upheld.

5 The ratio of fixed assets to turnover gives a measure of the capacity usage of the fixed assets. This can only be implied by comparison.

6 Gross profit ratio. This expresses the profit gained per £100 of sales over cost of sales. In retail businesses it can be stable from year to year, and variations can usually be traced to competitive conditions. In a manufacturing business, less reliance can be placed on it for two main reasons:

(a) The elements of cost are not necessarily sensitive to sales volume by any mathematical association.

(b) The production of a 'trading account' in traditional form usually involves the manipulation of cost figures to conform with the accounting concepts and conventions in a way which would not arise should an adequate costing system be in force.

7 The net profit ratio expresses the amount of net profit per hundred pounds of sales.

This may not be very stable, due to the variety of expenses charged against profits and the discretionary nature of so many of them.

8 Rates of return are the final tests of how well a company is being managed.

Links with other topics

Interpretation of accounts brings together virtually all other areas of study, including preparation of accounts, conventions, sources of finance, stock valuation, and depreciation, for example.

Students who really understand double-entry accounting and the effect figures have on one another will do well in the area of interpretation. Those who just learn that figures need to be shown in a certain way and do not fully appreciate their meaning, and consequently fail to 'see beyond the figures', will be all too apparent when attempting questions such as those shown below:

Sample questions

1 The outline balance sheets of Nantred Trading Co Ltd were as shown below:

Balance sheets
as at 30 September

1985 £	£		1986 £	£
		Fixed assets (as written down values)		
40,000		Premises	98,000	
65,000		Plant and equipment	162,000	
	105,000			260,000
		Current assets		
31,200		Stock	95,300	
19,700		Trade debtors	30,700	
15,600		Bank and cash	26,500	
66,500			152,500	
		Current liabilities		
23,900		Trade creditors	55,800	
11,400		Corporation tax	13,100	
17,000		Proposed dividends	17,000	
52,300			85,900	
	14,200	Working capital		66,600
	119,200	Net assets employed		326,600
		Financed by:		
100,000		Ordinary share capital	200,000	
19,200		Reserves	26,600	
	119,200	Shareholders' funds		226,600
	–	7% Debentures		100,000
	119,200			326,600

The only other information available is that the turnover for the years ended 30 September 1985 and 1986 was £202,900 and £490,700 respectively, and that on 30 September 1984 reserves were £26,100.

ACCA Level 1

Required:

(a) Calculate for each of the two years six suitable ratios to highlight the financial stability, liquidity and profitability of the company.

(b) Comment on the situation revealed by the figures you have calculated.

Answer plan

This question requires students to select, calculate and interpret the appropriate ratios.

The ability to calculate the net profit before tax from a balance sheet only is necessary. The profits for the two years will be:

	1985 £	1986 £
Reserves at the end of year	19,200	26,600
Add back:		
Proposed dividends	17,000	17,000
Corporation tax	11,400	13,100
	47,600	56,700
Less reserves at end of previous year	26,100	19,200
Net profit before tax for current year	21,500	37,500

A choice of ratios is available, which could include the following:

	1985	1986
Current ratio	1.27:1	1.78:1
Quick ratio	0.67:1	0.67:1
Net profit to sales	10.6%	7.6%
Net profit to net assets employed	18.04%	11.48%
Sales to net assets employed	1.70	1.50
External liabilities to shareholders' funds	0.44	0.82

It will be apparent that financial stability has weakened. There is a greater reliance on external financing. The current ratio has shown an improvement, but the quick ratio reveals that the company is still dangerously illiquid.

Profitability has fallen drastically and it is very apparent that in 1986 the company expanded rapidly. The full effects of this programme will not be noticed until 1987 and later years.

2 O'Neill Ltd trades in musical instruments, hi-fi equipment and cassette tapes. Good profits have been made over the recent years and income statements (as per extracts below) for the years to 31 March 1985 and 1986 disclosed gross margins of £159,300 and £166,200 respectively.

The managing director is not particulary happy about the results for 1986, and has asked for a short report.

Required:

(a) Calculate an accounting ratio for each year which will reveal the extent of the problem.

(b) Write a report to the managing director stating five possible reasons for the difference in the ratio between those two years.

Extract from income statement

	£ 1985	£ 1986
Opening stock	25,000	38,000
Purchases	278,700	318,300
Available stock	303,700	356,300
Closing stock	38,000	22,500
Cost of sales	265,700	333,800
Sales	425,000	500,000
Gross margin	159,300	166,200

ACCA Level 1

Answer plan

This question centres on the gross profit margin. The drop in rate from 1985 is in excess of 4 per cent (37.4 per cent to 33.2 per cent).

There may be reasons why the reduction in profit per £ of sales has occurred, and of which the management are fully aware, but this question suggests otherwise and the following comments should be incorporated into a formal report:

(a) Inaccurate stock valuations at both the beginning and end of each year.

(b) Price increase of goods which have not been passed on to customers.

(c) Invoices dated prior to year end for goods supplied which were not received until early in 1987.

(d) Sales despatched to customers prior to the end of 1986 but not invoiced until 1987. (It is important to mention the cut-off procedures which must be adhered to at the year end.)

(e) Pilferage, either by staff or customers.

(f) A change in the sales mix. A breakdown of sales between the two years may reveal reasons for lower profit margins being made.

3 You are given below, in summarized form, the accounts of Algernon Ltd for 1986 and 1987.

1986 Balance Sheet

	Cost £	Depn £	Net £
Plant	10,000	4,000	6,000
Building	50,000	10,000	40,000
			46,000
Investments at cost			50,000
Land			43,000
Stock			55,000
Debtors			40,000
Bank			3,000
			237,000
Ordinary shares £1 each			40,000
Share premium			12,000
Revaluation reserve			—
Profit and loss account			25,000
10% Debentures			100,000
Creditors			40,000
Proposed dividend			20,000
Bank			—
			237,000

1987 Balance Sheet

	Cost £	Depn £	Net £
Plant	11,000	5,000	6,000
Building	90,000	11,000	79,000
			85,000
Investments at cost			80,000
Land			63,000
Stock			65,000
Debtors			50,000
Bank			—
			343,000
Ordinary shares £1 each			50,000
Share premium			14,000
Revaluation reserve			20,000
Profit and loss account			25,000
10% Debentures			150,000
Creditors			60,000
Proposed dividend			20,000
Bank			4,000
			343,000

	1986 Profit and loss a/c £	1987 Profit and loss a/c £
Sales	200,000	200,000
Cost of sales	100,000	120,000
	100,000	80,000
Expenses	60,000	60,000
	40,000	20,000
Dividends	20,000	20,000
	20,000	—
Balance b/f	5,000	25,000
Balance c/f	25,000	25,000

Required:

Calculate for Algernon Ltd, for 1986 and 1987, the following ratios:

Return on capital employed;

Return on owners' equity (return on shareholders' funds);

Debtors turnover;   Creditors turnover;

Current ratio;   Quick assets (acid test) ratio;

Gross profit percentage;   Net profit percentage;

Dividend cover;

Gearing ratio.

ACCA Level 1

Answer plan

This is a straightforward ratio analysis question providing the correct figures are used to calculate the various ratios and percentages. Do you agree the following?

	1986	1987
ROCE	28%	14%
Debtors turnover	5 times	4 times
Creditors turnover	2½ times	2 times
Current ratio	1:6:1	1.4:1
Acid-test ratio	0.7:1	0.6:1
Gross profit percentage	50%	40%
Net profit percentage	20%	10%
Dividend cover	2 times	1 times
Gearing ratio	56%	58%

4 The summarized balance sheets of Ritt Ltd at the end of two consecutive financial years were as shown below.

Summarized balance sheets as at 31 March

1986 £000	1986 £000		1987 £000	1987 £000
		Fixed assets (at written down values)		
50		Premises	48	
115		Plant and equipment	196	
42		Vehicles	81	
	207			325
		Current assets		
86		Stock	177	
49		Debtors and prepayments	62	
53		Bank and cash	30	
188			269	
		Current liabilities		
72		Creditors and accruals	132	
20		Proposed dividends	30	
92			162	
	96	**Working capital**		107
	303	**Net assets employed**		432
		Financed by		
250		Ordinary share capital	250	
53		Reserves	82	
	303	Shareholders' funds		332
	—	Loan capital: 7% debentures		100
	303			432

Turnover was £541,000 and £675,000 for the years ended 31 March 1986 and 1987, respectively. Corresponding figures for cost of sales were £369,000 and £481,000 respectively.

At 31 March 1985, reserves had totalled £21,000. Ordinary share capital was the same at the end of 1985 as at the end of 1986.

Required:
(a) Calculate, for each of the two years, the ratios listed below:
   Gross profit/Turnover percentage
   Net profit/Turnover percentage
   Turnover/Net assets employed
   Net profit/Net assets employed percentage
   Current assets/Current liabilities
   Quick assets/Current liabilities

   (Calculations should be correct to one decimal place.)

(b) Comment on each of the figures you have calculated in (a), giving probable reasons for the differences between the two years.

ACCA Level 1

Answer plan

Part (a)

This question is slightly different to most in that you are not given any profit and loss account figures. Profits for the years, therefore, have to be calculated from the balance sheets. To do this a thorough understanding of the profit and loss appropriation account is essential. You should find that the net profit for 1986 is £52,000 and that for 1987 is £59,000.

Once this is done the calculation of the ratios is fairly straightforward and you should find the following:

	1986	1987
Gross profit/Turnover	31.8%	28.7%
Net profit/Turnover	9.6%	8.7%
Turnover/Net assets employed	17.2%	13.7%
Current ratio	2.0:1	1.7:1
Quick ratio	1.1:1	0.6:1

Part (b)

Some possible reasons for the variations between the two years:

1 A rise in purchase prices not passed on in increased selling prices and/or a change in sales mix.

2 Higher administration and/or sales expenses.

3 The full year effect of the increased investment has not yet materialized.

4 The increased investment has produced a liquidity problem of great magnitude.

Many other comments are possible and would be marked on their merits.

5 John Bright has provided his son, Thomas, with all the capital required in the setting up of a business on 1 April 1985 and its subsequent development. Thomas has now produced the following summarized accounts as a basis for discussing the business's progress with his father:

Trading and profit and loss accounts

Year ended	31 March 1986	31 March 1987
	£000	£000
Sales	100	140
Cost of sales	60	90
Gross profit	40	50
Overheads: Variable	20	35
Fixed	12	16
	32	51
Net profit/(net loss)	8	(1)

Balance Sheets

As at	1 April 1985	31 March 1986	31 March 1987
	£000	£000	£000
Fixed assets	70	70	80
Net current assets			
Stock	5	7	8
Debtors	—	11	24
Bank balance/(overdraft)	13	2	(4)
(Creditors)	(3)	(5)	(8)
	15	15	20
Net capital employed	85	85	100

Thomas is keen for his father to increase the capital employed in the business and has drawn his father's attention to the following favourable matters revealed in the accounts:

1 A £15,000 increase in net capital employed can be linked with a £40,000 increase in sales during the past year.

2 The rate of stock turnover during the past year has been 12 as compared with 10 in the previous year.

3 The increased fixed overheads last year is due to the renting of larger premises; however these new premises would be adequate for a turnover of £200,000.

John Bright is not pleased with the results of his son's business.
Thomas Bright can easily obtain employment offering a salary of £10,000 per annum and John Bright can obtain 10 per cent per annum from a bank deposit account.

Required:

(a) Calculate for each of the years ended 31 March 1986 and 1987 four financial ratios which draw attention to matters which could give John Bright cause for concern. Note: State clearly the formula or basis of each ratio used.

(b) Outline three reasons for closing the business and one reason in favour of its continuance.

(c) Outline the importance of distinguishing between fixed and variable overheads.

AAT

Answer plan

Calculating ratios is usually not too difficult but being able to give recommendations on courses of action to be taken is far more demanding. A full answer is given to this question to show what examiners look for in this area.

Part (a)

Re: Thomas Bright's business

Year ended	31 March 1986	31 March 1987
$\dfrac{Net\ profit}{Net\ capital\ employed}$	$\dfrac{£8,000}{£85,000} = 9.4\%$	$\dfrac{(£1,000)}{£100,000} = \text{Loss } 1\%$
$\dfrac{Net\ profit}{Sales}$	$\dfrac{£8,000}{£100,000} = 8.0\%$	$\dfrac{(£1,000)}{£140,000} = \text{Loss } 0.7\%$
$\dfrac{Gross\ profit}{Sales}$	$\dfrac{£40,000}{£100,000} = 40.0\%$	$\dfrac{£50,000}{£140,000} = 35.7\%$
Working capital $= \dfrac{Current\ assets}{Current\ liabilities}$	$\dfrac{£20,000}{£5,000} = 400.0\%$	$\dfrac{£32,000}{£12,000} = 266.7\%$
$\dfrac{Debtors}{Sales}$	$\dfrac{£11,000}{£100,000} = 11\%$	$\dfrac{£24,000}{£140,000} = 17.1\%$

(**Note:** the question only requires four ratios to be given.)

Part (b)

Reasons for closing the business:

1 Thomas Bright could obtain a greater return for his services by taking up employment at £10,000 per annum.

2 John Bright could invest his money in a bank deposit account offering a return of 10 per cent per annum.

3 The business has produced significantly poorer results in the second year of its existence.

4 Thomas Bright does not appear to be sufficiently aware of the factors which make for business success – refer to the 'favourable' factors identified by him in the question.

(**Note:** the question only requires three reasons to be given.)

Reasons in favour of continuance

1 Business still in formative stages. Difficulties appear to be largely associated with unprofitable growth in second year.

2 Job satisfaction can be an important factor to be considered; however the business must be viable.

(**Note:** the question only requires one reason to be given.)

Part (c)
Importance of distinguishing between fixed and variable overheads:
When considering plans for future it is important to know how costs will change with increased or decreased activity.

The distinction is important in determining break-even point.

In certain cases it may be beneficial for a business to accept orders which will produce revenue in excess of variable costs but not covering total costs.

Further reading

A. Pizzey *Accounting and Finance – a Firm Foundation* (Holt Rinehart & Winston), second edition, chapter 23.

13 Problems of liquidity

13.1 Insolvency

Whenever a company declares itself insolvent, there is invariably a reaction of amazement from the various interested parties. When either a receiver or a liquidator is appointed, the usual misinformed assumption is made that the company has suffered a dramatic collapse resulting from a single disaster which, of course, no one could have foreseen, whether managing director or key supplier.

Unfortunately, both these assumptions are seldom true. People may well be surprised when the crunch of insolvency is made public, but often many should have seen it coming, but shut their eyes to it.

Collapse is seldom sudden and is seldom the result of a single disaster. It is usually the result of a number of weaknesses which are present in the enterprise which add up to failure. It is not necessarily the same weaknesses which contribute to the insolvency of all companies. There are, however, a number of key pointers which should be easy to see from the outside, and which when they accumulate in any business must be danger signals of possible future insolvency.

Some types of business are more vulnerable than others to becoming 'lame ducks', and construction businesses are usually near the top of the annual 'league table' of insolvencies. Also, a large percentage of insolvencies are of comparatively newly-formed businesses.

It is arguable that all insolvencies are the result of bad management. The unforeseen should have been foreseen and risks in a particular project should have been evident, and avoided.

Questions concerning the down-turn in a company's performance over a number of years are closely linked with the previous chapter. Ratio analysis will highlight apparent abnormalities and, coupled with further background knowledge, will allow you to tackle the case study-type questions which can usually be found in most examinations at this level. Being able to offer advice and recommending appropriate action through the eyes of, say, a bank manager to the directors of an ailing company are common examination fare.

13.2 Reasons for possible insolvency

A list of various reasons for possible insolvency, although not necessarily an exhaustive list, is examined below.

The list is divided into three areas, management, trading and accounting.

13.2.1 Management

1 Board composition and balance.
2 Collective responsibility of board.
3 Chain of responsibility and middle management.

Does the 'balance' of the board of directors represent all the fundamental parts of the business, is there adequate finance representation, in particular, and are there suitable non-executive directors, who have no axe to grind? Clearly it is not right for a phalanx of accountants to attempt to manage a manufacturing concern, nor for engineers alone to be formulating a marketing strategy without representation from the selling side of an organization. It may seem facile to point to a lack of balance on a board of directors as a corporate weakness. However, it occurs quite frequently in apparently thriving concerns. It is only afterwards that one can see such imbalance as being symptomatic of one of the corporate illnesses which led to insolvency.

The managing director, although leader, should not be treating the business as a one-man band. There is a limit to the amount of work any individual can do; and to whom is he answerable? The board which does not involve itself with decision-making collectively will not have the necessary powers to avoid insolvency when it threatens, and the board which lacks the machinery of middle management will not be able to ensure that its decisions are properly implemented.

13.2.2 Trading

1 Overtrading

Overtrading is commonly regarded as the most usual cause of insolvency, and is really the only 'legitimate' way to run out of cash. For this reason it is often made a scapegoat for failure which has occurred from other causes, and is often advanced as a reason by management who have treated sales expansion as being the absolute objective, without having stopped to consider the costs of such expansion. Too frequently, managers ignore profit in the search for turnover, and ignore cash in the search for profit. Simply to expand a trade on the same terms will require proportionately more working capital; higher sales means higher debtors, and almost certainly increased stock holdings. Sufficient working capital has to be found, and 'overtrading' merely describes the management who have not planned where the cash is going to come from.

2 Inflation and high interest rates

Even with a modest rate of inflation of, say, 5 per cent per annum, just to stand still requires that much more working capital. How difficult firms must have found trading conditions not many years ago, when inflation rates exceeded 20 per cent per annum for long periods.

3 Competitive quoting, or serious erosion of margins

In the search for expansion, it is common to see the effects of competitive quoting on a business. To obtain increased turnover and activity a company may quote at marginal cost, plus a small profit for additional business, which is much less than on the original sales. Word then gets around the customers, and the company begins to lose some of its original sales at the old margins; these sales are replaced by sales at the new competitive, and less profitable, level. The result is increased activity, with all the attendant need for increased working capital, and much lower profits available to meet the cash need.

4 Outsize project

Many insolvencies, and some firms which have been household names, have been blamed on one particular scheme or project which has turned sour, lost money and dragged down either the rest of the company or the rest of the group. As a rule of thumb, a company should not enter into any commitment that it could not write off in its entirety, and still stay alive. This may be an impractical and extreme view, as many will point to commitments to some mammoth project which has not turned sour, and which has given their company the solid foundation on which it has been able to build subsequently. Nevertheless, there can be no doubt that embarkation on an outsize project must raise doubts in the mind concerning the possible effects if it goes wrong.

5 High gearing

In times of economic depression, and in particular in times of high interest rates and probably lower profits, it becomes more important than ever to examine company gearing. When the first two-thirds of the work activity in a year is merely going to service a company's borrowings, what happens if demand and activity should drop by 40 per cent? Pay-back periods are crucial. Conversely, however, one could say that monies borrowed today will be paid back at tomorrow's inflated earnings.

6 Resistance to change or technological advance

It is important to consider the attitudes of a company, as well as its specific actions. Inaction can be as damaging as wrong action, although in the context of resistance to change, it may be less spectacular. The 'traditional' business which resists any change and shuns technological advance may not go bust as quickly as one that has all the latest methods which it cannot afford, but it will nevertheless drift down, with little hope of ultimate survival, in a competitive environment. Thus it is necessary to consider whether a company is keeping up to date, whether it is being overtaken and its markets eroded by younger and more virile companies, to the extent that it will ultimately be unable to survive.

In the UK, managers tend to have a strong motive for short-term profits, and there is a lack of investment in research and development. Both these factors could have long-term negative effects.

7 Borrowing short and lending long, or shorter-term borrowing for longer-term assets

It may scarcely be credible to imagine a quoted company acquiring land for development purposes effectively financed by ninety-day bills, but such has been the case. Lack of a solid fixed capital base is frequently the cause of downfall, particularly of smaller companies.

8 Deterioration of service

Inevitably, prior to failure, perhaps only immediately prior to failure, it will become apparent that the company's service is deteriorating. Either deliveries are not met, or after-sales service falls off, or possibly the product is just not such good value. When this danger sign appears, it is imperative to act with the utmost speed, because failure is imminent. This is not to say that where service deteriorates, insolvency is inevitable, but in all insolvencies this will be a late danger sign, as the company struggles to survive.

13.2.3 Accounting

1 Inadequate, erroneous or out of date methods

It is in the field of accounting that it is possible to be more specific about corporate weaknesses, but some of the 'danger signs' which are highlighted in this area may again be ones which are present in successful and solvent companies.

Almost invariably in insolvency, the receiver and liquidator uncover a totally inadequate system of accounting, or may even be unable to uncover any system at all. It is symptomatic of corporate insolvency that accounting is insufficient. The best management in the world cannot make proper and corrective decisions and monitor progress, if it has inadequate information to work on. In general, the suspicion of out-of-date or inadequate accounting must ring danger bells of possible future insolvency.

2 Lack of cash-flow budgets

In particular, it is widely held that the absence of cash-flow statements and budgets is a serious deficiency in a company's accounting. It can be argued that such cash-flow budgets, measuring actual performance against forecast, are essential in businesses of all sizes. They should be aimed not only at the short-term, but also at a year ahead at least, to describe to management the future effects of present policies, and to give early warning of the results of overtrading or increase, say, in seasonal business.

3 Unsystematic payment of creditors and collection of debtors

It is a simple fact that no company faced with insolvency will continue to part with cash in the same regular way that it did when its cash balances did not give rise to concern.

Similarly, it must be expected that an air of desperation will creep into cash collection: the easiest debts to collect are pressed for, while the difficult ones may be ignored.

4 Creative accounting and beneficial adjustments

At the beginning of this chapter, it was mentioned that even the most sensible of managers will close their eyes to potential insolvency, or will refuse to admit that it could happen. Frequently, management resorts to what can loosely be described as 'creative accounting', which may take the form of various sorts of self-delusion, or alternatively of deliberate attempts to cover up the true position in order to persuade lenders to extend or increase their lending facilities. Assets are revalued, bases of stock valuation are changed and apparently justified; expenditure is carried forward, and/or liabilities are ignored or omitted. The results of these manoeuvres may at first be difficult to detect, even by the most diligent auditors. The Companies Acts make it an offence for directors to deliberately mislead auditors.

Creative accounting can only be described as a kind of fraud. But theft of assets, particularly these days by means of computers, is today's crime growth area, with potentially serious effects on companies' well being.

A single one of the above signs or factors, or even a combination, will seldom be sufficient to bring a company down, but a high score must give rise to doubt; while any one insolvent company reviewed in retrospect will inevitably display a large number of the above weaknesses.

Links with other topics

This topic links directly with interpretation of accounts, as ratio analysis forms the cornerstone of problems of liquidity. Control of working capital, funds flow and gearing are also closely linked.

Sample questions

Case studies are an ideal medium for this topic. Students can show their skills by sorting information and being able to decide the major factors which are perhaps causing a cash crisis. Being able to recommend possible courses of action to alleviate the problem, usually in the form of a report, is an essential part of case study work.

1 Trendy Fashions Limited

Mr Fletcher, the managing director of Trendy Fashions Ltd, carefully perused each item on the list of creditors owing at the end of 198X which had been compiled by Mr Price, his accountant.

The company had failed to anticipate the market demand for male teenage casual clothes, and had experienced two very difficult years. Sales had decreased and losses incurred.

A re-equipment programme to take account of new technology put into action some three years ago had been curtailed, and some short-term finance totalling £130,000 secured to finance the programme was due for repayment in the following year.

There was, however, one ray of hope for Mr Fletcher. A young female designer, Sarah Orme, had recently commenced employment with the firm. Even old John Perry, the chief designer, had become excited by the flair present in Sarah's work.

Orders were on the increase, and Mr Price anticipated a small profit for next year. The outlook was, indeed, brighter.

Trendy Fashions Ltd Budgeted profit and loss account 198X

	£	£
Sales		556,400
Less: Cost of goods sold	239,900	
Wages and salaries	226,740	
Advertising	19,300	
Light, heating and power	19,940	
Insurances	740	
Repairs and maintenance	16,300	
Goodwill written off	10,000	
Depreciation	10,500	
*Loss on sale of plant and machinery	8,000	551,420
Profit for year		4,980

After deliberating for a while, Mr Fletcher decided that he wasn't too concerned about completing the capital programme in 198X. What really worried him was a

* This arises from the proposed sale of old plant, with a book value of £224,000, for £216,000. The cash received would be used to complete the re-equipment programme by buying a new batch of modern sewing machines at a cost of £114,000.

suspicion that the firm would not be able to pay off next year's maturing liabilities, and maintain the present operating cash balance of £15,000.

Mr Fletcher felt sure that Mr Price would be able to help him with this particular problem.

Required:

(a) Assuming you are Mr Price, draw up a statement and report to Mr Fletcher whether Trendy Fashions Ltd. could, in fact, complete the re-equipment programme, pay off the loans and maintain an operating cash balance of £15,000 in 198X.

(b) State what advice you would give to Mr Fletcher if all the objectives outlined in (a) could not be achieved next year.

BTEC

Answer plan

The ability to be able to construct a forecast cash statement for 198X, with particular emphasis on the non-cash items contained in the budgeted profit statement, is essential in answering the questions raised by Mr Fletcher. It could take the following form:

Trendy Fashions Ltd
Forecast cash statement at end of 198X

	£	£	£
Cash balance at end of 198X			15,000
Add: Cash receipts – 198X			
Cash from sale of plant		216,000	
Non-cash expenses:			
Depreciation	10,500		
Goodwill	10,000		
Loss on sale	8,000		
		28,500	
Profit for year		4,980	
			249,480
			264,480
Deduct proposed payment 198X			
New machinery		114,000	
Loans		130,000	
			244,000
			20,480
Less: Mr Fletcher's cash requirements			15,000
			5,480

Options open to Mr Fletcher could include:

(a) Possible renegotiation of the loans for a short period.

(b) Spreading the cost of the new machinery over a longer period of time, or trying to obtain longer credit facilities.

2 Prepare a report on the Dunn & Williams Canning Co Ltd for the managing director, Mr Keegan, who is concerned over the increase in bank borrowings at the end of 198X.

You are provided with canning industry ratios for 198X, and you are required to calculate and include in your report similar ratios for the Dunn & Williams Canning Co Ltd for 198X and 198Y.

Canning industry ratios 198X *

Liquidity	1.0
Current ratio	2.7
Stock turnover	7 times
Days sales in debtors	32 days
Return in capital employed (shareholders' equity)	18%
Net profit percentage	3.5%
Efficiency in the use of fixed assets	13

* Based on year-end balance sheet figures.

The Dunn & Williams Canning Co Ltd
balance sheets – 31 December

	198X £	198Y £
Ordinary shares of £1 each	459,000	459,000
Retained profits	438,600	489,600
Mortgages	51,000	45,900
Trade creditors	193,800	382,500
Accrued expenses	71,400	96,900
Bank overdraft	127,500	357,000
	1,341,300	1,830,900
Land and buildings	163,200	153,000
Machinery	158,100	135,100
Stock	637,500	1,032,800
Debtors	346,800	484,500
Cash	35,700	25,500
	1,341,300	1,830,900

Profits statements for the years ended 31 December

	198X £	198Y £
Net sales	3,442,500	3,570,000
Cost of goods sold	2,754,000	2,856,000
Gross operating profit	688,500	714,000
General administration and selling expenses	280,500	306,000
Depreciation	127,500	153,000
Miscellaneous expenses	107,100	153,000
Net profit before tax	173,400	102,000
Taxation	86,700	51,000
Net profit after tax	86,700	51,000
Retained profits b/fwd	351,900	438,600
	438,600	489,600

Assume tax is paid on a current basis, i.e. not included in creditors.

BTEC

Answer plan

By calculating the ratios in line with those of the canning industry, the conclusion will be reached that the reasons for the increase in the bank overdraft can be summarized as follows:

(a) Decline in profitability, so less cash from sales is retained in the business.

(b) Large fixed asset purchased financed from the bank overdraft.

(c) Massive build-up of stocks which have not been sold, although purchases still must be paid for.

(d) Debtors taking longer to settle their bills. If the bank were to call in the bank overdraft now, the company would be forced to sell some of their assets to remain in business.

3 Using the summarized accounts of Algernon Ltd as shown in chapter 12, question 3, and the ratios prepared for that question, comment on the position, progress and direction of Algernon Ltd.

ACCA Level 1

Answer plan

From the ratios the company appears to be trying to expand unsuccessfully. Generally, ratios of all types are changing adversely. We are not told what expansion actually took place; benefits may not have yet appeared. However, even allowing for this possibility, this adverse movement in profitability is deeply worrying.

4 Company financial statements including profit and loss accounts, balance sheets and statements of source and application of funds are used by a variety of individuals and institutions for a wide variety of purposes.

Required:
Specify six different types of users of financial statements and explain in each case the aspects of performance or position in which they are interested.

ACCA Level 1

Answer plan

Any six of the following types of individual/institution could be used in your answer:

User	Scope of interest
Suppliers	Stability of company and its ability to pay short-term liabilities.
Lenders	Ability of company to pay interest and to repay principal on due dates.
Customers	Security of supply.
Employees	Ability to meet wage demands.
Government	Tax collections, statistics.
Business consultants	Long- and short-term strengths and weaknesses.
Competitors	Assessment of comparative performance and position.
Shareholders (actual and potential)	Profit and profitability, stability, growth.

5 John Timpson, an established retail trader, who is very pleased with the expansion of his business during the past financial year, has been warned by his accountant that he must not simply concentrate his attention on profit growth. John Timpson recognizes that a legacy from his late father has made an important contribution to the recent development of his business.

The following summarized information relates to John Timpson's business during the years ended 30 September 1986 and 1987:

Summarized balance sheets

As at 30 September	1986		1987	
	£	£	£	£
Fixed assets				
At cost		280,000		350,000
Less depreciation provision		80,000		50,000
		200,000		300,000
Current assets				
Stock	40,000		147,000	
Debtors	45,000		58,000	
Balance at bank	35,000		5,000	
	120,000		210,000	
Less current liabilities				
Creditors	50,000	70,000	84,000	126,000
		270,000		426,000
Less long term loan – 10% pa		30,000		50,000
		240,000		376,000

Year ended 30 September	1986	1987
	£	£
Sales	200,000	300,000
Gross profit	60,000	108,000
Net profit	30,000	37,600

Required:

(a) Brief notes in support of John Timpson's optimistic view of the progress of his business.

(b) Brief notes in support of the accountant's warning concerning developments in John Timpson's business.

Note: Answers should be supported by the use of appropriate financial ratios.

AAT

Answer plan

From the information given, the following ratios should be calculated for 1986 and 1987:

> Gross profit to sales
> Current ratios
> Debtors collection period
> Net profit to sales
> Stock turnover
> Return on net capital employed
> Liquidity (quick or acid-test ratio)

John Timpson's business
Results years ended 30 September 1986 and 1987

Part (a)

Ratios in support of John Timpson's optimism

		1985–86	1986–87
1	$\dfrac{\text{Gross profit}}{\text{Sales}}$	30%	36%
2	$\dfrac{\text{Current assets}}{\text{Current liabilities}}$	2.4 times	2.5 times
3 (a)	Debtor's turnover ratio $= \dfrac{\text{Credit sales}}{\text{Year end debtors}}$	4.4 : 1	5.2 : 1
(b)	Debtors' collection period $= \dfrac{360}{\text{Debtors' turnover ratio}}$	81 days	69.6 days

John Timpson can point to:

1 increased rate of gross profit to sales;

2 improved working capital;

3 reduction in debtors' collection period;

4 increases in sales, gross profit and net profit.

Part (b)

The accountant will draw attention to the following ratios.

		1985–86	1986–87
1	Return on net capital employed $= \dfrac{\text{Net profit}}{\text{Net capital employed}}$	$12\frac{1}{2}$%	10%
2	Liquidity (quick ratio) $= \dfrac{\text{Balance at bank + debtors}}{\text{Creditors}}$	160%	75%
3	$\dfrac{\text{Net profit}}{\text{Sales}}$	15%	12.5%
4	$\dfrac{\text{Sales}}{\text{Net capital employed}}$	83.3%	79.8%
5	Stock turnover (using closing stock)	3.5 times	1.3 times
6	Great increase in creditors, evidence of possible extended credit being taken.		

The accountant can point to:

1 falling return on capital employed;

2 disastrous decline in liquidity;

3 fall in net profit/sales percentage;

4 poorer utilization of capital employed in trading activities;

5 effect of capital expenditure incurred in 1986–87 on liquidity position;

6 doubtful justification for increased loan at 10 per cent per annum.

7 doubtful justification for capital expenditure in 1986–87 (note: capital expenditure more than £70,000).

Further reading

M. W. E. Glautier and B. Underdown *Accounting Theory and Practice* (Pitman), chapter 4.

A. Pizzey *Accounting and Finance – a Firm Foundation* (Holt Rinehart & Winston), second edition, chapter 23.

14 Sources of finance

In order to start up, expand, pay expenses or invest for the future, a business require **finance**. Many firms fail to survive, not because they are not profitable, but becaus they have insufficient funds to settle their debts. Therefore the selection of a appropriate source of finance is essential.

Most questions on finance are of the essay type: either general questions on th subject, or particular types of finance problem which must be solved in the context c specific circumstances. Also, the topic may be part of other questions o interpretation and analysis.

14.1 Elements of the finance problem

Firms must consider three elements of their finance requirements:

1 the amount required;
2 how the finance is to be used, and for how long;
3 the source, and its associated period of time.

These elements are common to all finance decisions. If a large amount is require then external sources, outside the firm, may have to be used. This may require change in company ownership or liquidity, if external sources are used. If the finan is to be used for a long time, some sources may prove to be expensive, or simply n available.

14.2 Time periods

It is vitally important that consideration is given to the period of time for which th finance is needed. If a long-term need is financed from a short-term source, then func may not be available for a sufficient length of time to complete the activity that being financed. Either a new source will have to be found, or the activity abandone Many firms have found their existence threatened under these circumstances.

Finance sources may be classified into the following time-periods:

Short-term: less than one year
Medium-term: between one and five years
Long-term: over five years

Additionally, there are some finance sources which are never repaid, for exampl share capital; they are a permanent feature of the firm's capital structures. Suc sources are usually classified as long-term sources.

14.2.1 Short-term sources

A firm may look to sources of short-term finance within itself, or to outside source therefore a useful classification is internal and external sources.

1 Internal

Retained profits represent the profits available after all costs have been pai dividends distributed and transfers to reserves carried out.

Cash management is the efficient control of receipts from debtors and payments t creditors. Procedures can be established to speed up incoming cash, e.g. strict cred collection routines, which help to reduce bad debts. The payment of cash to credito may be deferred by delaying payments by a few days without risking the loss c discounts.

2 External

Trade credit is an arrangement between a firm and its suppliers, whereby the supplier delivers goods and then agrees to payment being deferred until a later date. The normal credit period is one month, but practice varies between industries.

A **credit sale** is a means of purchasing goods and paying by instalments. Ownership of the goods passes to the purchaser immediately; the length of the credit period is normally six months.

Bill finance settles debts between parties by means of a bill of exchange. This is a form of cheque which is post-dated 30, 90, or 180 days forward. It is a promise to pay the bearer a sum of money stated on the bill on a specific date. The seller of goods (drawer) draws up a bill addressed to the buyer (drawee) who 'accepts' the bill by writing across it 'accepted', and signing it. The drawee thereby accepts liability to pay the bill on the due date.

A bank bill is a bill backed by a financial institution which assumes responsibility for payment of the bill upon maturity. The drawer (seller of the goods) can either wait for the maturity date to receive the money, or may sell the bill to a third party at a rate less than the face value. This is known as **bill discounting** and is commonly undertaken by banks and discount houses.

Bank credit may take the form either of an overdraft or a short-term loan. An overdraft is where a bank agrees to honour cheques drawn on a current account, up to a stated sum beyond the point at which the account has sufficient funds to meet such cheques. Interest is charged on the total funds used.

A loan is where an account is credited with a stated amount, for a given period of time. Interest is charged on the total amount provided, and the arrangement is therefore more expensive than an overdraft. The loan is repaid in regular instalments.

The majority of companies are expected to give credit when selling to trade customers. If a company expands quickly, it may find itself unable to provide credit to a rapidly increasing customer base. Much of its working capital would then be tied up in credit to customers, when it could more profitably be used in expanding the business. **Factoring companies** specialize in purchasing firms' debts of this sort. Usually up to 80 per cent of the debt is paid immediately, with the balance being paid when the customers pay the factor, or after an agreed period. Thus the company has immediate access to cash that it might not normally receive for up to three months. Factoring companies give a choice between a recourse service, which gives complete protection on all approved sales, and a non-recourse service whereby the factor is able to recover a bad debt from the company in the event of a customer defaulting on payment. The cost of factoring is between 0.5 per cent and 2.5 per cent of gross annual turnover and is restricted to those companies with an annual turnover in excess of £100,000. An example of the effect of factoring on the balance sheet would be as follows:

	Before factoring £	£	After factoring £	£
Current assets				
Debtors	220,000		47,000	
Stocks	170,000	390,000	180,000	227,000
Current liabilities				
Bank overdraft	95,000		45,000	
Trade creditors	190,000		90,000	
Other creditors	38,000	323,000	25,000	160,000
Working capital		67,000		67,000

Source: The Association of British Factors

Receipt of an initial 80 per cent prepayment of £173,000 reduces creditors by £100,000; stocks increased by £10,000; the bank overdraft is reduced by £50,000, and other creditors are reduced by £13,000.

Factoring companies also offer services such as sales accounting and collection, screening of potential customers, and help for exporters.

If a company does not require the full factoring service, **invoice discounting** may be used to provide cash through the sale of specific or all sales invoices. It is usually carried out on a non-recourse basis.

Other short-term methods of raising finance include **goods discounting**, whereby [a] firm sells its goods to a specialist organization, and **loans from customers**, whic[h] enable the supplier to purchase the raw materials needed for goods which will [be] delivered to the customer.

14.2.2   Medium-term source

The sources of medium-term finance available include retained profits (internal), an[d] three external sources, leasing, hire purchase, and loans.

Retained profits have already been discussed as a short-term source. Leasin[g] companies provide finance for specific assets, by purchasing the assets and the[n] renting them to their customers. It is a way for the customer to acquire substanti[al] assets without high initial outlay. Until the 1984 Finance Act and SSAP 21, leasin[g] had certain tax and disclosure advantages, and allowed companies to keep the[ir] gearing down, because leased assets did not have to be shown on the balance shee[t.] The Finance Act 1984 introduced a process of gradual change to capital allowance[s] which has now been completed. Consequently, the tax advantages to the lessor [of] leasing have been greatly diminished, and the finance charges in lease payments ha[ve] been increased accordingly. Also SSAP 21 requires a lessee to show leased assets [on] their balance sheet. Instead of leasing, it may well now be cheaper for firms to borro[w] at a commercial rate of interest and to buy equipment.

Hire purchase enables the buyer to own the asset after paying a deposit and repayi[ng] the balance in equal instalments over a specified period. The asset is purchased by t[he] finance company, and the customer can exercise the right to purchase upon fin[al] payment of a nominal sum.

Loans may be offered by clearing banks or other financial institutions. A fixed sum [is] advanced over an agreed period at a fixed rate of interest, and is repaid in regul[ar] instalments. Many financial institutions are offering varying terms and conditions, [to] fit the particular circumstances of each firm. Repayment 'holidays', or low initi[al] interest charges may be offered.

14.2.3   Long-term sources

Again, retained profits are an internal source of funding, in the long term as in oth[er] time-spans.

In the long term, there are the following types of external sources of finance:

Share capital is available only to limited companies, and only public companies a[re] able to tap the large financial markets; issuing costs may be prohibitive for small an[d] medium-sized firms. This method of finance has the advantage that no fixed returns [to] shareholders are required, and there is no fixed repayment period. However, th[e] control of existing shareholders is weakened by the issue of new shares, and dividen[d] payments are not tax deductible.

Loans are normally in the form of a **debenture**, which is usually secured on an asset [of] the firm. This gives the debenture-holder the right to seize the asset, should the fir[m] not repay the loan plus interest at the specified time. Each debenture holder is given [a] debenture deed, which is in multiples of £100 or perhaps £1,000. The deed carries [a] fixed rate of interest and a specified repayment date. There are no voting righ[ts] attached to the debenture.

Sale and lease-back occurs when a firm decides to sell its premises to a speciali[st] property organization which undertakes to lease back the property to the seller for [a] long period of time. The seller receives a sum of money immediately, to use whe[n] required. The purchaser receives the title to the property and a negotiated annu[al] rental. Leases vary from 40 to 50 years, sometimes longer. Firms such as Woolwor[th] plc have successfully used this method in the past.

14.3   Government policy

There are many government-backed sources available to companies.

14.3.1   New projects

In order to encourage new projects, which otherwise might not have been financed [or] even identified, the Government fully or partly subsidizes the cost of feasibility studi[es] carried out by private-sector consultants. The areas in which a business may apply for help are as follows:

1 information technology;
2 growing businesses;
3 regional and development programmes;
4 inward and outward overseas investment;
5 research and development;
6 manufacturing;
7 personnel and training;
8 marketing and exporting;
9 distribution;
10 service functions.

Government and EC support for information technology extends to the encouragement of significant products and processes which otherwise would not materialize.

The Alvey committee has identified four main areas that the Government wishes to encourage, namely software, engineering, the man-machine interface, intelligent knowledge-based systems, and very large scale integrated microchips.

A major government scheme, with the theme 'how to make your business grow' has been instigated to stimulate investment in businesses with growth potential. The business expansion scheme offers tax incentives for private individuals investing in expanding and new businesses.

Regional and local development programmes encourage and assist fledgling firms and potential new investors within certain local authority areas.

Advice is available on research and development projects requiring a specific expertise, and limited advice is available on product design. The Manufacturing Advisory Service helps to accelerate the introduction of new and improved methods into factories. This help involves the provision of experienced specialists, initially free of charge and subsequently at half cost, on new projects in the manufacturing field.

The Manpower Services Commission (MSC) provides free recruitment services to employers through its national network of jobcentres. For a fee, an additional service for the recruitment of professional, administrative, managerial, executive, technical and scientific staff is provided through the professional and executive register.

Advice on marketing is available free, or on a subsidized basis, from the Institute of Marketing, the Confederation of British Industry, and the small firms service of the Department of Trade and Industry. This comprises an export intelligence service, help to find overseas agents, and the financing of export market research.

Advice can be obtained from the Department of Transport by businesses interested in developing distribution, through either the railway network or inland waterways.

Service industries are encouraged to set up in assisted areas by the provision of advice on locations for office development and grants towards the cost of feasibility studies into the location of projects in assisted areas.

14.3.2 Setting-up schemes

The enterprise allowance scheme helps unemployed people wishing to start their own business. Qualifying persons are paid £40 per week, for up to 52 weeks. Advice and guidance to participants is provided by the small firms service of the DTI.

14.3.3 Tax incentives

Relief from capital gains tax is possible by claiming rollover relief. This relief is intended to encourage firms to reinvest the proceeds from the sale of assets. If any gain arising from the sale of an asset is used to finance the purchase of a new asset, the tax due on the gain can be deferred for up to 10 years.

At the time of writing, capital allowances are still available for expenditure on plant and machinery. Taxable profits may be reduced by a given proportion of expenditure on fixed assets to be used in the business, thereby reducing a business's tax bill.

The business expansion scheme offers tax relief at their highest rate of income tax to individuals who invest in new projects started by qualifying companies. The tax relief is only available to outside investors, and is intended to encourage a greate supply of outside finance for growing businesses. The scheme works by allowing a individual to set against taxable income the cost of shares in qualifying companies.

The venture capital scheme allows any losses incurred by an individual investor t be set off against general income.

14.3.4 Joint scheme with private financial institutions

The Loan Guarantee Scheme is available to small businesses, whereby the governmen will guarantee 80 per cent of medium-term loans made by participating financia institutions. Sole proprietors, partnerships, cooperatives or limited companies ar eligible.

Summary

1 Finance sources may be classified into short, medium and long-term.

2 Each time-period comprises internal and external sources.

3 The Government and the European Community provide support for the financir of new projects.

Links with other topics

Chapter 15 looks at the relationship between fixed interest and equity sources finance, and the effect on profits, liquidity and performance, in capital structure an gearing. Many of the sources of finance mentioned in this chapter will appear on th funds statements in chapter 16, and in chapter 10 on company annual reports.

Sample questions

1 Compare hire purchase with equipment leasing.

First-year Business Studies degree, Staffordshire Polytechn

Answer

A short explanation of each source is required first, then a comparison with regard ownership, cost, tax benefits etc.

Ownership: with hire purchase, the asset is eventually owned by the firm, but wit leasing the asset commonly reverts back to the lessor.

Cost-leased assets are more expensive, sometimes up to 40 per cent above th purchase price.

Tax position: hire-purchase interest is tax deductible, and capital allowances ar available on a proportion of the asset cost. It is possible to offset the whole of th lease payment against taxable profits.

Effect on cash flow: hire purchase companies require a deposit, usually percentage of the purchase price, and the remaining sum plus interest is repaid ove three to five years in equal instalments. Leasing does not usually require a deposit, bt if it does, this comprises two months' rent in advance, equal payments being mac over the period of the lease.

2 Outline the major methods of raising long-term finance for a manufacturir company whose shares are quoted on the Stock Exchange.

First-year Business Studies degree, Staffordshire Polytechn

Answer

The candidate must explain in detail the following:
(a) retained profits;
(b) share capital;
(c) loans;
(d) sale and leaseback.

Then the possibility of government help may be considered, the most relevar aspects of which are listed below. These are only guidelines and the candidate wou have to evaluate each and then assess whether it is suitable for the company i question.

Information Technology
Regional and Development Programmes
Inward and Outward Overseas Investment
Research and Development
Manufacturing
Personnel and Training
Marketing and Exporting

A candidate would be heavily penalized for including short or medium-term sources.

3 A firm is considering modernizing its factory equipment. Critically evaluate the various ways in which the firm may finance the exercise.

First-year Business Studies degree, Staffordshire Polytechnic

Answer

The financing of factory equipment is mainly a medium-term task. If the firm is heavily committed to equipment, there is a possibility that some of the long-term sources may be tapped.
The following must be included:

(a) leasing;

(b) hire-purchase;

(c) loans;

(d) retained profits.

4 Set out the advice you would give to the following:

(a) a sole proprietor wishing to expand;

(b) a private company wishing to renew its machinery;

(c) a public company experiencing working capital difficulties.

First-year Business Studies degree, Staffordshire Polytechnic

Answer

(a) Firstly, indicate those sources not available, such as share capital, probably not leasing or sale and leaseback. So sources such as loans (long and medium-term), leasing, hire purchase and retained profits should be included.

(b) This company may use the sources mentioned in (a), plus the possibility of selling shares if the amount involved is substantial. It is essentially a medium-term problem.

(c) This problem requires short-term solutions.
Internal: retained profits and cash management.
External: trade credit, bill finance, bank overdraft, factoring, invoice discounting.

Further reading

Assisting Small Firms (published by Staffordshire Polytechnic, Dept of Economics).
Finance for New Projects in the UK (published by Peat Marwick McLintock).
Factoring of Trade Debts (published by the Association of British Factors).

15 Financial structure

The theory of company finance is based on the assumption that the objective management is to maximize the wealth of the firm's ordinary shareholders. A busine is likely to be financed by a combination of preference shares, ordinary share retained profits, medium and long-term loans and current liabilities, as shown chapter 14. The business will endeavour to raise a combination of finance from the different sources at the least possible average cost, and thereby help to genera surplus funds for the proprietors. Raising finance as cheaply as possible wi therefore, increase the value of the proprietors' interest and help towards maximizi their wealth.

An ideal, or optimum, financial structure will have been achieved when the busine has minimized the average cost of the different sources of finance. The business w need to bear in mind the risks attached to the introduction, or increase in, fix interest capital. This is mainly due to the fact that all interest must be paid, whatev profits or losses are made. It is a charge in the profit and loss account. If the busine fails to pay the interest, it runs the risk of being made bankrupt or wound up. This more likely if the provider of the loans have some security for their investment in t form of a mortgage on the business's assets. The finance manager will need continuously monitor and evaluate the proportion of funds it raises from the differe sources, in response to the changing financial environment. If, for example, there w a general decrease in interest rates, it might be preferable for a business to raise a new finance required in the form of loans rather than shares.

The financial structure of the business will therefore need to be as flexible possible, although it should be recognized that many of the decisions on the type a size of finance raised are of a medium and long-term nature. The various componen of the financial structure are shown in the following diagram:

Financial structure →	Preference share capital Ordinary share capital Reserves Medium and long-term loans
	Plus Short-term sources Creditors

The Group balance sheet for ICI as at 31 December 1987 shows that their tot assets of £8,787m have been financed as follows:

	£m
Creditors due within one year	2,970
Creditors due after more than one year	1,581
Provisions for liabilities and charges	295
Deferred income	139
Minority interests	357
Ordinary shares	676
Reserves	2,769
	8,787

In this chapter we will examine the kind of factors that determined the financial structure of ICI, exploring the answers to such questions as:

1 Why do short-term creditors finance total assets by a greater percentage (33.8 per cent) than medium and long-term creditors (18 per cent)?

2 Why is there no preference share capital in the existing financial structure?

3 Why do reserves form the second largest component (31.5 per cent) of the financial structure, and which particular reserve is the most important source of finance?

4 Why is the ordinary share capital such an insignificant proportion (7.7 per cent) of the total financial structure etc?

The main points that will be covered in this chapter are:

1 Features of the various sources of finance which are relevant to financial structure decisions.

2 Major factors in attempting to determine an 'ideal' financial structure.

3 Gearing ratios.

The gearing ratios outlined in this chapter are all traditional measures used with financial information taken directly from the balance sheet and profit and loss account. An alternative measure is to use the market value of the debt and equity which may more closely represent the economic value of the firm. It is important to understand the differences between the measures and to be consistent with whichever one(s) you use.

Questions may be asked about the main characteristics of, and the relationships between, the different sources of finance within the financial structure of a business. This may require a descriptive answer about the different sources as far as cost, availability etc. are concerned, or a numerical calculation of the relationship between the sources of finance, in the form of gearing ratios or percentages, and comments on your findings. The findings would include analysis of profit performance, adequacy of cash flow and liquidity, potential security, control aspects, risk profile, etc. relevant to the particular financial structure being employed or proposed.

15.1 Sources of finance and structure decisions

15.1.1 Preference shares

Preference shares generally form only a small percentage of most business sources of finance, and are therefore not very important in financial structure decisions. Nevertheless, many businesses still have in their balance sheet preference shares which were issued many years ago, although in other cases the shares have been converted to ordinary shares or loan capital, or simply redeemed.

Raising finance in the form of loans is more popular, because the interest payable on loans is chargeable for tax purposes. This means that if a business raises loan capital at, say, 13 per cent, this will only cost the company 8.45 per cent net of tax, if the corporation tax rate is 35 per cent. The dividend payable to preference shareholders is an appropriation of profits and, therefore, is not tax deductible. The rate of dividend payable will almost certainly be fixed, and its level will depend on circumstances when it was raised. Its cost would almost certainly exceed the net cost of loan interest. In the period from 1981 to 1986, only 3 per cent of the total issues of new money raised by UK Stock Exchange-listed security companies was in the form of preference shares, compared with 37 per cent in the form of loans.

On 31 December 1987, ICI had no preference shares in its financial structure.

15.1.2 Ordinary shares

Ordinary shareholders provide the main risk-bearing capital of companies. They are the main risk bearers, ranking after preference shareholders for dividend distribution purposes, and after the interest payable to loan capital holders. As shown in chapter 10, interest payable on loans is a charge in the profit and loss account, whereas dividends are on appropriation of profits. If there are insufficient profits, the ordinary shareholder stands the risk of not being paid any dividend. In the period from 1981 to

1986, for example, the issue of ordinary shares provided 60 per cent of new money raised by UK Stock Exchange-listed security companies. Most of these monies were raised in the form of rights issues. In 1986, of the total new money raised on the UK stock market (£9,148m), 83.6 per cent was in ordinary shares (75.7 per cent of which were in the form of rights issues), 3.5 per cent was in preference shares, and 12.9 per cent in loan capital.

The cost of ordinary share capital to a business would be any dividends paid, which are an appropriation of profits. The level of dividend paid, if any, would be dependent mainly upon the level, consistency and growth of profits, and also on any available reserves, cash levels, profitable investment opportunities, management attitudes, etc.

On 31 December 1987, ICI had £676m of called-up and fully-paid share capital in its financial structure, as shown previously, all of which was in the form of ordinary stock of £1 units. The ordinary share capital of £676m represented 7.7 per cent of the total assets of £8,787m.

15.1.3   Retained profits

Profits ploughed back into businesses are a major source of funds as shown in chapter 14. Nevertheless, internally generated funds have declined over recent years as a result of a number of factors, including the incidence of tax, inflation and recessions. Retained profits have no 'direct' cost in the form of dividends (or interest) payable, but there is an opportunity cost.

Ploughing back profits and raising money from an ordinary share issue will increase a business's potential to borrow funds. This is because the new equity will generate extra earnings and cash flow, together with an increase in net assets, which would form a basis for extra borrowing.

On 31 December 1987, ICI had £2,769m of reserves, as shown previously, of which £1,964m was the balance on the profit and loss account. The reserves of £2,769m represented 31.5 per cent of the total assets of £8,787m, the profit and loss account being 22.4 per cent of this.

15.1.4   Loan capital

Loan capital is an important source of finance for businesses, as indicated previously. The amount of new money raised by UK companies in the form of debt has varied with the changing financial environment. In 1981, for example, the debt totalled £4,404m (16.5 per cent of total issues), whereas in 1986 this had increased considerably.

The interest on loan capital is a charge against the profits of a business. The business will therefore have to ensure that it has sufficient profits, cash flow and security to support the level of debt it has chosen. If a business fails to meet its interest commitment, the trustee for the debenture holders will take action against the business.

On 31 December 1987, ICI had £1,557m of loans (£124m secured and £1,433m unsecured). The loans represented 17.7 per cent of the total assets of £8,787m.

15.1.5   Current liabilities

The size and make-up of current liabilities varies considerably between different businesses. The major components of current liabilities are usually trade creditors and bank loans or overdrafts. Current liabilities are an important, continuous short-term source of finance, because they are continually being re-created. Some of the components could, however, be considered to have a longer-term nature, particularly bank borrowings and overdrafts. Until current liabilities are discharged, the business is using the credit extended to it, but this would have a cost.

The cost could be any discount lost by not paying before a certain date, loss of goodwill for the same reason, extra interest payable on some debts, etc. The business will, therefore, have to take these possible costs into account when any financial structure decisions are made. On 31 December 1987 ICI had creditors due within one year of £2,970m as shown previously, which formed 33.8 per cent of the total assets of £8,787m.

15.2 'Optimum' financial structure

The following are the major factors that a business will take into account when it is planning its financial structure:

1 The **amount** of capital needed.

2 The **attitudes** of the different providers of finance.

3 The existing **borrowing level** of the business and of its competitors within the same industry.

4 Whether there is sufficient **cash flowing** through the business to enable the loan interest, dividend payments, and any repayments of capital, to be made on time.

5 Whether a high enough proportion of the business assets is financed by the proprietor's capital to avoid the **control** of the business falling into the hands of third parties.

6 The **cost** of each component of the financial structure (and its weighted averaged) in the form of dividends, interest, opportunity cost, etc.

7 The possible effects of **inflation**.

8 The likely trend in **interest rates**, and its effects on borrowing, short or long-term etc.

9 The level and consistency of **profits** to cover adequately the interest and dividends payable. If the level of profits fluctuates, as perhaps in a seasonal business, the business may not be able to borrow as much as in a situation where the profits are at a more consistent level (see example below).

10 The **repayment**, redemption or conversion provisions for any of the sources of finance.

11 Whether the business has suitable assets to offer as **security** for any monies borrowed. The business will have to offer some form of security to its lenders, in most cases.

12 The **risk** attached to any projects that the business is proposing.

13 The effects that **taxation** might have on the different available sources of capital.

14 The **timing**, with careful consideration being given to when capital is needed.

15 The **financial risk** that the equity shareholders are prepared to accept. Rational investors are risk averse and they will require compensation in the form of bigger returns for the extra risk of introducing, or increasing, the amount of debt in the capital structure.

All the factors are influenced and shaped by the wider economic and political environment, and as this changes, so does the relative importance of each of the factors and the impact that they have on the financial structures of businesses.

15.3 Gearing ratios

The relationship between ordinary shareholders' funds and any fixed interest capital in a financial structure is known as **gearing**.

Gearing can be calculated in a number of different ways. One method is simply to express the ordinary shareholders' funds as a percentage of the ordinary shareholders' funds plus any fixed interest capital:

$$\frac{\text{Ordinary shareholders' funds}}{\text{Ordinary shareholders' funds plus fixed interest capital}} \times \frac{100}{1} = \text{Gearing \%}$$

ICI ratio for 1987 was 61.9%

This percentage shows how much of the net capital employed in the business is in the form of ordinary shareholders' funds, and will give some indication of the financial strength of the company. If the percentage is low, this could indicate that the ordinary shareholders could lose control of the company. The risks are much greater in this kind of situation, as far as the equity shareholder is concerned, but the rewards could be consequently higher.

A second method of expressing the gearing relationship is to exclude the reserves from the equation, i.e.:

$$\frac{\text{Ordinary share capital}}{\text{Ordinary share capital plus fixed interest capital}} \times \frac{100}{1} = \text{Gearing \%}$$

ICI ratio for 1987 was 24.2%

Thirdly, the ordinary share capital can be related to the fixed interest capital, i.e.:

$$\frac{\text{Ordinary share capital}}{\text{Fixed interest capital}} \times \frac{100}{1} = \text{Gearing \%}$$

ICI ratio for 1987 was 31.9%

All these ratios are based on book values, but it is possible to use market values instead. The use of market values would reflect up-to-date values and take into account, amongst other things, current interest rates and yields. In addition to these three alternative (capital) gearing percentages, it is also possible to calculate an **income gearing ratio/percentage**, whereby the business can investigate whether the returns payable to the fixed interest capital are adequately covered by earnings. This ratio is calculated by taking the earnings before interest and tax and dividing them by the interest, i.e.:

$$\frac{\text{Earnings before interest and tax (EBIT)}}{\text{Interest}} = \frac{\text{No. of times}}{\text{interest is covered}}$$

ICI cover for 1987 was 7.2

A business will require the interest payable to be covered from perhaps 4 to 7 times, depending upon the company, its commercial sector, and the economic and political environment at the time.

A second method of calculating the income gearing is to express the gross interest as a percentage of the earnings before interest and tax, i.e.:

$$\frac{\text{Gross interest}}{\text{Earnings before interest and tax}} \times \frac{100}{1} = \text{income gearing \%}$$

ICI percentage for 1987 was 13.8%

ICC Business Ratios, a division of ICC Information Group Ltd, publish business ratio reports, and they include three financial structure ratios in the reports, namely borrowing ratio, an **equity gearing ratio** and an **income gearing percentage**. These terms are defined as follows:

Borrowing ratio: Total debt expressed as a ratio of net worth.

Equity gearing: Shareholders' funds expressed as a ratio of total liabilities.

Income gearing: Gross interest paid as a percentage of pre-interest, pre-tax profits.

Total debt: The sum of the short-term loans and the long-term loans.

Net worth: Equal to the shareholders' funds, less the intangible assets.

Shareholders' funds: The issued ordinary and preference share capital, capital and revenue reserves, profit and loss account balance, as well as government grants.

Total liabilities: The sum of capital employed and total current liabilities.

Capital employed: The net assets employed by a firm.

The borrowing and equity gearing ratios are similar to the gearing ratios already covered, and the income gearing ratio is identical to the one outlined previously. These three ratios are shown for ICI at the end of this section.

The gearing level that any business has will depend on many different factors, as outlined in Section 15.2. These include **costs, time periods, profit levels, cash flow, security, control, size, type of business,** etc. A business which has consistent and adequate earnings, a satisfactory cash flow, and can offer security to lenders, will be able to 'afford' a much higher gearing level than one that does not have these features.

A large retail business in the local high street may well have these features and this will enable it to borrow substantial amounts and thereby increase its profits and its returns to the ordinary shareholder. A business which has fluctuating or uncertain profits and cash flows, and/or few assets to offer as security, will not be able to borrow to the same level.

Businesses with a large proportion of fixed interest capital are said to be **highly geared** whilst those with a small proportion of fixed interest capital are **lowly geared**. A business can use its fixed interest capital to **lever up** the rate of return on its proprietor's funds, over and above that achieved on the total capital employed. As long as a business is able to do this, it can introduce more fixed interest capital into its financial structure.

The following example illustrates these principles. The financial structures of three companies are as follows:

	A Ltd	B Ltd	C Ltd
	£	£	£
Ordinary shares of £1 each	25,000	20,000	10,000
Reserves	25,000	15,000	5,000
13% loan capital	—	15,000	35,000
	50,000	50,000	50,000

The companies all have capital employed of £50,000, and they all have the same annual earning before tax of £10,000.

If the following formula is used:

$$\frac{\text{Ordinary shareholders' funds}}{\text{Ordinary shareholders' funds} + \text{loan capital}} \times \frac{100}{1} = \text{Gearing \%}$$

The gearing percentages are as follows:

A Ltd = 50,000/50,000 = 100%

B Ltd = 35,000/50,000 = 70%

C Ltd = 15,000/50,000 = 30%

The three companies have no gearing, medium gearing, and high gearing respectively. The return to the ordinary shareholders will increase as the businesses are progressively more highly geared, providing the average return on the total capital employed exceeds the average return to the fixed interest capital.

In this example, all the businesses earn 20 per cent before tax on total capital employed, i.e.:

$$\frac{10,000}{50,000} \times \frac{100}{1} = 20\%$$

The average return payable to the fixed interest capital (loans) is only 13%.

The following figures show how the business with the most highly-geared financial structure (C Ltd) will produce the highest return to the ordinary shareholders:

	A Ltd	B Ltd	C Ltd
	£	£	£
Earnings before tax	10,000	10,000	10,000
13% Loan interest	—	1,950	4,550
Earnings after loan interest	10,000	8,050	5,450
Tax (assume 35% corporation tax rate)	3,500	2,818	1,908
Earnings after tax available to ordinary shareholders	6,500	5,232	3,542
Return on equity as a %	13%	14.9%	23.6%

If the annual profit figure fell to £5,000 though, the return to the shareholders of C Ltd would decrease considerably, indicating the risk(s) attached to the policy of high gearing:

	A Ltd	B Ltd	C Ltd
Earnings before tax	5,000	5,000	5,000
13% Loan interest	—	1,950	4,550
Earnings after loan interest	5,000	3,050	450
Tax (assume 35% corporation tax rate)	1,750	1,068	158
Earnings after tax available to ordinary shareholders	3,250	1,982	292
Return on equity as a %	6.5%	5.66%	1.95%

The **borrowing, equity gearing** and **income gearing ratios and percentages** for ICI for the years ending 31 December 1985 and 1986 are shown in the ICC Business Ratios publication, and are as follows:

	1986	1985
Borrowing ratio	54.3	51.0
Equity gearing	0.4	0.4
Income gearing	16.6	18.9

The ratios indicate that there was very little change in ICI's finance structure as regards the level of borrowing over the two years 1985 and 1986. A borrowing ratio of 54.3 suggests that about 54 per cent of the net worth of the business was financed by debt, and the other 46 per cent, therefore, financed by the ordinary shareholders' funds. This ratio could be compared with the industrial average figures for the relevant sector, and constructive comments could then be made on whether or not ICI was more or less highly-geared than the 'average' company in the same sector, and the possible reasons for this. The income gearing figure indicates that the interest, as a percentage of the pre-interest, pre-tax profit figure, declined by about 12 per cent in 1986 compared with 1985. The reason for this is the increase in pre-interest, pre-tax profits in 1986 to £1,218m, from £1,124m in 1985, and the reduction in interest in 1986 to £202m, from £212m in 1985.

The gearing measures shown in this section are useful for companies when planning their financial structure. In addition to considering the different finance sources available, a company's financial structure may be altered in a number of other different ways, such as the issue of bonus shares, capital reorganization or reconstruction, and capital reduction.

Links with other topics

Financial structure links with topics in a number of other chapters. It links most closely with the last three chapters, 12, 13 and 14. Financial structure decisions are an important aspect when analysing and assessing business performance, and link therefore, with the topics covered in chapters 12 and 13 which concern analysis, and how to assess a company's performance.

Sample questions

1 When the amount of ordinary share capital is small in relation to the long-term loans in the financial structure of a business, it is said to be highly geared. One of the effects of this is that the ordinary share capital is sensitive to any fluctuations in profits.

Comment on the above statement with the aid of suitable illustration(s).

First-year Business Studies degree level

Understanding the question

It is essential to understand the nature of gearing and how fluctuations in profits can have a dramatic effect on the return to ordinary shareholders. It will be necessary to illustrate your answer with suitable figures, preferably choosing a low, medium and highly-geared company, and show the effect of, say, two different levels of profit, one level of profit which shows the benefit of high gearing/leverage and one which highlights the risk attached to a lower level of profit.

Answer plan

Comments are required on the statement showing your knowledge of gearing – the relationship between equity capital and fixed interest capital. Companies can be low, medium or highly geared and there are a number of gearing ratios that can be calculated to show this relationship.

An illustration would include, say, three different companies with nil/low, medium and highly geared structures, but with the same total capital employed. The financial structures would include ordinary share capital and loan capital.

Two or more different levels of profit would then be chosen, one showing an increasing return to the ordinary shareholders in the highly geared structure and one, with a much lower level of profit, which would show a considerably decreased return to the highly geared structure. This would indicate the risks attached to highly geared structures and the sensitivity of business with these kinds of financial structures to fluctuations in profits.

2 The following are extracts from the accounts of three limited companies in the same industry:

	H Ltd		O Ltd		T Ltd	
	£000s	£000s	£000s	£000s	£000s	£000s
Fixed assets		160		280		1,300
Current assets	140		180		1,200	
Less current liabilities	120		140		500	
(Creditors)		20		40		700
		180		320		2,000
Ordinary share capital		40		100		600
Revenue reserves		120		160		600
14% loan capital		20		60		800
		180		320		2,000
Earnings after tax		28		38		180

(Assume corporation tax at 35%)

You are required to compare the three companies by calculating the borrowing ratio, equity gearing and income gearing, and comment on your findings.

First-year Business Studies degree level

Understanding the question

This is a straightforward question requiring the calculation of three gearing ratios. It will be necessary to know the relevant formulae, but alternative simplified ones could also be acceptable. The important thing is to show a clear understanding of what the calculated ratios mean, so that comparative comments can be made.

Answer plan

The three calculations are as follows:

Borrowing ratio: Total debt expressed as a ratio of net worth

H Ltd	O Ltd	T Ltd
20/160 = 0.13	60/260 = 0.23	800/1,200 = 0.67

Equity gearing: Shareholders' funds expressed as a ratio of total liabilities

160/300 = 0.53	260/460 = 0.56	1,200/2,500 = 0.48

Income gearing: Gross interest paid as a percentage of the preinterest, pretax profit

2.8/45.88 × 100/1 =	8.4/66.86 × 100/1 =	112/388.9 × 100/1 =
6.1%	12.56%	28.8%

Comments required on the findings.

All these ratios indicate T Ltd's higher gearing. The income gearing, for example shows 28.8 per cent of pre-interest; pre-tax profit is taken up by the interest.

3 An extract from the balance sheet and income statement at 31 December 1987 of HOT Ltd shows the following:

Extract from balance sheet

Ordinary share capital in £1 shares   £1.5m

Extract from profit and loss account

Earnings before tax   £250,000
(Assume corporation tax rate is 35%)

The directors are considering the possibility of keeping the same level of capital employed, £1.5m, but introducing borrowing into the financial structure for the year starting 1 January 1988. Ordinary share capital would be reduced (and repaid) and replaced by borrowings.

The proposed financial structure would appear as follows:

Ordinary share capital	£750,000
12% debentures	£400,000
13% unsecured loans	£350,000

You are required to:

(a) Calculate the gearing ratio for HOT Ltd for the proposed financial structure using the formula:

Ordinary share capital/ordinary share capital + debentures + unsecured loans.

(b) Assuming that the earnings before tax and interest for 1988 remains at £250,000 calculate the income gearing as a percentage.

(c) Calculate the return to ordinary share capital for 1988 under the proposed financial structure and compare this with the return for 1987 and discuss your findings.

First-year Business Studies degree level

Understanding the question

This is a fairly straightforward question, with calculations and comments required. The formula for the calculations in (a) is given. When the calculations are carried out for both (capital) gearing and income gearing for the present and proposed financial structure, it should be possible to show the benefits of leverage. That is, the return to equity shareholders should be 'levered up' as a result of introducing debt into the financial structure.

Answer plan

(a) Calculation required for the gearing ratio from the formula, which is given:

750,000/750,000 + 400,000 + 350,000 = 0.50

(b) Using the formula:

$$\frac{\text{Gross interest}}{\text{Earnings before interest and tax}} \times \frac{100}{1} = \text{Income gearing \%}$$

$$\frac{48,000 + 45,500}{250,000} \times \frac{100}{1} = 37.4\%$$

(c) An outline income statement will help to answer this part of the question:

		1988 £	1987 £
Earnings before tax		250,000	250,000
Interest	48,000		
Interest	45,500	93,500	—
Earnings after interest		156,500	250,000
Tax (35%)		54,775	87,500
		101,725	162,500
Return to ordinary shareholders		101,725	162,500
No. of shares		750,000 shares	1.5m shares
Earnings per share (EPS)		= 13.56p	= 10.83p

The introduction of gearing into the financial structure clearly shows the benefits of leverage. The proposed financial structure shows an increase of EPS from 10.83p to 13.56p.

4 The net assets of three unconnected companies are financed as follows, as at 31 December 1984:

	Company					
	X plc		Y plc		Z plc	
	£000	£000	£000	£000	£000	£000
Share capital authorized						
Ordinary shares of £1.00 per share		12,000		—		—
Ordinary shares of £0.25 per share		—		6,000		6,000
8% preference shares of £1.00 per share		—		4,000		4,000
		12,000		10,000		10,000
Called up and issued						
Ordinary shares of £1.00 per share £0.75 paid		6,000		—		—
Ordinary shares of £0.25 per share fully paid		—	4,000		1,000	
8% preference shares of £1.00 per share, fully paid		—	4,000		2,000	
		6,000		8,000		3,000
Reserves						
Share premium account (raised on issue of ordinary shares)				500		200
General reserve	1,000		—		1,300	
Fixed asset revaluation reserve	2,000		—		—	
Fixed asset replacement reserve	—		1,000		—	
Profit and loss account	1,000		500		1,500	
		4,000		2,000		3,000
Shareholders' funds		10,000		10,000		6,000
10% Debenture stock		—		—		4,000
		10,000		10,000		10,000

For all three companies, the profit before interest and tax is estimated at £5,000,000 for the next 12 months ended 31 December 1985. The capital structure of each company will remain unaltered.

Taxation on profits after interest is an effective rate of 40 per cent. Assume that an ordinary dividend of 12 per cent of the paid up share capital will be paid.

Required:
For each of the three companies,

(a) prepare the estimated profit and loss accounts for the year ended 31 December 1985,

(b) calculate
(i) basic earnings per share for the year ended 31 December 1985,
(ii) gearing ratio as at 31 December 1984,

(c) briefly explain, in relation to gearing, the effects on earnings of substantial changes in profit after tax.

Marks will be awarded for workings which must be shown.

ACCA Level 1

Understanding the question

The question requires you to prepare an estimated profit and loss account for three companies from year end balance sheets and a few extra items of information. This should be a fairly straightforward exercise after the work covered in earlier chapters. You are then required to calculate certain basic ratios and comment on the financial structure of the businesses as evidenced by the substantial differences in the level of earnings.

Answer plan

Part (a)

From the accounting information given, prepare estimated profit and loss accounts in a vertical form for each company in the following manner:

X/Y/Z plc
Profit and loss account for the year ended 31.12.85

	£000	£000
Profit before interest and tax,		____
Interest		
Profit before tax		
Taxation		____
Profit after tax		
Dividends:		
Preference		
Ordinary		____
		____
Retained profit		____

The retained profits for the year are X plc 2,280, Y plc 2,200 and Z plc 2,480 (£000s).

Part (b)

(i) The basic earnings per share are calculated by dividing the profit after tax and preference dividends by the number of ordinary shares issued (see SSAP 3).

The basic earnings per share are: X plc 37.5p;
           Y plc 16.75p;
           Z plc 65.0p.

(ii) The gearing ratio can be expressed as the ratio of all ordinary shareholders funds to all fixed return capital (preference shares and debentures).

The ratios so calculated are: X plc 0.00:1;
          Y plc 0.6:1;
          and Z plc 1.5:1

which range from zero to high gearing.

Part (c)

In a lowly geared company the EPS will basically change in proportion to the changes in profit levels, whereas, in a highly geared company, the returns to ordinary shareholders will increase and decrease disproportionately with fluctuating profit levels.

5 The assets employed by limited companies are financed by loans of various sorts and/or by shares.

All limited companies, apart from those limited by guarantee, must have a share capital. The two most common types of share are preference and ordinary (equity).

The authorised share capital is stated in each company's Memorandum of Association and appears in the balance sheet, together with the issued share capital, which may, or may not, be fully called up. Some of the share capital may be redeemable.

Required:

Answer the following questions which relate to the above statements.

(a) In what respects are the rights of preference shareholders preferential over the rights of ordinary shareholders?

(b) For what main reason may a company issue preference shares rather than ordinary shares?

(c) For what main reason may a company issue redeemable shares rather than those which are irredeemable?

(d) What form of remuneration do shareholders receive on their holdings?

(e) How is the remuneration in (d) accounted for in a company's profit and loss account?

(f) Under what main circumstance may a company's share capital be only partly called up?

(g) What is the main effect of a preference share issue on the capital structure of a company?

ACCA Level 1

Understanding the question

This is a fairly straightforward question which requires you to link the material in this chapter on financial structure with material on company annual reports and accounts contained in chapter 10.

The question is mainly concerned with your appreciation of the differences between the different types of capital in the financial structure.

Answer plan

(a) Rights of shareholders

Preference shareholders usually have a right to receive dividends out of profits before ordinary shareholders and if the company is wound up, preference shareholders will be repaid capital before ordinary shareholders.

(b) Preference versus ordinary share issue

The main reason for a company to issue preference rather than ordinary shares would be to attract potential shareholders who are more risk averse.

(c) Redeemable versus irredeemable issue

The main reason for a company to issue redeemable rather than irredeemable shares is to raise finance for a set period of, say, 10 to 15 years by which time the company could be in a position to redeem the shares. The availability and cost of other funds would also be important.

(d) Shareholders' remuneration

Shareholders receive their remuneration in the form of dividends, providing there are sufficient profits and/or distributable reserves.

(e) Accounting for dividends

Dividends, proposed and paid, are an appropriation of profits, not a charge. Therefore they should be shown in the appropriations section of the profit and loss account, not in the main body of the statement.

(f) Partly called up share capital

A company may not require the total amount of its called up share capital in its initial stages and it may wish to 'call up' (require payment of) the remaining capital at a later date. A number of well-known businesses which were privatized recently raised their monies in instalments.

(g) Preference shares' effect on capital structure

Preference shares are part of the fixed return capital of a company, therefore if new preference shares are raised the gearing of the company will increase.

Further reading

R. J. Briston *Introduction to Accountancy and Finance* (Macmillan), chapter 6.

M. W. E. Glautier and B. Underdown *Accounting Theory and Practice* (Pitman), chapter 9.

C. Nobes *Introduction to Financial Accounting* (Allen & Unwin), chapter 11.

R. H. Parker *Understanding Company Financial Statements* (Pelican), chapter 7.

16 Funds flow

The importance of a healthy cash flow to a business's ability to survive and prosper has already been discussed in chapter 12. A business must ensure that its cash flow follows, at worst, only a short way behind, if not actually 'hand in hand' with its profits.

One of the major causes of business failure is insufficient cash or working capital. A business may yet be profitable, but if it is short of cash it may not be able to pay wages at the end of the week, or pay trade creditors for materials bought, at the end of the month. A shortage of cash may therefore inhibit any internal or external expansion, and may even force the business into bankruptcy or liquidation.

Increasing attention has been paid to the control of this vital resource, cash, particularly since the financial crisis of the early 1970s. The preparation of cash flow statements by internal management assists considerably in the control of cash. Another statement which will assist in its control is the funds flow statement.

Funds are not defined in the relevant accounting standard, SSAP 10, but it has a much broader concept than just cash and incorporates the movement over all working capital items during the year. A cash flow account/statement would just record all the **cash** inflows and outflows in an accounting period, regardless of whether or not they referred to that particular accounting period. The funds statement, on the other hand, shows the total flow of funds into and out of the business over all its resources and is not just simply confined to the narrow concept of cash. The funds statement would, therefore, include the flow of funds from the change over the accounting period to debtors, stocks or creditors.

The main points which will be covered in this chapter are as follows:

1 cash flow statements;

2 funds flow statements – preparation and interpretation, and standard accounting practice;

3 funds flow statements in practice;

4 working capital statements.

Questions may be asked on the preparation of relatively simple funds flow statements at this level, from given financial data. This data may include the balance sheets of a business at the start and end of an accounting period, and the linking income statement. The preparation of funds flow statements for groups and related companies will be dealt with at a later stage in your studies.

In addition to the preparation of such statements, you may be required to comment on them. This will involve analysing where funds have been raised and used over a particular accounting period. Your findings may be required to be linked with the analysis of the financial condition, progress and management of resources by the business as a whole. This topic links closely with those in chapters 12 and 13.

An alternative type of question is one where the funds flow statement is already prepared for you for one or more accounting periods, possibly with other financial statements, and you are required to comment on the financial condition and progress of the business, along the lines indicated in the previous paragraph.

16.1 Cash-flow statements

These statements can be prepared for past activities showing the opening balance of cash, a record of the receipts and payments over an accounting period, and showing the balance of cash at the end.

Opening cash balance
Plus
Receipts during the period
Less
Payments during the period
Equals
Closing cash balance
(plus or minus)

This kind of statement will be of use to the internal management to help them to analyse the past movements of cash and to answer such questions as:

1 What were the major sources of cash during the year?

2 Why was there a 'negative' balance at the end of (say) July?

3 Has the business taken advantage of certain cash discounts that were available during the year?

4 How is it that the cash balance has reduced over the period, whilst at the same time the business has made a profit? etc. etc.

It is much more useful for internal control purposes, however, to prepare budgeted/forecast cash flow statements. This enables internal management to make comparisons between forecast and actual statements and thereby seek explanations for any differences, to assist in the control of cash in the future. Cash budgets/forecasts will not be outlined in this chapter, which deals with the wider concept of funds. Cash budgets/forecasts will be covered in your studies of cost and management accounting.

16.2 Funds-flow statements

Funds-flow statements show an alternative but more embracing approach to cash flow. They are not confined just to cash movements, but incorporate a broader concept to funds. Funds-flow statements show the changes in working capital over the accounting period in question. They assist users in interpreting the financial condition and progress of a business, and answer some of the questions that cannot so easily be answered by examining income statements and balance sheets.

During the 1960s there was a trend in the USA towards an audited funds-flow statement as part of the financial reporting package. The objective was to supplement the traditional financial statements showing how the business had acquired funds and how it had used them. An increasing number of companies in the United Kingdom eventually followed these practices.

Funds-flow statements show any movements in the business's assets, liabilities and capital in the accounting period and the effect this had on the net liquid funds. They provide a link between the opening and closing balance sheets and the relevant income statement. No new financial data is used; it is simply a process of selecting, reclassification and presentation of the same information that is already contained in the traditional profit and loss account and balance sheet.

In this country the ASC issued an exposure draft, No. 13, in April 1974 and an Accounting Standard, SSAP 10, in July 1975, applicable to all businesses with a turnover or gross income of £25,000 or over. The standard includes illustrations in its appendix of how a statement could be drawn up by a business, both in a group and non-group situation.

The statements contain these basic sections as follows:

1 The sources of funds
e.g. (a) Profit generated from operations;
    (b) shares issued.

2 The application of funds
e.g. (a) Purchase of fixed assets;
    (b) payment of dividends;
    (c) payment of taxation.

3 The changes in working capital items including movement in net liquid funds
e.g. (a) Movement in stocks;
    (b) movement in debtors;
    (c) movement in creditors;
    (d) movement in net liquid funds.

The standard defines what is meant by net liquid funds, and it is basically cash/bank balances, and short-term investments.

16.3 Preparation of funds-flow statements

The following section shows how a funds-flow statement is prepared, using the layout outlined in the appendix of SSAP 10, from a profit and loss account for Year 2 and a balance sheet for Year 1 and Year 2.

The following are the summarized final accounts of a company:

Profit and loss account for year ending 31 December – Year 2

	£	£	
Trading profit		460,000	
Less cost of sales		300,000	
		160,000	
Expenses	81,000		
Depreciation on plant and equipment	17,000	98,000	
Profit before taxation		62,000	← Source
Corporation tax		22,000	← Application
		40,000	
Preference dividend paid	4,000		← Application
Ordinary dividend proposed	16,000	20,000	← Application
Retained profit		20,000	

Balance Sheet as at 31 December

		Year 2		Year 1	
	£	£	£	£	
Fixed assets					
Land and Buildings		130,000		34,000	← Application
Plant and equipment (net)		115,000		88,000	← Application
		245,000		122,000	
Current assets					
Stock	68,000		82,000		← Source
Debtors	38,000		50,000		← Source
Bank	nil		13,000		← Source
	106,000		145,000		
Less creditors and amounts falling due within one year					
Trade creditors	29,000		25,000		← Source
Bank	10,000		nil		← Source
Taxation	22,000		18,000		← Application
Dividend	16,000		15,000		← Application
	77,000		58,000		
Net current assets		29,000		87,000	
Total assets minus current liabilities		274,000		209,000	
Creditors – amounts falling due after more than one year					
Loan capital		26,000		30,000	← Application
		248,000		179,000	

(cont'd.)

(cont'd.)	£	£	£	£
Share capital and reserves				
Preference shares		69,000		20,000 ← *Source*
Ordinary shares		85,000		85,000
Profit and loss account		94,000		74,000
		248,000		179,000

16.3.1 Stage one of preparation

Sources of funds – generated from operations

The first step in preparing the funds-flow statement is to calculate the funds generated from the operations of the business over the year's trading. This will be the major source of funds for most companies. The profit before tax figure, £62,000, will be found in the income statement. Any expense or income items that have been entered in the income statement before the pre-tax profit figure which have not involved the movement of any funds must be adjusted. Adjustments are required for these items, because no funds have been received or expended. It is necessary, therefore, to add back any non-movement of funds expense items and deduct any non-movement of funds income/profit items from the profit figure. Elimination of these non-movement of funds items will result in a 'genuine' figure for funds generated from operations. The charge for depreciation, £17,000, in this example, is an example of an item which does not involve the movement of any funds and must, therefore, be added back to the profit before tax figure.

Other examples of items which would require adjustment in this manner include any adjustment for a provision for bad or doubtful debts, or the profit or loss on the sale of any fixed asset.

The profit or loss on the sale of any fixed asset is adjusted as a non-movement of funds item, as described above. This is because the total proceeds from the sale of a fixed asset are shown in the sources of funds section which follows. The total flow of funds from sources would not be correct if the item was not treated in this manner.

The funds-flow statement would be as follows, after stage one:

Sources of funds

	£	£
Profit before taxation		62,000
Add any items not involving the movement of funds:		
Depreciation on plant and equipment	17,000	17,000
Funds generated from operations		79,000

16.3.2 Stage two of preparation

Sources of funds – other sources

The next step in the preparation of the statement involves listing any other sources of finance that the business has raised during the year. This will include the issue of any new shares and/or loan stock, and the sale of any fixed assets. The amounts are found by examining the opening and closing balance sheets, linking income statement, and any notes that are attached.

In this instance the ordinary share capital has not altered, but the preference share capital has increased by £49,000. This amount will need to be listed as a source in the statement. There is no information on the sale of assets, and as the net figures for both land and buildings and plant and equipment have increased, the difference quite clearly represents the acquisition of more of these assets. This will be covered in a later section of the statement. If any of the assets had been sold in the year, the gross proceeds from the sale would be recorded in this section. Any profit or loss from these transactions appearing in the profit and loss account (before tax) would already have been dealt with in stage one, as indicated. The best way to deal with the adjustments of this nature is to prepare 'T' accounts, as shown in chapter 4.

The second stage entry would appear in the statement as follows:

Other sources

	£
Issue of preference shares	49,000

16.3.3 Stage three of preparation

Application of funds

The next step in the preparation of the statement is to list the application of funds. This will include the purchase of fixed assets, repayment of loans, payment of taxation and dividends, etc. This information can be obtained by examining all the financial statements and supplementary notes.

Purchase of fixed assets

From the balance sheets in this question, it can be seen that land and buildings have increased from £34,000 to £130,000. The difference of £96,000 represents the additions during the year. There is no depreciation charged on these assets and there is no reference to any sales during the year.

Plant and equipment have also increased from £88,000 to £115,000, a difference of £27,000. An examination of the income statement, however, shows that depreciation of £17,000 has been charged on these assets, to arrive at the net figure of £115,000. The depreciation will have to be added to the difference of £27,000, giving total purchases of plant and equipment in the year of £44,000. This figure would require further adjustment if there had been any sales during the year. The total purchases of fixed assets during the year are therefore:

	£
Land and buildings	96,000
Plant and equipment	44,000
	140,000

Repayment of loans

An examination of the balance sheets shows that the loan capital has decreased from £30,000 in Year 1 to £26,000 in Year 2. The difference of £4,000 represents a net repayment of £4,000, and must be listed in the statement.

Payment of taxation and dividends

An examination of the income statement shows a 'charge' against the second year's profit for taxation of £22,000, and this amount is shown as outstanding in the current liabilities in the balance sheet at the end of Year 2. This amount will be payable in nine months' time on 1 October, Year 3. The funds-flow statement has to include the actual payment of tax during the year in question, Year 2. This will be £18,000, the figure shown in the closing balance sheet for Year 1. Had this amount of £18,000 not been paid in Year 2, it would have been shown as still outstanding in the balance sheet at the end of that year, or if it had been written off, this would have been shown in the income statement. The important point is to make sure you calculate the **payment of tax during the year**, and list this in the funds-flow statement, and not simply the amount shown in the income statement.

A similar approach is necessary for the calculation of dividends. The income statement for Year 2 shows a preference dividend paid of £4,000 and a proposed ordinary dividend of £16,000. The proposed ordinary dividend of £16,000 is shown as a current liability in the balance sheet at the end of Year 2 and will be paid to shareholders in the first few weeks of Year 3. The amount of dividends actually paid in Year 2 will therefore be the figure shown as outstanding in the balance sheet at the end of Year 1, £15,000, plus the preference dividend paid in Year 2 of £4,000, a total of £19,000. Had the £15,000 outstanding at the end of Year 1 not been paid, it would have appeared in the current liabilities at the end of Year 2, along with Year 2's proposed dividend. Both the payment of taxation, £18,000, and the payment of dividends, £19,000, must be listed in the funds-flow statement.

The stage 3 entries would appear as follows:

Application of funds	£	£
Purchase of land and buildings	96,000	
Purchase of plant and equipment	44,000	140,000
Repayment of loans		4,000
Payment of taxation		18,000
Payment of dividends		
Preference	4,000	
Ordinary	15,000	19,000
		181,000

16.3.4 Stage four of preparation

Increase (decrease) of working capital

The last step is concerned with the section that shows the **movements over the accounting period of each working capital component**, i.e. stock, work in progress, debtors, creditors, and net liquid funds.

Net liquid funds comprise cash and bank balances and short-term investments. These movements can be obtained by calculating the differences between the opening and closing balance sheet figures and listing these in the statement as an application or a source.

In this question, the movements of working capital are therefore:

Increase (decrease) in working capital

	£	
Decrease in stocks	(14,000)	
Decrease in debtors	(12,000)	
Increase in creditors	(4,000)	
Movement in net liquid funds		
Increase in bank overdraft	(23,000)	
		(53,000)

The completed funds-flow statement will now appear as follows:

Funds-flow statement for year ending 31 December Year 2

Sources of funds	£	£
Profit before taxation		62,000
Add any items not involving the movement of funds:		
Depreciation on plant and equipment	17,000	17,000
Funds generated from operations		79,000
Other sources		
Issue of preference shares	49,000	49,000
		128,000
Application of funds		
Purchase of land and buildings	96,000	
Purchase of plant and equipment	44,000	
	140,000	
Repayment of loans	4,000	
Payment of taxation	18,000	
Payment of dividends:		
preference	4,000	
ordinary	15,000	181,000
		£(53,000)
Increase (decrease) in working capital		
Decrease in stocks	(14,000)	
Decrease in debtors	(12,000)	
Increase in creditors	(4,000)	
Movement in net liquid funds:		
Increase in bank overdraft	(23,000)	£(53,000)

16.4 Interpretation of funds-flow statements

The statement will assist the internal management, and particularly the external financial user, to answer a number of questions concerning the movement of funds in the business. These questions might include the following:

1 What are the total funds generated from within the business?
    (*Answer: £79,000.*)

2 Has the business obtained funds from any other source?
    (*Answer: yes, £49,000 from the issue of preference shares.*)

3 What are the total funds generated by the business over the relevant accounting period?
    (*Answer: £128,000.*)

4 Has the business generated sufficient funds in total to cover its applications?
    (*Answer: no, the total application of £181,000 exceeds the sources, £128,000, by £53,000.*)

5 Has the business generated sufficient funds from its own operations to finance the acquisition of net fixed assets? The answer will help to see whether or not the business is a viable and going concern, able to replace its assets without having to raise new capital.
    (*Answer: the profits of £79,000 were insufficient to finance the new acquisitions of assets totalling £140,000. This does not mean the business is not a viable going concern; other tests are necessary.*)

6 If the business did not generate enough funds from within to finance its fixed assets, how did it cover the deficiency – by raising new share capital, and/or borrowing and/or reducing working capital?
    (*Answer: the business raised £49,000 in preference share capital to assist its financing of new assets etc, and its remaining deficiency of £53,000 was covered by reducing working capital to this extent.*)

7 Has the working capital increased or decreased during the accounting period?
    (*Answer: as already indicated in 6 above, the working capital has decreased by £53,000. It would be helpful to calculate current and quick ratios to see whether or not working capital and liquidity levels are acceptable at the end of Year 2.*)

This links closely with the work in chapters 12 and 13. The current and quick ratios in this question are as follows:

	Year 1	Year 2
Current ratio	2.5	1.38
Quick ratio	1.09	0.49

These ratios indicate that the reduction in working capital of £53,000 has had quite a dramatic effect on the working capital and liquidity position, and further investigation would be required.

8 What have been the movements in the individual items of working capital, namely stocks, debtors and creditors?
    (*Answer: the stocks have decreased by £14,000, debtors by £12,000, and the creditors have increased by £4,000. It would be useful to calculate the stock turnover and average collection and payable periods at the end of Year 2, as shown in chapters 12 and 13. These periods should be compared with those at the end of Year 1, and then it can be seen whether or not the new periods are acceptable.*)

9 Has there been an increase or decrease in net liquid funds over the accounting period, and what is the overall liquidity position?
    (*Answer: there has been a decrease in net liquid funds of £23,000. The liquidity position has already been referred to in 7 above, which indicated that there are some liquidity problems.*)

10 What have been the movements of individual items of net liquid funds?

> (*Answer: the only net liquid fund item in this question is the bank, which ha[s] moved from a positive figure of £13,000 to a negative one of £10,000. If t[he] business had had short-term investments, it would have been possible to hav[e] seen its policy in regard to these assets. The business might have sold them, f[or] example, to help overcome its liquidity problem.*)

11 How does the Year 2 pattern of sources and application of funds, bot[h] individually and collectively, relate to the trend over the past five years?

> (*Answer: only one year's figures are available in this example. If the previo[us] year's figures were available, it would assist users to assess the financi[al] condition and progress of the business. Trend analysis is an important area [of] interpretation in financial accounts. It would also be extremely useful [to] prepare a forecast funds-flow statement for Year 3 in this example, and the[n] compare it with the actual figures in due course.*)

12 Has the business generated enough funds to pay dividends and tax?

> (*Answer: the business has generated £79,000 from within the business a[nd] £49,000 from the issue of preference shares, which is obviously sufficient [to] pay the dividends of £19,000 and taxation of £18,000. The funds were al[so] used to purchase the fixed assets and repay the loans, however, and this has l[ed] to an overall deficiency of £53,000, as shown in 4 above.*)

16.5 Funds-flow statements in practice

As indicated previously, there are guidelines in the appendix of SSAP 10 on t[he] presentation and layout of the statements for companies in a group situation [or] otherwise. In practice, there has been a wide variety of presentation of the[se] statements over the years. ICI's statement of sources and application of group funds [is] shown in the appendix, and readers are advised to examine this and other publish[ed] funds-flow statements.

16.5.1 Working capital flow statements

The same financial data found in the funds-flow statement could be re-presented in [a] working capital flow statement, to emphasize the changes in working capital.

The statement could be historical or a forecast one; the latter would pro[ve] particularly useful for internal decision-making in this most important area. T[he] layout and presentation could take different forms, dependant upon the requiremen[ts] of management.

One possible presentation is as follows, using the figures in the question above:

Working capital flow statement for year ending 31 December Year 2

	£	£
Sources of working capital		
Trading profits		79,000
Preference shares		49,000
		128,000
Applications of working capital		
Purchase of fixed assets	140,000	
Repayment of loans	4,000	
Payment of taxation	18,000	
Payment of dividends	19,000	181,000
Reduction in working capital during the year		£53,000
Which can be analysed as follows:		
Reduction of stock	14,000	
Reduction of debtors	12,000	
Increase in creditors	4,000	
Increase of bank overdraft	23,000	
		£53,000

The statement shows quite clearly that the sources, totalling £128,000, a[re] insufficient to cover the applications of £181,000, by £53,000. The working capi[tal] has had to be squeezed (or 'milked') to cover this deficiency. It has been necessary reduce stocks, collect the debtors more quickly, delay payment to creditors and move from a cash in the bank position to an overdraft. It would be helpful to calculate the working capital ratio, current assets to current liabilities, from the balance sheets, as shown previously in the Interpretation section.

Links with other topics

Funds flow links most closely with the work covered in chapters 12 and 13. It also builds on the work in chapter 14, Sources of finance, and chapter 15, Financial structure. In addition, funds flow relates to chapter 9, Accounting standards, SSAP 10 being an example of one of the standards, and to chapter 10, Company annual reports and accounts. SSAP 10 is an important part of the financial reporting package.

Sample questions

1 You are required to prepare a funds-flow statement for H Ltd for the year ending 31 December 1987, from the financial information shown below:

Income statement for the year ending 31 December 1987

	£000	£000
Trading profit		300
(After charging depreciation of £50 on plant and equipment)		
Corporation tax		100
Profit after tax		200
Balance brought forward		190
		390
Transfer to plant and equipment reserve	40	
Proposed ordinary dividend	100	140
Retained profit		250

Balance sheets as at 31 December 1986 and 1987

	1987		1986	
Fixed assets	£000	£000	£000	£000
Land		950		500
Plant and equipment		500	—	350
		1,450		850
Current assets				
Stock in trade	200		160	
Debtors	170		130	
Cash at bank	70		10	
	440		300	
Less current liabilities				
Creditors and accruals	140		90	
Taxation	100		70	
Dividends	100		10	
	340		170	
Net current assets		100		130
14% loan capital		(280)		(10)
		1,270		970
Preference share capital		130		130
Ordinary share capital		800		600
Plant and equipment reserve		90		50
Income statement balance		250		190
		1,270		970

First-year Business Studies degree level

Understanding the question

This is a fairly straightforward question, requiring the preparation of a funds-flow statement from an opening and closing balance sheet for 1987, and the income statement that links them. The first stage requires the identification of the profit before tax in the income statement, and its listing in the funds-flow statement. The remainder of the answer follows the procedure outlined previously.

Answer plan

Stage one

Sources of funds	£000	£000
Profit before taxation		300
Add any items not involving the movement of funds		
Depreciation on plant and equipment	50	50
Funds generated from operations		350

Stage two

Funds from other sources	£000	£000
14% loan capital	270	
Issue of ordinary share capital	200	470

Stage three

Application of funds	£000	£000
Purchase of land	450	
*Purchase of plant and equipment	200	
Payment of taxation	70	
Payment of dividends	10	730

Stage four

Increase (decrease) in working capital	£000	£000
Increase in stocks	40	
Increase in debtors	40	
Increase in creditors	(50)	
Movement in net liquid funds:		
increase in cash/bank balances	60	
		90

The completed funds-flow statement will appear as follows:

H Ltd Funds-flow statement for year ending 31 December 1987

	£000	£000
Sources of funds		
Profit before taxation		300
Add any items not involving the movement of funds:		
Depreciation on plant and equipment	50	50
Funds generated from operations		350
Other sources		
14% loan capital	270	
Issue of ordinary share capital	200	470
		820
Application of funds		
Purchase of land	450	
Purchase of plant and equipment	200	
Payment of taxation	70	
Payment of dividend	10	
		730
		90

*£200 equals the difference between the opening (£350) and closing (£500) balances on the plant and equipment asset account, plus the depreciation of £50, which has been charged in the income statement during the year.

(cont'd.)

(cont'd.)	**Increase in working capital**	£000	£000
	Increase in stocks	40	
	Increase in debtors	40	
	Increase in creditors	(50)	
	Movement in net liquid funds:		
	Increase in cash balances	60	
			90

2 You are given below, in summarized form, the accounts of Algernon Ltd for 1986 and 1987.

	1986 Balance Sheet			1987 Balance Sheet		
	Cost	Depn	Net	Cost	Depn	Net
	£	£	£	£	£	£
Plant	10,000	4,000	6,000	11,000	5,000	6,000
Building	50,000	10,000	40,000	90,000	11,000	79,000
			46,000			85,000
Investments at cost			50,000			80,000
Land			43,000			63,000
Stock			55,000			65,000
Debtors			40,000			50,000
Bank			3,000			—
			237,000			343,000
Ordinary shares £1 each			40,000			50,000
Share premium			12,000			14,000
Revaluation reserve			—			20,000
Profit and loss account			25,000			25,000
10% Debentures			100,000			150,000
Creditors			40,000			60,000
Proposed dividend			20,000			20,000
Bank			—			4,000
			237,000			343,000

	1986 Profit and Loss A/c	1987 Profit and Loss A/c
	£	£
Sales	200,000	200,000
Cost of sales	100,000	120,000
	100,000	80,000
Expenses	60,000	60,000
	40,000	20,000
Dividends	20,000	20,000
	20,000	—
Balance b/f	5,000	25,000
Balance c/f	25,000	25,000

(a) Prepare a source and application of funds statement for Algernon Ltd for 1987, to explain as far as possible the movement in the bank balance.

(b) Using the summarized accounts given, and the statement you have just prepared, comment on the position and direction of Algernon Ltd.

(*Note:* The calculation of ratios is *not* required.) *ACCA Level 1*

Understanding the question

The answer to part (a) is fairly straightforward, requiring you to prepare a source and application of funds statement, but you are recommended to use the format outlined in this chapter and SSAP 10. One particular point to notice very carefully is the increase in land of £20,000. This is a revaluation, not a purchase, and does not therefore involve the movement of any funds.

In part (b) you are required to comment on the financial position of the company, and if you have prepared the statement correctly you should find no difficulty in noticing the significant features of the business, not forgetting to examine the balance sheets and profit and loss accounts in the question.

Answer plan

(a)

Stage one

	£000	£000
Sources of funds		
Profit before taxation		20
Add any items not involving the movement of funds		
Depreciation of plant and buildings	2	2
Funds generated from operations		22

Stage two

	£000	£000
Funds from other sources		
Issue of ordinary £1 shares at a premium	12	—
Issue of 10% debentures	50	62

Stage three

	£000	£000
Purchase of plant	1	
Purchase of buildings	40	
Purchase of investments	30	
Payments of dividends	20	91

Stage four

	£000	£000
Increase in stocks	10	
Increase in debtors	10	
Increase in creditors	(20)	
Decrease in bank	7	7

The completed sources and application of funds statement will appear as follows:

Algernon Ltd
Sources and application of funds statement for the year ending 31 December 1987

	£000	£000
Sources of funds		
Profit before taxation		20
Add any items not involving the movement of funds:		
Depreciation of plant and buildings		2
Funds generated from operations		22
Other sources		
Issue of ordinary shares at a premium	12	
Issue of 10% debentures	50	62
		84
Application of funds		
Purchase of plant	1	
Purchase of buildings	40	
Purchase of investments	30	
Payment of dividends	20	91
		(7)
Decrease in working capital		
Increase in stocks	10	
Increase in debtors	10	
Increase in creditors	(20)	
Decrease in bank	(7)	(7)

(b) The statement shows that the firm has expended £71,000 on new plant, buildings and investment, whilst it has only generated £22,000 from the operations of the business. In fact the income statements show that the turnover is static and the newly acquired assets will have to generate extra sales soon, or the company will be in financial trouble. The deficiency in funds has been covered by the issue of shares and loan stock amounting to £62,000. The total sources of £22,000 and £62,000 were still insufficient to cover the total applications of £91,000 and this has led to a decrease in working capital of £7,000. The increase in creditors, £20,000, has been matched by an increase in stocks and debtors, and the deficiency of £7,000 stems from the fact that the bank balance has been reduced from £3,000 to an overdraft of £4,000.

It would be useful, though not required by the question, to calculate liquidity and profitability ratios at this stage and it would show clearly the financial difficulties that Algernon Ltd are in.

3 O Ltd has made a profit for the year ending 31 December 1987, but its balance at the bank has fallen considerably during the year.

The managing director of the company has asked you, as a trainee accountant, to prepare a funds-flow statement for 1987 to help to explain to him how this has arisen.

You are presented with the balance sheet for 1986 and 1987.

Balance sheets as at:

	31. 12. 87				31. 12. 86	
	£000	£000	£000	£000	£000	£000
Fixed assets						
Intangible assets						
Goodwill		1,000			800	
Fixed assets						
Land and buildings		1,300			1,200	
Plant and motor vehicles (cost)	2,000			1,200		
Less accumulated depreciations	800			600		
		1,200	3,500		600	2,600
Current assets						
Stock in trade		700			400	
Debtors and prepayments		1,800			700	
Cash/bank		100			700	
		2,600			1,800	
Creditors – amounts falling due within one year						
Trade creditors		500			1,000	
Accruals		100			200	
Corporation tax		300			200	
Dividends		100			100	
		1,000			1,500	
Net current assets			1,600			300
Total assets – current liabilities			5,100			2,900
Creditors – Amounts falling due after more than one year						
15% Loan stock (secured)			(1,500)			(400)
			3,600			2,500
Share capital and reserves						
Ordinary shares			2,000			2,000
General reserves			550			300
Profit and loss account			1,050			200
			3,600			2,500

The figure of £1,050,000 for the profit and loss account for 1987 is made up a
follows:

Balance brought forward	£200,000
Profit after taxation and after the proposed dividend and the transfer to general reserves	850,000
	1,050,000

First year Business Studies degree course leve

Understanding the question

This is a slightly more difficult question. The calculations are not as straightforward
and comments will be required to explain how the business has made profits and ye
at the same time, has a reduction at the bank of £600,000.

A funds-flow statement should be prepared following the four stages indicate
previously, showing your workings clearly.

Answer plan

Stage one

		£000
*Profit before taxation		1,500
Add any items not involving the movement of funds		
Depreciation on plant and motor vehicles		200
		1,700

	£000	£000
Workings *Profit for year after tax, proposed dividends and increase in general reserves		£850
Add back taxation	300	
Proposed dividends	100	
Addition to general reserves	250	650
		1,500

Stage two

	£000	£000
Funds from other sources		
Issue of 15% loan capital	1,100	
		1,100

Stage three

	£000	
Application of funds		
Purchase of land and building	100	
Purchase of plant and motor vehicles	800	
Purchase of goodwill	200	
Payment of taxation	200	
Payment of dividends	100	
		1,400

Stage four

	£000	
Increase (decrease) in working capital		
Increase in stock in trade	300	
Increase in debtors and prepayments	1,100	
Decrease in trade creditors	500	
Decrease in accruals	100	
Movement in net liquid funds		
Decrease in cash/bank	(600)	
		1,400

The completed funds flow statement will now appear as follows:

O Ltd
Funds-flow statement for the year ending 31 December 1987

	£000	£000
Sources of funds		
Profit before taxation		1,500
Add any items not involving the movement of funds:		
Depreciation on plant and motor vehicles		200
Funds generated from operations		1,700
Other sources		
Issue of 15% loan capital	1,100	1,100
		2,800
Application of funds		
Purchase of land and buildings	100	
Purchase of plant and motor vehicles	800	
Purchase of goodwill	200	
Payment of taxation	200	
Payment of dividends	100	1,400
		1,400
Increase in working capital		
Increase in stock in trade	300	
Increase in debtors and prepayments	1,100	
Decrease in trade creditors	500	
Decrease in accruals	100	
Movement in net liquid funds:		
Decrease in cash/bank	(600)	
		1,400

Comments

The business generated funds from operations of £1,700,000, as shown in stage one. In addition to this there were additional sources of £1,100,000, giving a total of £2,800,000. The total applications were £1,400,000, the balance of £1,400,000 has gone towards increasing working capital. The business increased its stocks and debtors by a total of £1,400,000, and decreased its creditors and accruals at the same time by £600,000, a total of £2,000,000. This meant that the business required additional liquid funds of £600,000 (£2,000,000 − £1,400,000). This 'deficiency' of £600,000 was 'covered' by reducing the cash at the bank from £700,000 to £100,000.

The statement shows quite clearly how the company made a substantial profit and yet at the same time suffered a large reduction in its bank balance. It is possible to calculate profitability and liquidity ratios to see whether or not the respective levels are acceptable. The increase in working capital and the reduction at the bank, as shown above, are matters for management policy.

4 From the published accounts of ICI PLC, shown in the appendix, you are required to examine the statement of sources and application of group funds for 1986 and 1987, and comment on the flows of funds over the two years to assist in the analysis and assessment of the financial performance and progress of the company.

First year Business Studies degree course level

Understanding the question

In this question the statements are already prepared and it will be necessary to examine the movement of funds over the two years. This may require an examination of the remaining financial reporting package to obtain a full picture. Each source and use should be examined in the statements and suitable comments made about its size in relation to the total sources and uses and the changes over the two years.

Answer plan

The statements are for the group — so the figures and presentation are more comple[x]
than in the previous questions. Nevertheless the statements can be examined a stage [at]
a time and calculations and suitable comments made.

Stage one
Sources of funds

The trading profit has increased by £248m (23.6 per cent) to £1,297m in 1987 an[d]
after adjustments for non-movement of funds the total generated from operations ha[s]
increased by £313m (21.1 per cent) to £1,798m. The major non-movement of fund[s]
item was depreciation — £464m in 1987.

Stage two
Other sources of funds

The other sources of funds decreased by £104m to £110m in 1987. The movement [in]
short-term borrowings and cash and short-term investments have been included in t[he]
working capital section.

Stage three
Application of funds

The total amount expended on fixed assets decreased by £44m (3.8 per cent) [to]
£1,112m in 1987, whereas the amount applied to dividends and tax increased [by]
£34m (13.6 per cent) to £283m and by £51m (17.1 per cent) to £349m respectivel[y].

Stage four

A rearrangement of the short term borrowings and investments shows the followi[ng]
position for working capital.

Increase (Decrease) in Working Capital

	1987 £m	1986 £m
Stocks	169	(115)
Debtors	68	(45)
Creditors and provisions decrease	(50)	66
Short-term borrowings	(118)	70
Movement of net liquid funds:		
Cash and short-term investments	(46)	(105)
	23	(129)

This shows a decrease in working capital in 1986 and a small increase in 1987 an[d]
these two figures can be checked by listing the sources and taking the applicatio[n]
figures away. These comments can be developed further and, together with th[e]
profitability, current and liquidity ratios will assist in analysing and assessing th[e]
financial performance and progress of the company as a whole.

5 The following information relates to X plc. The company's accounting year end[s]
on 30 September.

Balance sheets of X plc at the end of

	1986 £000	1986 £000	1987 £000	1987 £00[0]
Tangible fixed assets (note 1)		945		1,66[ ]
Current assets:				
Stocks	1,225		1,488	
Debtors	700		787	
Short-term investments	175		262	
Cash at bank	184		186	
	2,284		2,723	

(cont'd[ )

(cont'd.)	£000	£000	£000	£000
Less:				
Creditors:				
amounts falling due within one year:				
Bank overdraft	52		105	
Trade creditors	525		735	
Expense creditors	9		10	
Taxation	140		228	
Proposed dividends	140		175	
	866		1,253	
Net current assets		1,418		1,470
Total assets less current liabilities		2,363		3,132
Creditors:				
amounts falling due after more than one year:				
long-term loan		525		700
		1,838		2,432
Capital and reserves:				
Called-up ordinary share capital		1,225		1,400
Share premium account		—		87
General reserve		525		787
Profit and loss account		88		158
		1,838		2,432

Summary profit and loss account
for the year ended 30 September 1987

	£000	£000
Profit on ordinary activities before taxation		735
Corporation tax		228
Profit on ordinary activities after taxation		507
Less:		
Proposed dividend	175	
Transfer to General reserve	262	
		437
		70
Retained profit brought forward		88
Retained profit carried forward		158

Note 1 – Schedule of tangible fixed assets:

	Freehold premises	Plant and machinery	Freehold premises	Plant and machinery
	1986		*1987*	
	£000	£000	£000	£000
At cost	560	455	560	718
Additions during the year	—	263	280	700
	560	718	840	1,418
Less depreciation	35	298	53	543
Net book value	525	420	787	875

You are required to:

(a) prepare a sources and application of funds statement for X plc, for the year ended 30 September 1987, conforming to the requirements of Statement of Standard Accounting Practice No. 10, insofar as this is possible from the information given;

(b) write a short commentary on the statement prepared in (a) above.

CIMA Stage 2

Understanding the question

This is a fairly straightforward question requiring you to prepare a statement of sources and application of funds statement in part (a) conforming as far as possible with the layout recommended in Appendix 1 of SSAP 10. If you follow the steps recommended in the preparation of these statements in this chapter, you should have no difficulty, bearing in mind that this question has been set at the Stage 2 level. In part (b) you are required to interpret briefly the statement you have prepared in part (a).

Answer plan

Part (a)

Stage one – Sources of funds

	£000	£000
Profit before taxation		735
Add any items not involving the movement of funds		
Depreciation of fixed assets		
Freehold premises (53 − 35)	18	
Plant and machinery (543 − 298)	245	263
Funds generated from operations		998

Stage two – Funds from other sources

	£000	£000	£000
Issue of ordinary shares at a premium			
(1,400 − 1,225)	175		
(87 − 0)	87	262	
Issue of long term loans (700 − 525)		175	
			437

Stage three

	£000	£000
Purchase of freehold premises	280	
Purchase of plant and machinery	700	
Dividends paid	140	
Taxation paid	140	
		1,260

Stage four

	£000	£000
Increase in stocks	263	
Increase in debtors	87	
Increase in expense and trade creditors	(211)	
Movement in net liquid funds:		
Increase in S.T. investments	87	
Increase in cash	2	
Increase in bank overdraft	(53)	
		175

The completed sources and application of funds statement would appear as follows

X plc
Sources of application of funds statement
for year ending 30 September 1987

Sources of funds	£000	£000
Profit before taxation		735
Add any items not involving the movement of funds:		
Depreciation of fixed assets		263
Funds generated from operations		998

(cont'd

(cont'd.)

	£000	£000
Other sources		
Issue of ordinary shares at a premium	262	
Issue of long term loans	175	437
		1,435
Application of funds		
Purchase of fixed assets	980	
Dividends paid	140	
Taxation paid	140	(1,260)
		175
Increase in working capital		
Increase in stocks	263	
Increase in debtors	87	
Increase in creditors	(211)	
Movement in net liquid funds		
Increase in S.T. investments	87	
Increase in cash	2	
Increase in bank overdraft	(53)	
		175

Part (b)

An examination of the statement you have prepared shows that the business has generated almost £1m within the business. To finance its activities, it has raised £437,000 from 'outside' the business in the form of new shares at a premium (£262,000) and long term loans (£175,000).

These total funds, £1,435,000, have enabled the business to acquire almost £1m of new assets as well as pay the outstanding dividends (£140,000) and taxation (£140,000), leaving sufficient to increase working capital by £175,000.

Part of the working capital requirements have been financed by an increase in creditors and bank overdraft which may be a relatively cheap source. All these figures indicate an increase in activity.

It would be possible to calculate a number of ratios, as shown in chapters 12 and 13, to help to make further comments on the financial condition and progress of the company. The availability of the 1986 profit and loss account would help the analysis considerably.

Further reading

G. A. Lee *Modern Financial Accounting* (Nelson), fourth edition, chapter 12.

R. Lewis and M. Firth *Foundations in Accounting 2* (Prentice Hall International), second edition, chapter 9.

F. Wood *Business Accounting 2* (Pitman), fifth edition, chapter 23.

17 Working capital control

Every year thousands of firms, be they sole traders, partnerships, or limited companies, cease to trade and either a trustee in bankruptcy (in the case of non-limited companies), or a liquidator (in the case of limited companies) is appointed.

In the strict sense of the word, few of these firms will be 'bankrupt': their assets will still exceed liabilities, but the proportion of fixed assets to current assets will be out of phase.

We have seen in chapter 12 how to measure the current ratio and 'acid test' ratio, and in chapter 13 we have seen ways in which firms can run into liquidity crises.

17.1   Control of the main elements of working capital

Cash is but one element of the working capital cycle. Stock and work-in-progress represent the first stage of the flow cycle. Turnover of stock must be maintained if liquidity margins are not to be put in danger. A bottleneck of slow-moving stock is often the cause of financial problems.

The purchase of materials must be monitored carefully. A fine balance is sometimes necessary between bulk buying at more advantageous prices, and the tying-up of funds. An efficient stock control system, whereby waste is minimized, requisitions are carefully controlled, and storage is planned so as to avoid damage, is essential.

Next in the cycle is finished stock. Comparing how long such stock is held in store from one period to another is important.

The next point on the working capital cycle is trade debtors. This is where risk is greatest. Once goods have been delivered to customers and invoices despatched as promptly as possible, one hopes customers will pay within the stipulated period allowed for credit.

Although most customers will probably make efforts to meet settlement dates, some will deliberately take extra credit and pay only when pressed. Others may be in some financial difficulty and unable to pay on time and a further, though fortunately small, number of customers, will become bankrupt, and despite the efforts of a trustee in bankruptcy, no payments to unsecured creditors will ever be made.

All unsecured creditors rank third in line as to who gets paid when a bankruptcy petition is served. Secured creditors, usually the lenders of finance, have security in the form of a charge on an asset, and rank in priority to anyone else. Secondly come preferential creditors who, as one might suspect, are mainly government and local government departments.

In business, one acts as an unpaid tax collector in many areas. PAYE, national insurance and VAT are good examples of how the government expects regular payments (monthly or quarterly) to be made. It must be very tempting if liquidity problems arise to use money to pay creditors which is not yours to use! Hence the preferential creditors are only taking their money, which was never yours in the first place.

Next come the rank and file unsecured creditors, and lastly the owners of the bankrupt business can reclaim their investment, if anything remains.

Slow payers are an embarrassment to a business operating with a low liquidity ratio (see chapter 12), and debtors taking longer to pay will further highlight this problem.

Credit control is an important area of concern for every business selling goods on credit terms, and regular monitoring of sales ledger accounts should be a vital feature of any financial control.

Inter-firm comparisons will give some ideas as to how many times items such as stock and debtors turn over, on average. These figures will vary from one industry to another, but there are plenty of statistics available to give comparisons from company to company within a particular area of trade.

Ratio analysis within a firm can point to trends in the movement of working capital, and overall increases and decreases in working capital can be shown in the sources and application of funds statement.

Firms which do go under usually are not bankrupt in the accepted sense of owing more liabilities than they have assets to cover. The lack of cash to pay immediate needs, wages for example, is the cause of most company failures. Rolls-Royce and Laker Enterprises would come under this category.

Look again at chapter 13 on problems of liquidity as to the causes of financial problems.

Accountants responsible for the financial management of small businesses will usually have to accept that the resources available for operating financial control and reporting systems are strictly limited.

17.2   Valuation problems

Working capital must work for the business. Stock must turnover as quickly as possible, always allowing of course for minimum levels to maintain continuity of sales. Debtors must be pressed, if necessary, to meet credit deadlines, and maximum credit must be taken from the suppliers of goods and services.

But the problem does not end there. The annual accounts are expected to give a 'true and fair view' of the company's position at a given date. Certainly most judgment in the preparation of balance sheets and profit and loss accounts centres on stock and debtors.

Stock can be valued on many bases. LIFO (last in, first out) and FIFO (first in, first out) are probably the best known methods, and consistency of application is essential from one year to the next. This should, in theory, present no problem. But the golden rule that stock should be valued at the 'lower cost or market value' is sometimes difficult to achieve. What is 'market value', for example? What does one do about old and obsolete stock? In the case of manufacturing companies, three kinds of stock exist at the balance sheet date, namely raw materials, partly-finished goods, and finished goods, all to be valued at the varying stages of production. What proportion of overheads is to be included at these stages can be a difficult problem.

As mentioned before, apart from obvious bad debts, which most businesses incur from time to time (inevitable from the actual number of bankruptcies each year), other debts can prove difficult to collect. Bankruptcy does not happen overnight. It is a gradual process, highlighted by increasing difficulty in meeting debts as they fall due. One cannot write off a debt as 'bad' until it is quite clear that any balance owing is totally irrecoverable. This does not prevent a 'specific reserve' being made against named debts, of that part of an amount outstanding which is deemed unlikely to be recovered. This is good prudent accounting practice and one which is acceptable to the Inland Revenue when assessing profits to tax. Adjustments to this reserve can be made annually, according to circumstances prevailing with debtors.

Links with other topics

This subject links closely with ratio analysis and funds-flow statements. Working capital trends can be plotted with the help of suitable ratios, and overall changes in working capital can be analysed through the medium source and application of funds statement.

Problems causing liquidity difficulties also link with this topic, and underpinning everything are conventions and concepts (prudence, for example).

Sample questions

1 After stocktaking for the year ended 31 May 198X had taken place, the closing stock of Cobden Ltd was aggregated to a figure of £87,612.

During the course of the audit which followed, the facts listed below were discovered:

(a) Some goods stored outside had been included at their normal price of £570. They had, however, deteriorated and would require an estimated £120 to be spent to restore them to their original condition, after which they could be sold for £800.

(b) Some goods had been damaged and were now unsaleable. They could, however, be sold for £110 as spares, after repairs estimated at £40 had been carried out. They had originally cost £200.

(c) One stock sheet had been over-added by £126 and another under-added by £72.

(d) Cobden Ltd had received goods costing £2,010 during the last week of May 198X but because the invoices did not arrive until June 198X they have not been included in stock.

(e) A stock sheet total of £1,234 had been transferred to the summary sheet as £1,243.

(f) Invoices totalling £638 arrived during the last week of May 198X (and were included in purchases and creditors) but because of transport delays, the goods did not arrive until late June 198X and were not included in closing stock.

(g) Portable generators on hire from another company at a charge of £347 were included, at this figure, in stock.

(h) Free samples sent to Cobden Ltd by various suppliers had been included in stock at the catalogue price of £63.

(i) Goods costing £418 sent to customers on a sale or return basis had been included in stock by Cobden Ltd at their selling price, £602.

(j) Goods sent on a sale or return basis to Cobden Ltd had been included in stock at the amount payable (£267) if retained. No decision to retain had been made.

Required:
Using such of the above information as is relevant, prepare a schedule amending the stock figure as at 31 May 198X. State your reason for each amendment.

ACCA Level 1

Answer plan

This is a test of ability to recognize cut-off points and act upon relevant information at a closing stock figure.

The problem of matching revenues and expenditures within a given accounting period is fundamental in answering this question. Year-end adjustments are somewhat artificial as business does not cease on the evening of a particular day and commence afresh the next.

The adjustments required to the stock figure of £87,612 will be as follows:

		Increase £	Decrease £
A	Cost is lower than net realizable value	—	—
B	Net realizable value	—	130
C		72	126
D		2,010	—
E		—	9
F		638	—
G		—	347
H	Hired item	—	63
I	Reduced to cost	—	184
J		—	267
		2,720	1,126
		(1,126)	
		1,594	

Making a total stock figure of £89,206

2 From the two balance sheets of Moorland Products Ltd shown below, calculate the change in working capital over the year and show how this change has arisen.

Moorland Products Ltd
Balance Sheets: 31 December

	1987 £	1988 £		1987 £	1988 £
Share Capital	60,000	65,000	Freehold land and buildings	23,000	26,000
General reserve	5,000	6,000			
Undistributed profit	13,000	15,000	Plant and machinery	39,000	41,000
Debentures	–	60,000		62,000	67,000
Current liabilities:			**Current assets:**		
			Stocks	17,000	80,000
Creditors	23,000	26,000	Debtors	10,000	13,000
Dividend	8,000	10,000	Cash	20,000	22,000
	109,000	182,000		109,000	182,000

ACCA Level 1

Answer

Moorland Products Ltd

	1987 £	1988 £	Change £
Current assets:			
Stocks	17,000	80,000	+ 63,000
Debtors	10,000	13,000	+ 3,000
Cash	20,000	22,000	+ 2,000
	47,000	115,000	

	1987		1988			Change
Current liabilities:						
Creditors	23,000		26,000			+ 3,000
Dividends proposed	8,000		10,000			+ 2,000
		31,000		36,000		
Working capital		16,000		79,000		

The major factor in the change in working capital is the increase in stocks. Small increases in debtors and cash are matched by an increase in current liabilities. The stock appears to have been financed by the long-term loan for the most part.

The other type of question which may be set at this level requires the presentation of current cost profit and loss accounts and current cost balance sheets. Questions requiring the calculation of current cost accounting adjustments are of a more advanced nature and may be set at the second or third level of your finance accounting studies. Another aspect to bear in mind is that the last standard on this topic, SSAP16, is no longer mandatory and the nature and type of adjustments have varied slightly over the various recommendations.

3 A business sells, *inter alia*, two items of stock – X and Y. During one trading period, the sales and purchases of those two commodities were:

Commodity	Purchases	Sales on Credit
X	10 Units at £4 each 15 Units at £4.50 each 20 Units at £5 each	30 Units at £6 each
Y	15 Units at £2 each 10 Units at £3 each	20 Units at £4 each

At the end of the trading period, it was known that the purchase price of further stocks of X would be at £6 per unit, and of Y at £2.50 per unit. The sales of Y were discovered to have been made to a customer where there was a high risk of default, and no payment has been received during the period.

Required:

(a) Draw up a table showing the gross and net profit on X and Y, and the value of the closing stock of each commodity.

(b) Explain clearly the basis for your answer to (a), stating what accounting principles you have applied.

ACCA Level 1

Answer plan

The first point to recognize is that stock is required to be valued at 'the lower of cost or realizable value'. Cost is a rather ambiguous term but is conventionally taken to mean a figure based on historic or actual cost rather than some notional future value such as replacement cost. A common interpretation of historic cost is to apply a first-in-first-out (FIFO) method of valuation to arrive at the cost of sales and, hence, closing stock.

Can you agree that profit on commodity X is £47.50 and that for commodity Y £35 (less any amount deemed to be uncertain of collection)?

4 You are given the following balances at 1 January 1901: Debtors £10,000; Bank overdraft £5,000; Provisions for doubtful debts £400. You ascertain the following information:

	£
Sales for the year 1901 (all on credit)	100,000
Sales returns for the year 1901	1,000
Receipts from customers during 1901	90,000
Bad debts written off during 1901	500
Discounts allowed during 1901	400

At the end of 1901 the provision for doubtful debts is required to be 5 per cent of debtors, after making a specific provision for a debt of £200 from a customer who has gone bankrupt.

	£
Sales for the year 1902 (90% on credit)	100,000
Sales returns for the year 1902 (90% relating to credit customers)	2,000
Receipts from credit customers during 1902	95,000
Debtor balances settled by contra against creditor balances during 1902	3,000
Bad debts written off during 1902 (including 50% of the debt due from the customer who had gone bankrupt, the other 50% having been received in cash during 1902)	1,500
Discounts allowed during 1902	500

At the end of 1902 the provision for doubtful debts is still required to be 5 per cent of debtors.

Required:
Write up the debtors and provision for doubtful debts accounts for 1901 and 1902 bringing down the balances at the end of each year and showing in those accounts the double entry for each item.

ACCA Level

Answer plan

An extremely useful question in that the ability to understand the working capital cycle and the necessity to value debtors currently at the year end is coupled with the actual ledger entries. (A good chance to recap on previous work.)

If correctly answered, the debtors figure at the end of 1901 is £18,100 and at the end of 1902, £6,300. The provision for doubtful debts is £1,095 at the end of 1901 and £315 at the end of 1902.

5 The accounts of Fine Spindles Limited are prepared on a quarterly basis. Owing to very severe staff shortage at 31 March 1987, the usual stock taking was not undertaken.

However, the following information has now been produced:

1 The accounts for the quarter ended 31 December 1986 showed stock in trade, at cost, at that date of £16,824.

2 An error, only now discovered, in the stock sheets for 31 December 1986 shows an overcast of £2,000.

3 Goods invoiced to customers during the quarter ended 31 March 1987 totalled £54,210; however this includes goods invoiced at £1,040 despatched to customers in December 1986.

4 Goods invoiced to customers at £3,900 in April 1987 were despatched by Fine Spindles Limited in March 1987.

5 Goods purchased by the company during the quarter ended 31 March 1987 amounted to £46,680, at invoice prices.

6 A burglary at the company's stores in March 1987 resulted in stock costing £8,000 being stolen.

7 In March 1987, it was decided that a quantity of stock, which would normally be sold for £1,950, will only realize half cost price. This stock was unsold at 31 March 1987.

8 Credit notes totalling £4,550 were issued to customers for returns inwards during the quarter ended 31 March 1987.

9 The company normally obtains a gross profit of 30 per cent on cost price on all sales.

Required:
(a) A computation of the stock valuation at 31 March 1987.
(b) The trading account for the quarter ended 31 March 1987.

AAT

Answer plan

Part (a)

Take each point and work out the effect on stock valuation and/or the trading account. Then show the adjustments which have to be made in a reasonable statement as follows:

Stock valuation at 31 March 1987

	£	£
Stock valuation at 31 December 1986 per accounts		16,824
Less overcast error		(2,000)
		14,824
Plus purchases quarter ended 31 March 1987		46,680
		61,504
Less burglary loss		(8,000)
		53,504
Less sales quarter ended 31 March 1987		
Goods invoiced to customers	54,210	
Less December 1986 despatches invoiced January 1987	(1,040)	
	53,170	
Plus March 1987 despatches invoiced April 1987	3,900	
	57,070	
Less sales returns quarter ended 31 March 1987	(4,550)	
Cost price of sales 10/13 × £52,520	52,520	40,400
(reducing the sales to cost price)		13,104
Less stock reduced to half cost price		
($\frac{1}{2}$ × 10/13 × £1,950)		750
Stock valuation at 31 March 1987		12,354

Part (b)

Trading account for the quarter ended 31 March 1987

	£	£
Sales		52,520
Less cost of sales:		
Opening stock	16,824	
Purchases	46,680	
	63,504	
Less closing stock	12,354	
	51,150	
Less burglary loss	8000	43,150
Gross profit		9,370

Further reading

M. W. E. Glautier and B. Underdown *Accounting Theory and Practice* (Pitman) chapter 7.

Alan Pizzey *Accounting and Finance – a Firm Foundation* (Holt Rinehart and Winston), second edition, chapter 7.

18 Accounting for changing prices

Historical cost accounting conventions arose during the expansion of business enterprises and activities during the last century, with shareholders and other financial reporting users requiring more and more accounting information. Whilst the information provided to users did have some limitations, as indicated in previous chapters, the relatively small changes in price levels added very little to the existing distortion of accounting results.

The changes in price levels from the middle of the 17th century to early in this century had been only gradual, and movement had been both up and down. Since about 1914, however, the changes in price levels have been more predictable, and with a strong tendency to move in the same direction, upwards. The pattern continued into the 1970s, when the changing price level, as measured by the Retail Price Index (RPI), increased to almost 25 per cent in 1974, when compared with 1973. The rate has since declined fairly sharply, even if not evenly, and at the time of writing it is about 6 per cent.

The path of inflation rates from 1970 to 1988

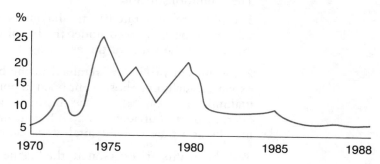

Discussions on accounting for changing price levels started in earnest in the 1940s, but it was not until the 1960s, when the rate of inflation started a more definite upward trend and there was a demand for more useful information for decision-making purposes, that more practical attempts were made to prepare and present accounts for changing price levels.

It was generally considered that accounts prepared under the historical cost accounting conventions were misleading, and could lead to unsatisfactory financial and accounting decisions. There was therefore increasing pressure to examine more closely the limitations of the conventions, in particular, the money convention, the myth that the pound or franc are unchanging units of measurement, like the miles on the motorway or kilometres on an autoroute.

This chapter is concerned with the whole problem of accounting for changing price levels. It initially looks at the limitations of historical cost accounting and then at some of the partial solutions that businesses have adopted over the years. The final part of the chapter covers the various, more comprehensive, recommendations that have been made in the 1970s and 1980s, mainly by the Accounting Standards Committee (ASC).

The structure of the chapter will, therefore, be as follows:

1 Limitations of historical cost accounting in periods of changing price levels.
2 Partial solutions used by some businesses to the problems caused by changing price levels.
3 More comprehensive recommendations proposed by the ASC in the 1970s and 1980s to the problems caused by changing price levels.

Questions on accounting for changing price levels range from the fairly descriptive to others which require the calculation and presentation of accounts adjusted for inflation. The descriptive questions could include ones which require you to:

1 Discuss the limitations of accounts prepared under the historical cost convention

or

2 Compare and contrast alternative methods of accounting for price level changes such as current cost accounting and the current purchasing power of the pound method.

18.1 Limitations of historical cost accounting in periods of changing price levels

Historical cost accounting's greatest advantage over the years has always been its simplicity and objectivity. The information required to prepare such accounts is relatively easy to obtain and verify.

Even under a system of historical accounting, the accountant does not stick rigidly to objectively determined facts, however, as shown in previous chapters. It is necessary to estimate certain items that are included in the income statement and balance sheet. An example of this would be depreciation, as shown in chapter 8, when £464m was shown as charged in ICI's 1987 accounts. This amount will have been estimated, as indeed will have been many other items in the accounts, such as the value of stocks, the provision for bad debts etc. In addition to these problems changing price levels cause further problems in the form of limitations to accounting information, principally concerned with the way profits are measured and assets valued.

The limitations include:

1 Profits are overstated in the income statement, because depreciation and cost of sales have been charged under the historical cost convention and are an inadequate measure of the value of the assets used.

2 Insufficient profits are retained in the business, because of the understatement of expenses, including those mentioned in point 1. The retentions could be inadequate to maintain the capital of the business intact. Overstated profits could lead to overpayment of dividends, and if the business has to raise new capital in lieu of this, may be at a time when capital is scarce, and therefore expensive.

3 If the profits are overstated, the business could be liable for more taxation than the profit had been calculated after accounting for changes in price levels.

4 The assets are often shown in the balance sheet at unrealistic values. The balance sheet then becomes even more like a collection of debit balances, not yet written off and not a statement showing a true and fair view of the financial position of the business.

5 Historical cost accounting does not disclose the gains that a business will obtain by holding a net monetary position or losses on holding a net monetary asset position which arise during an increase in price levels.

A net monetary liability position arises when a business owes more to its creditors, bank, etc. than it owns in the form of monetary assets such as cash, bank, and stock. A net monetary asset position arises when the business's monetary assets exceed its monetary liabilities.

6 When making comparisons over a number of accounting periods, it will be necessary to adjust the historic cost accounting figures by the relevant changing price levels, to make any kind of comparison meaningful.

Historical cost accounting information, without any adjustment for changing price levels, can, therefore, be very misleading.

18.2 Partial solutions used by some businesses for the problems caused by changing price levels.

Many businesses did not wait for the first full mandatory accounting standard on inflation, SSAP 16, before attempting to take into account changing price levels

These businesses pursued what could be considered to be partial solutions, and they modified, and in many cases have continued to do so, their historical accounts by some or all of the following adjustments:

1 Charging depreciation in their income statements on a current/replacement cost basis. This extra charge reduces the net profit, or increases the net loss. The reserves are thereby increased, and this would help businesses to meet the increased cost of replacing their fixed assets.

2 Using the last-in-first-out method of stock valuation, a method shown in chapter 17. This adjustment has similar effects and benefits to 1 above, producing a more conservative profit figure.

3 The revaluation from time to time of fixed assets in the balance sheet to market value or current/replacement cost. This will show the assets in the balance sheet at a much more realistic figure. The return on capital employed (see chapter 12) will give a better guide to the 'real' rate of return when based on current values.

In many cases these adjustments, and other similar ones, have accounted for a large part, or the whole, of the effect of changing price levels in the period from the 1950s to the 1980s, on the particular business in question. In some instances, however, partial solutions have caused inconsistency between accounting periods and between businesses. The revaluation of fixed assets have often been irregular, and the last-in-first-out method of stock valuation does not have the same impact on the balance sheet as on the income statement.

18.3 Recommendations proposed by the ASC in the 1970s and 1980s

As a result of the increasing price level changes in the early 1970s, and the consequent problems this brought for both preparers and users of accounting information, the ASC issued an exposure draft (No. 8) in 1974, accounting for changes in the current purchasing power of the pound (CPP).

The main purpose of CPP accounting was to remove the effects that changes in the general purchasing power of money had on historic accounts. It looked at the enterprise from the point of view of purchasing power and showed the impact of increasing prices. The measure used was the RPI, which was considered to be the best available to indicate the change in the general purchasing power of money. As a result of ED 8, the first accounting standard on this subject, SSAP 7, was issued, in May 1974. The main features of this standard were:

1 Companies to continue to keep basic annual accounts in historic £s.

2 Listed companies to prepare a supplementary statement in terms of the value of the £ at the end of the period to which the accounts relate.

3 Conversion by means of a general index of the purchasing power of the £.

The CPP method of accounting had considerable virtues, being simple to apply and objective. The use of the RPI attracted a great deal of criticism, however, and the government of the day were concerned about the general indexation of wages and prices, and the possible perpetuation of inflation. At the same time, 1973 to 1975, there was a growing financial crisis in the country, with the FT Index registering an all-time low. This emphasized the need to look more closely at accounting for changing price levels, with prices rising at almost 25 per cent per annum. As already indicated, profits were being overstated when calculated on the historical cost basis and dividends were being paid, in some instances, out of non-existing profits, just paper profits in fact. Business had insufficient cash flow to carry out the necessary replacement of fixed assets, which were constantly increasing in price. There were big increases in the prices of raw materials, and consequently the financing of an ever-increasing working capital, to just stand still, compounded the problem. The cost of borrowing was high and companies had difficulty raising new monies, either as equity or loans.

It was against this background that in 1974 the government set up a committtee of inquiry, under Francis Sandilands, to examine accounting for price level changes. SSAP 7 had been issued in the mean time, but only as a provisional standard. This standard had only a very short life, and only a few companies complied with it.

The Sandilands committee reported in September 1975 and rejected the CPP method of accounting. The report criticized the use of the RPI and the unit of measurement used. It also stated that most of the users of accounts would find the information difficult to understand and, because it was in a supplementary statement to the main accounts, it would have little impact.

The committee recommended current cost accounting as the main method of accounting for price level changes. The committee identified the need to maintain the operating capacity of businesses, the key criterion in determining the current costs of consuming assets. It also recognized the need to take account of the impact of changing price levels on the working capital needs of businesses.

The principal features of the current cost accounting system advocated were:

1 Accounts to be continued to be drawn up in terms of monetary units.

2 Accounts to show the 'value to the business' of assets at the balance sheet date.

3 The profit (or loss) for the year should consist of the business operating gains and should exclude any holding gains.

4 The accounts drawn up in this way should become the basic published accounts for the business. The historical cost of assets to be shown in the notes.

The Sandilands report was accepted by the government, and the ASC published another exposure draft, ED 18 *Current Cost Accounting*, in November 1976.

The exposure draft's proposals followed the Sandilands recommendations fairly closely, requiring businesses to put historical cost accounting to one side. The ED was opposed by many different groups and individuals, however, for various reasons, including:

1 The complicated nature of the proposals.

2 Criticism of some of the individual detailed proposals, and the need to distinguish between the operating profits and the profits available for distribution to shareholders.

3 Continuing support for alternative accounting systems for price level changes, particularly CPP accounting.

4 The big impact that current cost accounting would have on the profits of most businesses and the effect that this might have on dividends and share prices.

ED 18 was eventually withdrawn in 1977, and the ASC set up a committee under the chairmanship of William Hyde to recommend some interim guidelines until the ASC could publish some new proposals. The Hyde committee published a set of interim guidelines in November 1977 which it hoped would form a basis for a new, more simplified accounting standard on current cost accounting in due course. The guidelines recommended that listed and large unlisted companies should include in their annual financial report a 'voluntary' separate current cost profit and loss account, as from the year ended 31 December 1977. The account would show the historic cost profit amended by three adjustments on the following lines:

1 A depreciation adjustment: this would represent the difference between depreciation based on the historic and current cost of fixed assets consumed in the period.

2 A cost of sales adjustment: this would represent the difference between the amount charged in the computing the historic and current cost of stock at the date of sale.

3 A gearing adjustment: this would credit back to the profit and loss account the relevant proportion of the two adjustments, above, based on the premise that the shareholders would not meet the full cost of maintaining the operating capacity of the business, but part of it would usually be financed by borrowing. This adjustment would obviously not arise if the business had no borrowings.

There was no requirement in the guidelines for a current cost balance sheet, which ED 18 had required, and only the historic cost accounts would be subject to a true and fair view examination by the auditor.

A large number of companies followed these non-mandatory guidelines, along with other companies which calculated, and presented, current cost accounting information in other forms. In April 1979 the ASC published a third ED, on this topic, No. 24, *Current Cost Accounting*. This ED built on the work of the Hyde guidelines but included other requirements, namely a further adjustment to the current cost profit and loss account, a current cost balance sheet, and the calculation of a current cost earnings per share figure. The ED emphasized the objective of maintaining the physical capital of businesses.

ED 24 became a full accounting standard in March 1980, SSAP 16 *Current Cost Accounting*, which set out the principles on which published accounts should be adjusted for the impact of changing price levels on the businesses operating capability. The standard related to accounting periods starting on, or after, 1 January 1980, and broadly applied to all listed companies, unless they were authorized insurers, property companies or investment companies. It also applied to all other companies, unless they satisfied two of the following criteria:

1 Turnover of less than £5m per annum.

2 Historical cost balance sheet total of less than £2.5m.

3 Average number of UK employees less than 250.

The approach was based upon the idea that a profit can only be earned once provision has been made out of current income for the maintenance of a company's productive capability. This provision was to be made at current levels of cost, rather than at historic cost levels. This would give an indication of the level of retentions required in order to replace assets at current prices.

The method of achieving these objectives initially involves the making of three adjustments to the historic cost accounting profit, for fixed assets, stocks, and monetary working capital.

Businesses were required to include in their published accounts a current cost profit and loss account and a current cost balance sheet with notes aimed at illustrating the impact of specific price changes, rather than general price changes, on the business. This was to be achieved by using either historic or current cost figures, as the main accounts and the other figures in the notes.

The **first level** of profit in the current cost profit and loss account was called the current cost operating profit, and was the trading profit from the historic cost accounts, adjusted for the impact of price level changes by making three adjustments, namely:

1 a depreciation adjustment;

2 a cost of sales adjustment;

3 a monetary working capital adjustment.

The **second level** of profit was called the current cost profit to shareholders. This was calculated by deducting any interest payable, and taxation, from the current cost operating profit, and by making a further adjustment, for gearing. This adjustment arises to the extent that a business may be financed partly by borrowing, and recognized that the burden of maintaining the business capability would fall partly on the lenders. A proportionate reduction was therefore made to the first three current cost accounting adjustments above. The purpose of the gearing adjustment was to adjust the current cost operating profit to show the impact of increasing price level changes on the shareholders' interest, after taking into account the need to repay any loans the business may have had.

An example of a current cost profit and loss account is as follows:

	£000	£000
Turnover		30,000
Historical cost trading profit before interest		4,000
Less current cost accounting adjustments:		
Cost of sales	700	
Depreciation	1,000	
Monetary working capital	300	2,000

(*cont'd.*)

(cont'd.)		£000	£000
First level Current cost operating profit			2,000
Interest on borrowing		400	
Gearing adjustment		(300)	100
Current cost profit before tax			1,900
Taxation			1,000
Second level Current cost profit attributable to shareholders			900
Dividends			500
Retained current cost profit for the year			400

The accompanying current cost balance sheet would show the same assets as in the historic cost balance sheet, but on a current cost basis, which corresponded with those used in calculating the current cost profit and loss account. All non-monetary assets, excluding goodwill, would be shown at the value which would reflect the change in price levels which had occurred since the assets were purchased. Monetary assets, e.g. debtors and creditors, would remain at historic cost values as they would have arisen at, or near to, the balance sheet date. A **current cost reserve** would also be required to show the effect of the various current cost adjustments that had been made.

SSAP 16 was expected to last for a minimum three-year experimental period, during which no alterations would be made to it. A monitoring working party was established by the ASC to monitor the success, or otherwise, of the standard. Although the standard was mandatory, an increasing number of companies did not comply with it. It became the most disregarded of the accounting standards for a number of different reasons. These reasons included the doubts about preparing two sets of accounts on different bases. Very few companies, in fact, presented current cost accounts as their main ones. Other reasons included:

1 Many companies thought that the current cost accounting information was of little use for decision making, despite the fact that this was one of the main reasons for this system of accounting.

2 Unsuitability for specialized companies.

3 Companies wishing to show higher profits during periods of recession, which historic cost accounting generally enabled them to do.

4 The fact that the rate of inflation fell during the experimental period from 13 per cent per annum in 1980 to 4.7 per cent per annum in 1984 and subsequently to just above 3 per cent, before increasing to about 6 per cent at the time of writing.

By 1983/84 it was recognized that SSAP 16 would require considerable revision, following on the increasing non-compliance and general lack of support. The three-year experimental life was extended until another new ED could be issued. A SOI was issued in March 1984 which preceded the next initiative, a fourth ED on this topic, No. 35 *Accounting for the effects of changing prices*. The proposals, to take effect from 1 January 1985, were a compromise solution to the problem of changing price levels, but continued with the principles of current cost accounting. The scope of the ED was considerably narrowed, compared to SSAP 16, and applied only to public companies that were neither value-based nor wholly-owned subsidiaries, with the size test abandoned. Current cost information was to be given in the main accounts, either in note form, or as a part of full current cost accounts, and compliance would be essential to give a true and fair view.

The financial statement would show the effects of changing price levels on the operating capability and financing of the company by giving, *inter alia* the following current cost information:

1 a depreciation adjustment;

2 a cost of sales adjustment;

3 a monetary working capital adjustment;

4 a gearing adjustment, but with greater flexibility on its calculation than hitherto;

5 any other material adjustments to the profit and loss on ordinary activities, consistent with the current cost convention.

No current cost balance sheet was required, but the accounts had to show the gross and net current cost of fixed assets and accumulated depreciation and the current cost of stocks.

Many companies chose to comply with ED 35 but a number of other groups did not fully support it. The criticism of the ED included:

1 that it was too flexible;

2 dissatisfaction about the inclusion of the current cost accounting adjustments in the true and fair view requirement;

3 the exclusion of value-based companies.

In the meantime, mandatory status of SSAP 16 was suspended in June 1985, and the SSAP was later withdrawn.

In view of the criticism and lack of support for ED 35, the ASC reviewed it, and then withdrew it in March 1985. They intend to recommend new proposals, in due course, after extensive consultation with many different bodies. In the mean time, businesses are encouraged to provide information on the impact of price level changes on their results in their annual report and accounts. Very few companies are presenting reports of this kind.

The ASC accepts that there is no single answer to accounting for price level changes, but encourages companies to produce information, in their annual report and accounts, to show its impact.

Links with other topics

Accounting for changing prices links with most of the other chapters in this text. The historic cost convention is covered in chapter 7, and can be linked to the current cost accounting principles developed in this chapter. The four recommended current cost accounting adjustments for the depreciation, cost of sales, working capital and gearing, can usefully be linked with the three relevant chapters on these topics. The initiatives pursued by the ASC through SOIs, EDs and SSAPs can be linked to chapter 9 and to chapter 10. This topic can also be linked to chapter 12 and chapter 13. These two chapters, and chapter 18, will enable you to determine the effect, if any, of changing price levels on the financial position and performance of a business.

Sample questions

1 Describe the main limitations of preparing balance sheets and profit and loss accounts on an historic cost accounting basis in times of inflation.

CIMA Stage 1

Answer plan

The main limitations would include:

(a) Depreciation based on historic costs inadequate.

(b) The proportion of historic gross profit of which holding gain is not disclosed.

(c) Historic cost accounts could lead to over-taxation.

(d) Fixed assets values are outdated.

(e) Gains on holding a net monetary liability position, or losses on holding a net monetary asset position are not disclosed.

(f) The depletion of capital arising from the increasing price level changes is not reflected in the statements.

(g) Comparison of results over time can be difficult unless the figures are adjusted for changes in price levels, etc.

2 You are required to outline the main principles of the current cost accounting system that has been recommended by the ASC in its various exposure drafts and accounting standards in the United Kingdom in the 1970s and 1980s.

First-year Business Studies degree level

Answer plan

The current cost accounting system is based upon a concept of capital which is represented by the net operating assets of a business. These net operating assets (fixed assets plus stock and monetary working capital) are the same as those included in historic cost accounts, but in the current cost accounts the fixed assets and stock are normally expressed at current cost.

A change in the input prices of goods and services used and financed by the business will affect the amount of funds required to maintain the operating capability of the net operating assets; current cost accounts are designed to reflect this in the determination of profit and in the balance sheet.

The basic objective of current cost accounts is to provide more useful information than that available from historic cost accounts alone for the guidance of the management of the business, the shareholders and others on such matters as:

(a) the financial viability of the business;

(b) return on investment;

(c) pricing, cost control and distribution decisions;

(d) gearing.

3 SSAP 16 and ED 35 recommended that there should be four current cost accounting adjustments to be made to the historic cost profit. Describe briefly the nature and purpose of these four adjustments.

First-year Business Studies degree level

Answer plan

Depreciation adjustment: allows for the impact of price changes when determining the charge against revenue for the part of fixed assets consumed in the period.

Cost of sales adjustments: allows for the impact of price changes when determining the charge against revenue for stock consumed in the period.

Monetary working capital adjustment: represents the amount of additional (or reduced) finance needed for monetary working capital as a result of changes in the input prices of goods and services used and financed by the business.

Gearing adjustment: indicates the benefit or cost to shareholders which is realized in the period, measured by the extent to which a proportion of the net operating assets are financed by borrowing. ED 35 allowed alternative methods of calculating the gearing adjustment. These adjustments could include figures for illustration purposes.

4 During a period of inflation, many accountants believe that financial reports prepared under the historical cost convention are subject to the following major limitations:

1 stocks are undervalued:

2 depreciation is understated;

3 gains and losses on net monetary assets are undisclosed;

4 balance sheet values are unrealistic;

5 meaningful periodic comparisons are difficult to make.

Required:
Explain briefly the limitations of historical cost accounting in periods of inflation with reference to each of the items listed above.

AAT Final membership examination

Answer plan

You are required to explain briefly the main limitations of historical cost accounting. The five main limitations are listed for you in the question and each has been briefly discussed in this chapter.

1 Stocks undervalued

During periods of increasing prices stocks will be undervalued at the end of the accounting period unless some system of accounting for price level changes i provided. The use of the last-in-first-out (LIFO) method of stock valuation would help, but the use of a replacement or current cost index system can overcome the problem.

The undervaluation of stock would result in distortion of the profit and capital employed figures in the balance sheet and the financial position of the business would be misrepresented. Rising prices would make it increasingly difficult for the business to finance its extra working capital requirements.

2 Depreciation understated

If depreciation charged in the profit and loss account is based on the historic cost of fixed assets, the profits will be overstated. If such profits are withdrawn or paid out the business will have insufficient funds to replace its fixed assets. Depreciation based on current or replacement cost would overcome this problem, provided that the funds generated are managed accordingly.

3 Gains/losses on net monetary assets

Business make gains and losses on net monetary assets but these are not reported in the annual reports based on the historic cost convention. If the business borrows to finance its activities at a fixed rate of interest, during periods of rising prices it will make a gain and vice versa if it lends monies. Under the various systems recommended for accounting for price level changes, these gains/losses would be reported and financial report users could find the data very useful.

4 Balance sheet values unrealistic

Fixed assets are usually recorded in the balance sheet at historic cost, which may differ considerably from their replacement or current cost. This would result in a reduced capital employed figure and a misrepresentation of the financial position of the business. To overcome this problem, some businesses revalue their fixed assets from time to time. Others increase their fixed assets figures by the use of indexes.

5 Periodic comparisons

Comparisons of financial results over time become very difficult if they are not adjusted for price level changes. Companies prepare 5 to 10 year summaries of their results and a comparison of (say) the figures for 1988 with those from 1979 would be almost meaningless unless you adjust for the inflation of the intervening years. Some companies do indeed adjust the figures accordingly and you should examine very carefully any data given to you for comparison purposes for indications of such adjustments.

Further reading

M. Harvey and F. Keer *Financial Accounting Theory and Standards* (Prentice Hall), second edition, chapters 6 and 7.

G. A. Lee *Modern Financial Accounting* (Nelson), fourth edition, chapters 6 and 7.

Mallinson *Understanding Current Cost Accounting* (Butterworths).

Appendix of figures extracted from ICI's Annual Report for 1987

GROUP PROFIT AND LOSS ACCOUNT

For the year ended 31 December 1987

	Notes	1987 £m	1986 £m
TURNOVER		**11,123**	10,136
Operating costs	4	(10,001)	(9,232)
Other operating income	4	175	145
TRADING PROFIT	4	**1,297**	1,049
Share of profits less losses of related companies	5	157	95
Net interest payable	6	(142)	(128)
PROFIT ON ORDINARY ACTIVITIES BEFORE TAXATION		**1,312**	1,016
Tax on profit on ordinary activities	7	(504)	(382)
PROFIT ON ORDINARY ACTIVITIES AFTER TAXATION		808	634
Attributable to minorities		(48)	(34)
NET PROFIT ATTRIBUTABLE TO PARENT COMPANY		760	600
Extraordinary item	8	—	(43)
NET PROFIT FOR THE FINANCIAL YEAR		760	557
Dividends	9	(277)	(238)
PROFIT RETAINED FOR YEAR		483	319
EARNINGS PER £1 ORDINARY STOCK	10	**113.6p**	92.0p

GROUP RESERVES ATTRIBUTABLE TO PARENT COMPANY

	Note	1987 £m	1986 £m
At beginning of year		3,008	2,838
Profit retained for year: Company		389	137
Subsidiaries		38	182
Related companies		56	—
		483	319
Amounts taken direct to reserves		(722)	(14)
At end of year	11	**2,769**	3,008

Figures in brackets represent deductions; £m means millions of pounds sterling.

BALANCE SHEETS

At 31 December 1987

	Notes	GROUP 1987 £m	GROUP 1986 £m	COMPANY 1987 £m	COMPANY 1986 £m
ASSETS EMPLOYED					
FIXED ASSETS					
Tangible assets	12	3,750	3,912	1,621	1,527
Investments: Subsidiaries	13			2,478	2,985
Related and other companies	14	417	333	152	153
		4,167	4,245	4,251	4,665
CURRENT ASSETS					
Stocks	15	1,812	1,734	707	631
Debtors	16	2,162	2,015	824	372
Investments and short-term deposits	17	494	471	25	29
Cash	17	152	221	9	40
		4,620	4,441	1,565	1,072
TOTAL ASSETS		8,787	8,686	5,816	5,737
CREDITORS DUE WITHIN ONE YEAR					
Short-term borrowings	18	(559)	(441)	(6)	(77)
Current instalments of loans	21	(46)	(74)	—	(2)
Other creditors	19	(2,365)	(2,022)	(1,470)	(1,396)
		(2,970)	(2,537)	(1,476)	(1,475)
NET CURRENT ASSETS (LIABILITIES)		1,650	1,904	89	(403)
TOTAL ASSETS LESS CURRENT LIABILITIES		5,817	6,149	4,340	4,262
FINANCED BY					
CREDITORS DUES AFTER MORE THAN ONE YEAR					
Loans	21	1,511	1,538	578	478
Other creditors	19	70	83	549	733
		1,581	1,621	1,127	1,211
PROVISIONS FOR LIABILITIES AND CHARGES	20	295	276	12	25
DEFERRED INCOME: Grants not yet credited to profit		139	183	97	114
MINORITY INTERESTS		357	404		
CAPITAL AND RESERVES ATTRIBUTABLE TO PARENT COMPANY					
Called-up share capital	22	676	657	676	657
Reserves: Share premium account		236	115	236	115
Revaluation reserve		78	84	6	6
Other reserves		316	368	425	823
Profit and loss account		1,964	2,476	1,761	1,311
Related companies' reserves		175	(35)		
Total reserves	11	2,769	3,008	2,428	2,255
Total capital and reserves attributable to parent company		3,445	3,665	3,104	2,912
		5,817	6,149	4,340	4,262

The accounts on pages 32 to 53 were approved by the Board of Directors on 7 March 1988 and were signed on its behalf by:

D. H. Henderson *Director*

A. W. Clements *Director*

J. T. Harrison *Chief Financial Officer*

STATEMENT OF SOURCES AND APPLICATIONS
OF GROUP FUNDS

For the year ended 31 December 1987

	Notes	1987 £m	1986 £m
SOURCES			
FUNDS GENERATED FROM OPERATIONS			
Trading profit		1,297	1,049
Depreciation		464	491
Petroleum revenue tax paid, less provided			(42)
Government grants credited to profit, less received		(19)	(9)
Dividends from related companies		65	56
Miscellaneous items, including exchange		(9)	(60)
		1,798	1,485
LESS: INTEREST AND TAXATION PAID DURING YEAR			
Interest (net)		(141)	(125)
Taxation		(349)	(298)
SOURCES NET OF INTEREST AND TAXATION		1,308	1,062
APPLICATIONS			
DIVIDENDS PAID DURING YEAR			
Parent company		254	222
Subsidiaries to minority shareholders		29	27
		283	249
FIXED ASSETS			
Tangible assets		708	643
Disposals of tangible assets		(26)	(35)
Acquisitions and new investments	24	544	578
Disposals of subsidiaries and related company investments	24	(114)	(30)
		1,112	1,156
WORKING CAPITAL CHANGES			
Stocks increase (1986 decrease)		169	(115)
Debtors increase (1986 decrease)		68	(45)
Creditors and provisions increase (excluding dividends and taxation) (1986 decrease)		(50)	66
		187	(94)
TOTAL APPLICATIONS		1,582	1,311
DEFICIT		(274)	(249)
FINANCED BY			
Issues of ICI Ordinary Stock		140	50
Repayment of ICI Preference Stock			(7)
Other external finance		(6)	(7)
Net repayment of loans (1986 net new borrowings)		(24)	178
Increase in short-term borrowings (1986 decrease)	*	118	(70)
Decrease in cash and short-term investments	*	46	105
		274	249

*Movements in these items represent the differences between amounts shown in the opening and closing balance sheets. Movements in other items do not correspond to the change in balance sheet amounts, due to effects of acquisitions and disposals of subsidiaries and effects of retranslating opening currency balances of overseas subsidiaries at closing exchange rates.

ACCOUNTING POLICIES

The accounts have been prepared under the historical cost convention and in accordance with the Companies Act 1985. Group accounting policies conform with UK Accounting Standards; the following paragraphs describe the main policies. The accounting policies of some overseas subsidiaries do not conform with UK Accounting Standards and, where appropriate, adjustments are made on consolidation in order to present the Group accounts on a consistent basis.

DEPRECIATION

The Group's policy is to write off the book value of each tangible fixed asset evenly over its estimated remaining life. Reviews are made periodically of the estimated remaining lives of individual productive assets, taking account of commercial and technological obsolescence as well as normal wear and tear. Under this policy it becomes impracticable to calculate average asset lives exactly; however, the total lives approximate to 21 years for buildings and 14 years for plant and equipment. Depreciation of assets qualifying for grants is calculated on their full cost.

FOREIGN CURRENCIES

Profit and loss accounts in foreign currencies are translated into sterling at average rates for the relevant accounting period. Assets and liabilities are translated at exchange rates ruling at the date of the Group balance sheet.

Exchange differences on short-term currency borrowings and deposits are included with net interest payable. Exchange differences on all other transactions, except foreign currency loans, are taken to trading profit. In the Group accounts exchange differences arising on consolidation of the net investments in overseas subsidiary and related companies are taken to reserves, as are differences arising on equity investments denominated in foreign currencies in the Company accounts. Differences on foreign currency loans are taken to reserves and offset against the differences on net investments.

GOODWILL

On the acquisition of a business, fair values are attributed to the net assets acquired. Goodwill arises where the value of the consideration given for a business exceeds such net assets. UK Accounting Standards require that purchased goodwill be eliminated from the Group balance sheet either upon acquisition against reserves or by amortization over a period. Elimination against Group reserves has been selected as appropriate to the goodwill purchases made during 1986 and 1987.

GOVERNMENT GRANTS

Grants related to expenditure on tangible fixed assets are credited to profit over a period approximating to the lives of qualifying assets. The grants shown in the balance sheets consist of the total grants receivable to date less the amounts so far credited to profit.

LEASES

All leases are accounted for as operating leases. The rentals due in each accounting period are charged to profit and loss account; no adjustments are made for notional depreciation or interest on finance leases.

PENSIONS FUNDING

The Company and most of its subsidiaries operate pension schemes which cover the majority of employees (including directors) in the Group. The amounts charged against profit are calculated with actuarial advice in accordance with local practice, and represent a proper charge to cover the accruing liabilities on a continuing basis. With minor exceptions these schemes are financed through separate trustee-administered funds.

RELATED COMPANIES

A related company is a company, not being a subsidiary, in which the Group has an interest of between 20 per cent and 50 per cent and on whose commercial and financial policy decisions the Group exercises significant influence. The Group's share of the profits less losses of all significant related companies is included in the Group profit and loss account on the equity accounting basis.

The holding value of significant related companies in the Group balance sheet is calculated by reference to the Group's equity in the net tangible assets of suc companies, as shown by the most recent accounts available, adjusted whe appropriate.

RESEARCH AND DEVELOPMENT

Research and development expenditure is charged to profit in the year in which it incurred.

STOCK VALUATION

Finished goods are stated at the lower of cost and net realizable value, raw materia and other stocks at the lower of cost and replacement price; the first in, first out or a average method of valuation is used. In determining cost for stock valuation purpose depreciation is included but selling expenses and certain overhead expenses a excluded.

TAXATION

The charge for taxation is based on the profit for the year and takes into accou taxation deferred because of timing differences between the treatment of certain item for taxation and for accounting purposes. However, no provision is made for taxatio deferred by reliefs unless there is reasonable evidence that such deferred taxation wi be payable in the future.

NOTES RELATING TO THE ACCOUNTS

3 CHANGES IN GROUP STRUCTURE (continued)

On 30 January 1987, the Group disposed of its subsidiaries in its Oil and Gas segmen to Enterprise Oil plc in exchange for a 25 per cent shareholding in that company. Th value placed on the Group's interest in Enterprise Oil plc (now a related compan) was equal to the book value of the consolidated net assets disposed of.

4 TRADING PROFIT

	1987 £m	198 £
TURNOVER	11,123	10,13
OPERATING COSTS		
Cost of sales	(6,908)	(6,47
Distribution costs	(791)	(73
Research and development	(461)	(39
Administrative and other expenses	(1,787)	(1,58
Employees' profit-sharing bonus	(54)	(5
	(10,001)	(9,23
OTHER OPERATING INCOME		
Government grants	31	3
Royalties	31	4
Other income	113	6
	175	14
TRADING PROFIT	1,297	1,04
Total charge for depreciation included above	464	49
Petroleum revenue tax included in cost of sales	5	3
Gross profit, as defined by the Companies Act 1985	4,215	3,65

5 SHARE OF PROFITS LESS LOSSES OF RELATED COMPANIES

SHARE OF PROFITS LESS LOSSES		
Dividend income	65	5
Share of undistributed profits less losses	91	3
Share of profits less losses before tax	156	8
GAINS ON DISPOSALS OF INVESTMENTS	9	
AMOUNTS WRITTEN OFF INVESTMENTS	(8)	(
	157	9

Total dividend income from shares in related companies comprised £15m (1986: £10m) from listed companies and £50m (£46m) from unlisted companies.

6 _NET INTEREST PAYABLE_

INTEREST PAYABLE AND SIMILAR CHARGES

Loan interest	150	135
Interest on short-term borrowings and other financing costs	60	67
	210	202

INTEREST RECEIVABLE AND SIMILAR INCOME FROM CURRENT ASSET INVESTMENTS

Listed redeemable securities	(11)	(15)
Short-term deposits	(48)	(54)
	(59)	(69)

EXCHANGE GAINS ON SHORT-TERM CURRENCY BORROWINGS AND DEPOSITS

	(9)	(5)
	142	128

Loan interest includes £126m (1986 £108m) on loans not wholly repayable within 5 years.

12 _TANGIBLE FIXED ASSETS_

	Land and buildings	Plant and equipment	Payments on account and assets in course of construction	Total
	£m	£m	£m	£m
GROUP				
COST OR AS REVALUED				
At beginning of year	1,375	6,055	511	7,941
Exchange adjustments	(130)	(373)	(36)	(539)
Revaluations and adjustments	(5)	(9)		(14)
New subsidiaries	31	133	3	167
Capital expenditure			708	708
Transfers	121	450	(571)	
Disposals and other movements*	(34)	(564)		(598)
At end of year	1,358	5,692	615	7,665
DEPRECIATION				
At beginning of year	509	3,520		4,029
Exchange adjustments	(35)	(168)		(203)
Revaluations and adjustments	(5)	(9)		(14)
Disposals and other movements*	(8)	(353)		(361)
Charge for year	56	408		464
At end of year	517	3,398		3,915
NET BOOK VALUE AT END 1987	841	2,294	615	3,750
Net book value at end 1986	866	2,535	511	3,912
COMPANY				
COST OR AS REVALUED				
At beginning of year	419	2,859	313	3,591
Capital expenditure			338	338
Transfers	33	234	(267)	
Disposals and other movements	(17)	(45)		(62)
At end of year	435	3,048	384	3,867
DEPRECIATION				
At beginning of year	201	1,863		2,064
Disposals and other movements	(3)	(36)		(39)
Charge for year	17	204		221
At end of year	215	2,031		2,246
NET BOOK VALUE AT END 1987	220	1,017	384	1,621
Net book value at end 1986	218	996	313	1,527

*Includes disposal of Oil and Gas assets.

	GROUP		COMPANY	
	1987 £m	1986 £m	1987 £m	1986 £m
The net book value of land and buildings comprised:				
Freeholds	812	834	217	214
Long leases (over 50 years unexpired)	9	11	2	2
Short leases	20	21	1	2
	841	866	220	218

21 LOANS

	Repayment dates	GROUP		COMPANY	
		1987 £m	1986 £m	1987 £m	1986 £m
SECURED LOANS					
US dollars ($5\frac{1}{2}$ to $10\frac{7}{8}$%)	1988/2012	40	30		
Australian dollars ($10\frac{1}{4}$ to 18.18%)	1988/97	59	73		
Other currencies	1988/2015	25	24		
TOTAL SECURED		124	127		
Secured by fixed charge		101	105		
Secured by floating charge		23	22		
UNSECURED LOANS					
Sterling:					
$7\frac{3}{4}$ and $8\frac{1}{2}$% Stocks	1988/93	109	109	109	109
$9\frac{3}{4}$ to $11\frac{1}{4}$% bonds	1992/2005	400	300	400	300
$11\frac{3}{8}$% Stock	1991/96	43	43	43	43
$8\frac{1}{2}$% convertible bonds*	1999	62	100		
$5\frac{7}{8}$% Stock	1994/2004	26	26	26	26
Others	1988/99	12	9		
		652	587	578	478
US dollars:					
$9\frac{3}{4}$% bonds*	1990	45	68		
$7\frac{1}{2}$ to $8\frac{1}{4}$% Eurodollar bonds	1988/96	61	95		
$6\frac{3}{4}$% convertible Eurodollar bonds*	1997	2	4		
$8\frac{1}{8}$ to 9.05% bonds	1988/2006	310	330		
5.3 to $8\frac{3}{8}$% loans	1988/2005	36	46		
Others	1988/98	15	17		2
		469	560		2
Canadian dollars ($10\frac{5}{8}$ to $14\frac{1}{2}$%)	1988/96	74	92		
Deutschmark ($6\frac{1}{2}$%)	1988/92	11	15		
Dutch florins ($6\frac{1}{4}$ to 9%)	1988/91	14	22		
Swiss francs ($3\frac{1}{2}$ to $4\frac{1}{4}$%)	1988/94	104	113		
Japanese yen (variable)	1989/95	14	7		
Other currencies	1988/98	95	49		
Multi-currency credit facility (variable interest; repayable and redrawable at borrower's option)			40		
TOTAL UNSECURED		1,433	1,485	578	480
TOTAL LOANS		1,557	1,612	578	480
Loans or instalments thereof are repayable:					
After 5 years from balance sheet date:					
Lump sums		688	697	325	300
Instalments		379	428	125	125
		1,067	1,125	450	425
From 2 to 5 years		390	356	128	53
From 1 to 2 years		54	57	—	—

(cont'd

(cont'd.)

	Repayment dates	GROUP 1987 £m	GROUP 1986 £m	COMPANY 1987 £m	COMPANY 1986 £m
TOTAL DUE AFTER MORE THAN ONE YEAR		1,511	1,538	578	478
TOTAL DUE WITHIN ONE YEAR		46	74	—	2
		1,557	1,612	578	480
Aggregate amount of loans repayable by instalments any of which fall due after 5 years		647	741	125	125

*Conversion rights attach to certain bonds, unless previously redeemed and subject to adjustment in certain events, as follows:

8½% sterling bonds, until 1 October 1999, into Ordinary Stock of the Company at 800 pence per £1 of Ordinary Stock (with an option to redeem on 15 October 1989 at a premium of 12%, giving rise to a contingent liability of £7m);

9¾% US dollar bonds, until 1 June 1990, into sterling bonds at a conversion rate of US$1.5773 = £1;

6¾% Eurodollar bonds, until 1 September 1997, into Ordinary Stock of the Company at 460 pence per £1 of Ordinary Stock (with a fixed rate of exchange applicable on conversion of the bonds of US$1.7423 = £1).

Loans from banks amounted to £135m (1986 £201m) in the Group of which £64m (£74m) was secured. New borrowings during the year included £100m 9¾% bonds due 2005 issued by the Company to be used for the general purposes of the ICI Group.

22 CALLED-UP SHARE CAPITAL OF PARENT COMPANY

	Authorized £m	Alloted, called-up and fully paid 1987 £m	Alloted, called-up and fully paid 1986 £m
Ordinary Stock (£1 units)	676	676	657
Unclassified shares (£1 each)	115		
	791	676	657

Ordinary Stock issued during the year totalled £19m comprising issues in respect of the Employees' Profit-Sharing Scheme £4m, the Company's share option schemes £2m and conversions of loan stock and exercise of warrants £13m.

Options outstanding at 31 December 1987 to subscribe for Ordinary shares of £1 under the Company's share option schemes for staff were:

Subscription price	Last date when options exercisable	Number of shares 1987	Number of shares 1986
£2.69	31 March 1987		209,458
£2.86	31 March 1988	229,587	1,193,985
£3.55	18 March 1987		11,000
£3.55	18 March 1988	15,000	33,000
£3.55	17 March 1989	27,000	58,000
£3.93	16 March 1990		25,000
£3.96	31 December 1988	572,960	601,870
£5.33	31 December 1989	558,936	581,554
£5.88	14 March 1991	37,000	131,000
£5.95	12 September 1994	671,600	1,150,600
£6.06	31 May 1991	1,299,212	1,354,446
£6.06	31 May 1993	287,773	298,228
£6.60	4 September 1995	98,700	98,700
£7.86	17 April 1995	530,600	562,100
£9.66	31 May 1992	1,362,495	1,403,995
£9.66	31 May 1994	272,593	277,384

(cont'd.)

(cont'd.)

Subscription price	Last date when options exercisable	Number of shares 1987	1986
£9.75	1 April 1996	1,310,900	1,354,200
£10.05	9 September 1996	175,400	175,400
£13.12	31 March 1997	155,600	
£13.81	31 May 1993	1,514,659	
£13.81	31 May 1995	267,454	
£15.12	1 September 1997	93,500	
		9,480,969	9,519,920

During 1987 movements in the number of shares under option comprised new options issued 2,043,265, options exercised 1,861,979 and options lapsed 220,237. At the end of 1987 there were 18,945,592 shares available for the granting of options (1986 20,823,904).

Warrants granting options to subscribe for 8,219,016 Ordinary shares of £1 each at 540p were exercised during the year, leaving a balance representing options over 1,945,359 shares exercisable until 1 June 1990.

Glossary

Account – contains the details of a payment, receipt, income or expenditure. Specific types are grouped together in the sales, purchases and general ledgers.

Accruals – payments made in arrears.

Appropriations – deductions made after net profit distributions to shareholders, reserves and payments made to the inland revenue.

Assets – the economic resources which a firm owns.

Balance sheet – list of the assets and liabilities of a business presented in such a way as to illustrate the company's financial position.

Book value – historic cost less depreciation charged to date.

Capital – the total value of the assets of a business less the total value of its liabilities, as at a specific date.

Concepts and conventions – the framework of ideas which surrounds the practice of accounting.

Control accounts – type of trial balance used to check the double entry accuracy of the sales and purchases ledgers.

Creative accounting – deliberate attempts to cover up the true financial position of a company.

Creditor (trade) – a supplier to whom the business owes money.

Creditor (secured) – usually applies to a lender of finance (e.g. a bank) where the security for the loan is in the form of deeds to land or the legal title to some other asset. Should the firm be unable to repay the loan then the lender can sell the asset to recover the value of the outstanding debt.

Current assets – short-term assets which are constantly changing in value.

Debentures – a long-term loan to a company repayable on a specific date. Holders usually have a charge on the company's assets and receive interest on an annual basis.

Debtor (trade) – customer who owes the firm money.

Depreciation – loss of value suffered by fixed assets. Defined in SSAP 12 as 'the measure of the wearing out, consumption or other reduction in the useful economic life of a fixed asset, whether arising from use, effluxion of time or obsolescence through technological or market changes'.

Direct taxes – taxes levied directly on the individual.

Drawings – withdrawal of money or goods by the firm's owners for their personal use.

Extraordinary items – anything that happens outside the ordinary activities of a company, which is significant to that company's financial position and is not expected to recur regularly or frequently.

Fixed assets – long-term resources of a company which do not fluctuate in value.

Folio – reference number indicating the location of an account entry.

Gearing – The relationship between the fixed return capital and ordinary shareholders' capital used to finance the business.

Going concern – a firm that it is assumed will continue in business for the foreseeable future.

Historic cost – the amount actually spent on an asset when purchased.

Income statement – structured list of income and expenditure illustrating the gross and net profit of a business.

Indirect taxes – taxes levied on the purchase of goods and services.

Journal – usually used in the book-keeping systems of larger businesses to record credit sales, purchases and returns. A separate journal is used for items such as disposal of assets, depreciation and the correction of errors.

Ledger – collection of accounts, usually divided into sales, purchases and general ledgers.

Liabilities – monies owed by the firm. Short-term liabilities are settled within one year, long-term liabilities, after more than one year.

Limited company – business formed under the Companies Acts. It is a separate legal entity, independent of the individual owners.

Liquidity – either the firm's ability to pay its debts or the ease with which an asset can be converted into cash.

Listed company – a company whose shares are quoted on the stock exchange.

Materiality – an item is material if its non-disclosure, mis-statement or omission would distort the view given by the accounts or other financial information.

Market value (of an asset) – the price which can be obtained from the sale of an asset in an 'arm's length' transaction on the open market.

Market value (of finished goods) – the price the firm would have to pay on the open market for goods which have been manufactured internally.

Monetary working capital – the total value of trade debtors, prepayments and trade bills receivable plus stocks not subject to a cost-of-sales adjustment, less trade creditors accruals and trade bills payable.

Net monetary assets position – the position of a business when its short-term assets exceed its short-term liabilities.

Net monetary liabilities position – the position of a business when its short-term liabilities exceed its short-term assets.

Net realizable value (of an asset) – the amount which could be gained from selling asset less any costs incurred in the sale.

Opportunity cost – the value of an asset had it been used for another purpose.

Partnership – a business jointly owned by between 2 and 20 persons.

Personal allowance – an individual's tax-free income: the amount which can be deducted from an individual's total annual income, income tax being payable on the remainder.

Prepayments – payments made in advance.

Prior year adjustments – adjustments made to the previous year's financial statements either to correct fundamental errors or because of changes in accounting policies.

Progressive taxes – variable rates of taxation under which the taxpayer's average tax rate rises as income rises.

Recoverable amount – the greater of the net realizable value of an asset and, where applicable, the amount recoverable from its further use.

Receiver – a person appointed to run the affairs of a company when it is in financial difficulties, usually at the request of secured creditors (e.g. banks).

Regressive tax – a tax paid by a taxpayer regardless of that taxpayer's income

Replacement value – the cost of replacing an asset.

Schedule D – the section of the Income and Corporation Taxes Act under which profits from trades and professions are assessed.

Scrap value – the break-up value of an asset.

Sinking fund technique – investments are made outside the business in order to provide funds to replace fixed assets at a future date (the end of those assets' lives)

Solvency – see **liquidity**.

Statement of affairs – list of the opening assets and liabilities of a business.

Sole proprietor – a business owned and controlled by one person.

Trial balance – list of balances extracted from the ledgers. The total debit balances must equal the total credit balances.

Trustee (in bankruptcy/liquidation) – person(s) appointed to wind up the affairs of business which is no longer solvent (able to pay its debts).

Value-added tax (VAT) – a tax levied on the increase in value of an item at every stage of production and/or sale.

Value of an asset to the business – the net current replacement cost or the recoverable amount of an asset.

Working capital – the value of current assets less current liabilities.

Work-in-progress – stock of partly finished goods (in a manufacturing business).

Writing down allowance – an annual allowance deductible from taxable profit following the purchase of most fixed assets.

Index